TIME OF NEED

BOOKS BY WILLIAM BARRETT

Time of Need
The Truants
The Illusion of Technique
Ego and Instinct (co-author, with Daniel Yankelovich)
What is Existentialism?
Irrational Man

William Barrett

Time of Need

Forms of Imagination
in the Twentieth Century

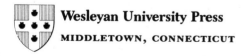 **Wesleyan University Press**
MIDDLETOWN, CONNECTICUT

ST. PHILIP'S COLLEGE LIBRARY

Copyright © 1972 by William Barrett

All rights reserved.

First published in the United States by Harper & Row, Inc., and in Canada by Fitzhenry & Whiteside Ltd., Toronto. First Harper & Row Torchbook edition published 1973.

Grateful acknowledgment is made for permission to quote excerpts from the following:

E. M. Forster, *Howards End* (New York: Alfred A. Knopf, Inc.). Reprinted by permission.

Samuel Beckett, *Waiting for Godot*, translated from the original French text by the author (New York: Grove Press, 1954). Copyright 1954 by Grove Press. Reprinted by permission of Grove Press and Faber and Faber Ltd.

Robert Frost, "Come In," from *The Poetry of Robert Frost,* ed. Edward Connery Lathem (New York: Holt, Rinehart and Winston, Inc., 1942). Copyright 1942 by Robert Frost. Copyright © 1970 by Lesley Frost Ballantine. Reprinted by permission of Holt, Rinehart and Winston, Inc., and Jonathan Cape Ltd.

Ernest Hemingway, *A Farewell to Arms* (New York: Charles Scribner's Sons). Reprinted by permission.

William Butler Yeats, "Under Ben Bulben" and "The Circus Animals' Desertion," from *Collected Poems* (New York: The Macmillan Company, 1940). Copyright 1940 by Georgie Yeats, renewed 1968 by Bertha Georgie Yeats, Michael Butler Yeats, and Anne Yeats. Reprinted by permission.

All inquiries and permissions requests should be addressed to the Publisher, Wesleyan University Press, 110 Mt. Vernon Street, Middletown, Connecticut 06457.

Distributed by Harper & Row Publishers, Keystone Industrial Park, Scranton, Pennsylvania 18512.

LIBRARY OF CONGRESS CATALOGING IN PUBLICATION DATA

Barrett, William, 1913–
    Time of need.
    Reprint. Originally published: 1st Harper torchbook ed. New York:
Harper & Row, 1973, c1972. Includes index.
    1. Civilization, Modern—20th century. 2. Arts and society.
3. Civilization—Philosophy. I. Title.
[CB425.B257 1984] 909.82 84-10416
ISBN 0-8195-6121-5 (pbk.: alk. paper)

Manufactured in the United States of America

Wesleyan Paperback, 1984

Contents

Illustrations

The time of need is long, it is the night of a world. The night must at long last gather to its own midpoint. At midnight the need reaches its peak. Then this famished time may become impotent even to feel its need. This impotence, which lets its own need get lost in the dark, is the starkest part of its need. . . . Perhaps the night of a world is now passing toward its midpoint. Perhaps our epoch is becoming completely such a time of need. Perhaps. But perhaps not, not yet, always not yet. . . .

—HEIDEGGER

Introduction

1. History Behind Our Backs

"History is what takes place behind our backs." So says Hegel, says Jean Paul Sartre. You may not find the exact words in Hegel. Sartre has a great gift for turning the insights of German philosophers into vivid and dramatic language, though sometimes their meaning becomes twisted to his own purposes. His paraphrase here, however, is entirely accurate to Hegel's thought. We may therefore take heart in setting out on these reflections under the sanction of a double quotation, which carries the authority of two very different philosophers.

History takes place behind our backs. We can see this clearly enough about the past. The men and women in history appear so often like actors striking out in the dark, buffeting each other amid shadows, "blind men battering blind men." Why did Napoleon invade Russia? It was the worst thing he could have done, and nothing compelled him to take that awful step. The Russians did not have ballistic missiles, and he was as far away from them as they from him and so had equally the protection of distance. Why didn't the Athenians and Spartans patch up their differences instead of dragging on a war from which ultimately neither side would recover? Pericles was a very enlightened statesman; and his famous speech on the Athenian war dead is one of the most intelligent eulogies of liberal civilization that has ever been made. But why couldn't he see that the virtues of Athenian life he praised had been nurtured by the city-state, and that this unique and precious institution would be so eroded by incessant local wars that it would at last be easily swept up into an empire like Alexander's? Thucydides tells us that both sides started the war for fear the other would

3

strike first. The words have an ominous ring for us today when each side fidgets at having to be the first to push the button. But of course we have good reason to fear, since the first strike could be the last one for its recipients, while the Athenians and Spartans, who had no atomic bombs, were being perfectly stupid. When we reflect on history, the blindness of its human actors appears indeed lamentable—but there always seem to be excuses for us.

We excuse ourselves, I think, mainly for two reasons. The first is the normal and natural sense of superiority the living must always feel toward the dead. We are alive and breathing and the people in history are not; and so we enjoy a privileged position in relation to all the kingdom of the dead. We are spectators who observe their follies from a sheltered position. Though we may be touched by their disasters, we are not part of them; and as we stand outside of their upheavals and turmoils, we unconsciously begin to feel that we must also be exempted from their short-sightedness and blindness.

The second reason, which is particular to our age and probably therefore more seductive, is our belief in our modern powers of information. Our journalism is so copious and proficient in digging up the facts, and our communications media so elaborate in broadcasting them, that news of what is happening anywhere in the world can flash before us on the screen at the mere switch of a dial. How could history be taking place behind our backs when we command such means of information? Besides, we have techniques for processing all that information: information systems, computers, social survey groups, Rand Corporations—they are all there ready to systematize, evaluate, and digest the great gobs of facts that are fed into them. Napoleon and Pericles may have been great men, but they had no such arsenals of information at their disposal. Of course, there are the old obstacles of human nature that will have to be overcome to make these powers of information effective. Vested interests or the passions of men may block the application of our knowledge. The inertia of negligence almost let our environment be destroyed before we took notice. But forewarned is forearmed, and nothing like that (so we assure ourselves) could happen again if we but stay resolutely well-informed. If we use all the resources of information, the historic process will not take place blindly behind our backs. Surely at last the ancient fates must give way to the instruments of modern knowledge.

So far this hope seems very remote. Perhaps it is our fate to live at the historic juncture where our agencies of information accumulate enough data to complicate matters but have not yet advanced to the point where they can resolve the complications they introduce. At any rate, there seems to be no definite ratio between the quantity of information fed into a computer and the wisdom of the decision that ensues. Probably more mountains of documents, more sheets of memoranda, more bulletins of information were consumed in order to produce our recent decisions in foreign policy than the whole Napoleonic administration handled through all the years of its reign. Yet the invasion of Cambodia and Laos does not seem to have been any wiser than Napoleon's march into Russia.

But without straying into the thickets of political controversy, we have more philosophic reasons to doubt that these powers of information will exempt us from the blindness of the past. Systems of information—and precisely to the degree that they seek to become more scientific—tend to lock themselves inside their own treadmill. The information will be more reliable the more it deals with hard facts. The harder the fact the more objective and measurable it must be; and thus the fact, to become sheer fact, must exclude everything that is not measured by its own self-imposed standards. So the fact becomes external, and therefore abstract. And the man perpetually buzzing after information usually misses what is really happening, especially in himself. That has been taking place in another region altogether—behind his back.

Art speaks to us from that other region, and at present it

ST. PHILIP'S COLLEGE LIBRARY

brings us a very different message from there. Contrary to the confidence in our powers of technology and information, the prevailing image of man we find in modern art is one of impotence, uncertainty, and self-doubt. Perhaps at no time in history has there been so glaring a contrast between the different ideas of itself that this age has fashioned in the two parts of its culture. Which is nearer the truth?

By modern art here we do not mean certain tendencies of the moment that now flourish in centers like New York. They represent an art of collapse and demoralization, which as so often happens in these cases can also mask itself behind a tasteless and boisterous self-assertion. Behind this temporary confusion there stands the great shadow of the modern movement in art, which is something else again. Perhaps we are not right to say it collapsed but that we of the present generation are no longer able to sustain its inner tensions. For what, in retrospect, was that art that came to be in the first half of this century but a perpetual questioning of its own tradition and even of the meaning and possibility of art itself? Time and again the artist seemed to push himself to the brink in order to find out whether art itself was still possible. There were the outbreaks of irritation in which it seemed that art itself must be rejected, like the mustache on the Mona Lisa or the stuffed monkey that Picabia exhibited as a "Portrait of Cézanne." But these displays of rejection were only part of the public vaudeville; secretly the artist was still hooked; the life of art in that period still lay in its inner tension with the forms of a tradition that it had to destroy in order to recast. The slate had to be wiped clean in order for art to be reborn. Naturally, this doubt of art could not stop there. Question any part of life insistently enough and the whole becomes involved; push art to the brink and the meaning of human life itself comes into question. No art of any period pushed so close—without succumbing—to the razor's edge of Nihilism.

In the same period, ironically enough, this question of Nihilism does not concern academic philosophers. In fact, it would seem rather naïve and gauche for a philosopher nowadays to ask, "Does life have a meaning?" Wittgenstein, one of the really important philosophers of the period, seems to have given the problem its *coup de grace*. The question cannot be properly stated, he tells us. The answer to the question of the meaning of life consists in the disappearance of the question. "Men to whom after long doubting the meaning of life became clear could not then say wherein this meaning consisted." He was quite right—at least for his thinking at that stage. The question cannot be stated in the language of facts. It cannot be fed into an information-system, which will then grind out an answer as one more item of information. A question of fact always returns us to the endless circle of facts, but this question lies outside that circle—in the realm of what Wittgenstein called, perhaps improperly, "the mystical."

What Wittgenstein means here may perhaps be made clear by a simple projection from the way things are now going. Imagine a society that has carried its information systems to the point where they can manage all the material data affecting its history. Here then at last we would have arrived at a stage where history can no longer happen behind our backs. But suppose further that this people begin to lose a sense of any meaning to the System or of their life generally. (One need not picture this world with the grimness of Orwell's *1984;* it might be as pleasantly bland as Disneyland.) They could not feed the question that assails them into their computers. The machine could record the material derangement in their life, but could not grasp the cause that brings it about. That would have crept up behind the back of both machines and men. This people could find no language to state what is afflicting them, which would thus become, quite literally, ineffable to them, and therefore belong to "the mystical."

Wittgenstein suffered this division in his own life. If he had merely dismissed the question as senseless, he might have been far more satisfying to orthodox positivism. Because he did not, he becomes a far more significant and representative modern spirit. The meaning of life was not for Wittgenstein the man, as for many positivists, a senseless and therefore pointless question. On the contrary, he held that questions of this kind are the most important ones a man can be concerned with. But he drew the line between the man and the philosopher within himself: philosophy could not speak with rigor about the things that concerned him most as a man and therefore philosophy must be silent about them. We are reminded of Kafka's strange figure of "the hunger artist" (whom we shall meet later) who starves himself for the probity of his art. When Wittgenstein said, "Of that whereof we cannot speak we must be silent," he really meant, unlike some philosophers who claim to follow him, that there was something to be silent about. And he persisted in the presence of that silence. He lived austerely in his chambers, and even had his meals there. Conversation with the other dons in the Commons dining room he found to be "neither of the heart nor of the head." Secretly he read Kierkegaard and thought him the greatest writer of the nineteenth century; but his own philosophy did not move in that direction. All his life he lived the question that he forbade philosophy to state.

But need we practice so cruel a self-mutilation? Need we take so narrow a view of philosophy? Must it deny itself a question which concerns us most as human beings? In any case, if philosophy cannot state this question art can express it. Art can bring before us the reality of individual characters who have lost or regained, or are in the process of losing or regaining, the meaning of life; and sometimes it brings before us the reality of the artist himself as he struggles at the edge of that meaning. The question here is no longer abstract but concrete. If philosophy is unable to state it formally, in art the question is nevertheless revealed as it is lived. And in the end philosophy has to bow to life and take notice. Through the means of art the nihilistic question can come out into the open and stand in the light. The philosopher has a chance to observe the human terrain out of which the question grows, and to follow the variety of shoots this subtle plant puts forth. For this he has to learn humility. He cannot force his conclusions. He cannot cerebrate but he must think—which means to let the work of art be what it is and follow it in its own terms. In doing so he may be surprised to learn that it will take him a good deal further than his cerebration might have gone on its own.

Accordingly, this book will try to follow the fortunes of Nihilism through some of its expressions in modern art. Of course, this century's art is too voluminous to be wrapped up in one package. We shall have to content ourselves with soundings here and there, mere random samples as it might seem. That they may not be too random we stick to fairly obvious and representative figures. And if we should seem therefore to be going over ground that is already well-trodden, at least we may have the reassurance that our conclusions about our age are not based on an eccentric choice of instances. But it would be a mistake to think these representative figures were chosen to fit into a general thesis, or even that they were consciously chosen at all. Rather, they clustered together out of the author's rather haphazard reading and looking, and the unifying ideas took shape from them.

No doubt, in all of this we shall be according a privileged position to the imagination and its powers. Not that we put forward art as a substitute for philosophy or religion; art simply opens the doors of our perception on the human phenomenology behind some of the questions of philosophy and religion. That is why the images of art provide us a deeper and more authentic record of an age than any factual history. In saying this we are only harking back to Aristotle's famous statement that "Poetry is more philosophical than history." But like many famous dicta of antiquity, this one has been repeated so often that we have forgotten its meaning, which we have to re-create for our own time. Aristotle's word *historia* has a wider scope than our "history": it would, for example, include all purely factual research into human behavior. We would thus have to recast his meaning in the form, "Poetry—or as we should prefer to say here, art—presents us a deeper truth about human life than all the researches of the behavioral sciences."

That is surely a bold claim, and a very disputable one; yet even our fact-minded culture admits in its clinical practices a privileged and revealing character to imagination. Dreams and fantasies may tell the psychiatrist more about the hidden depths of the patient's mind than do the external facts of his life. What the patient's imagination projects upon a few simple ink blots may reveal to the skilled diagnostician faults and clefts in the psychic substructure that have not yet erupted above the surface. The imagination of the artist goes beyond such idiosyncratic or clinical revelation. He creates a fantasy which holds and convinces other people; and which, so far as we all share it as art, expresses a truth valid for all of us. Art is thus quite literally, repeat literally, an expression of the collective soul of its time. The forms of imagination that any epoch produces are an ultimate datum on what that epoch is. Looking at these forms, we have to say this is truly what our age is, this is what we truly are. If the images of modern art may sometimes seem extreme to us, they really are not; the extremity is already in us but we have not yet come to recognize it.

I

The mortal form with which we shall mostly be dealing here is the novel. Here is a literary genre which, up till recent years, was held for its scope and flexibility to be the most adequate mirror of reality. Its readers saw within this mirror the boundless variety, tragic or comic or both as the case might be, of life itself. For a while even, during the nineteenth century, the novel almost overcame that chasm between the "two audiences"—lowbrow and highbrow—that yawns unpleasantly before all modern art. Dickens and Tolstoy, for example, undoubtedly belonged to great and serious literature, yet all who could read might be queuing up for the next installment from these authors. Moreover, as history, the novel is the literary form which, for certain periods at least, best re-created the actual quality of the life of its time. Dip into one of the Victorian novels, and that epoch comes to life more vividly than through the facts of any historical text. The novel was, in effect, the form of existential history *par excellence.*

The form reached its culmination in the realistic novel of the nineteenth century. Balzac, Stendhal, Flaubert, Zola in France; Turgenev, Dostoevsky, Tolstoy in Russia; in England Jane Austen, Dickens, Thackeray, George Eliot, Trollope. Varied as their individual visions are, they represent a triumph of realism over the older romance. True, the novel was a flexible enough form to permit the writer other effects, like fantasy or the grotesque; but those were fringe benefits, as it were, since the heart of the novel, its self-appointed destiny, had come to be its ability to portray the reality of everyday life more accurately than any other literary form.

We have spoken of it as a "mortal form"—and with good reason. Movies already usurp the place of the novel so far as the larger audience is concerned. A civilization that thirsts for immediacy, for instant meaning and instant sensation, finds expression in an art form that is far more immediate and instantaneous in its impact than the written word. But even apart from such external usurpation, there were internal tensions within the realistic novel that were to lead to its varied metamorphoses. We once took this novel so much for granted—as young readers the great examples of realistic fiction were almost our daily bread—that we tend to forget what a long history went into its making. People have always told stories as long as mankind had language, but not every narrative fits the requirements of realism. The realistic novel arose out of a number of special conditions that only modern Western society could provide. They are also the conditions from which all modern art develops.

Here we must go to the scholars for help. We take as our guide Erich Auerbach's *Mimesis*, one of the most remarkable works of literary interpretation in recent decades and perhaps the most penetrating history of the realistic novel yet written. Auerbach was a humanist in the older European sense of that word, which implies the combination of great learning and sensitivity. His book is also a work of touching piety. Though he suffered the upheavals of this century, forced as a Jew to flee Nazi Germany and take refuge in Turkey, where he taught and wrote for a long time in obscurity, his serene faith in the humanities and humane civilization nevertheless persisted through the dark years when it looked as if Fascism might take over all of Europe. The subtitle of his book, "The Representation of Reality in Western Literature," indicates its breadth. It also fits in with our present purposes. We are in search of the reality of the twentieth century as it appears in some of its representations. The two—reality and representation—necessarily go together. Neither without the other: reality is what we imagine it to be; and, conversely, the representation cannot be examined as a thing in itself apart from the reality it reveals. Auerbach sticks close to the text, but he is anything but a routine philologist. The text of the novel articulates its whole world. Everything in that world must be found in the words of the narrative itself—in the manner and matter of its telling. And so by interpreting texts, Auerbach can make abundantly clear how many diverse influences—religious and philosophical, social and political, aesthetic and stylistic—had to converge at that point where a great literary form like the realistic novel could be born.

Here is the gist of that history:

Neither the Greeks nor the Romans, from whom we got our other literary genres, possessed the form of the novel as we have known it. They had epic and tragedy, which dealt with heroic figures grander than life; ordinary men and women could only be subjects of comedy. Classical literature was thus built firmly upon the doctrine of the "two styles": the sublime and serious style proper to epic and tragedy; the low or "humble" style, which was to be exploited by comedy. In its aesthetic tastes, as well as its social attitudes, classical civilization remained thoroughly aristocratic despite all political fluctuations. Between the extraordinary and the ordinary man there appeared to them to be such a gulf that they would have thought it poor taste, a slighting of nature, to override the difference.

The Greeks could never have taken a play like Arthur Miller's *Death of a Salesman* as a genuine tragedy: the hero is too average and ordinary for his destruction to seem anything more than a grimly pathetic social statistic. To sound the tone of sublimity, tragedy must deal with noble and extraordinary individuals above the average run of mankind. Ordinary men die miserably every day, and we cannot be expected to feel pity and terror—the emotions of tragedy—for the passage of each. If we as an audience are to collaborate as spectators in the destruction of a man, we must at least feel we encounter someone in an exalted and interesting condition. As for the tragicomic, which makes up so much of the substance of our daily life, that is mere human muddle that the purity of art has to exclude. To mix tragedy and comedy would be as tasteless a performance as, to borrow Horace's image, the painting of a human face that ended in a fish's tail. We so often forget the differences that Christianity brought in that we overlook the gulf that separates us from the ancients. To modern tastes their aesthetic credo must appear almost brutally aristocratic.

The realistic novel is built upon a premise that is the exact opposite of this aristocratic doctrine of the "two styles." The novelist descends into the depths of ordinary life in order to find there material that can be serious, problematic, and tragic. By the nineteenth century this premise had been validated, in the only way aesthetic premises can be: great works had been produced according to its rules, and these works were impressive enough to be placed beside the grand works of the ancients. And though the medium of the novel was prose, it nevertheless could command resources of style that had their own peculiar resonance and sublimity.

What brought about this major revolution in imagination and taste? For one thing, Western civilization had also been formed by Biblical and Christian influences, which were far more democratic in spirit than the Greco-Roman inheritance. In Christianity, particularly, the whole of the historic drama had turned upon the life of one person, Jesus, who had been born among the poorest classes and recruited his followers there. The rise of Christianity and its sweep of the ancient world were testimony that history-shaking events could be initiated from what had been hitherto taken as the lower depths of mankind. God himself had taken on flesh and been born of woman amid these humble elements of society and therefore brought them at last into the purview of history. Here was the archetypical example to show that the sublime might also be found within the sphere of ordinary life. These transcendent possibilities of ordinary humanity had even been imparted to the women of the lower classes, and Dante toward the end of *The Divine Comedy* addresses his prayer to the Virgin:

> Thou art she who did so ennoble
> Human nature that its Creator did not disdain
> To become its creature.

Still, the classical principle of the two styles held out stubbornly against this Christian impulse. Literary men were formed within the classical mold, for to be literary one had to be at least literate, and to be literate then was to be steeped in the great works that had been handed down by the ancients. Cervantes is a good example of this division of mind in writers at the period when the novel was being born. His *Don Quixote* is often called the first realistic novel, since it gives an extraordinarily full-bodied picture of common life throughout the length and breadth of Spain toward the end of the sixteenth century. Yet Cervantes himself was a little puzzled by its enormous success with the public, and he continued to believe that his *Galatea,* which followed the form of the classical pastoral romance, was a greater achievement. Writers, even the greatest, can become riveted upon stylistic traditions. Cervantes was also a traditionalist on the matter of chivalry. Contrary to the common belief that he hated the romances of chivalry and wrote *Don Quixote* in order to demolish them, the fact is that he loved those romances and deplored only the bad ones written at his time. He himself had fought in the chivalric armies under Don Juan of Austria that defeated the Turks at Lepanto in 1571, and had almost lost his left hand in that battle. But history can take place behind the back even of the man who is making it, for despite its author's intentions *Don Quixote* did make chivalry ridiculous and hurry on its demise. The chivalric classes had to disappear before the appropriate conditions for the modern realistic novel could emerge. The democratizing fervor latent in Christianity had to become secularized through the gradual spread of egalitarian ideas and of democratic institutions.

More than this: the writer's consciousness of history itself had to be transformed. The novelist who would descend into his own time and depict realistically its actual conditions must feel that the present is unique and its particularities pregnant with meaning. If history moved in a circle, then the point on the wheel where he now stood was of peripheral importance; the wheel would continue turning in any case. The Greeks and Romans had regarded history largely as cycle and repetition: individual variations of men and events upon perennial types and themes. History, as Polybius put it, is "ethics teaching by examples." Only if the present repeats the past can one learn anything valuable from the examples provided by historical studies.

The Bible of the Hebrews, on the other hand, presented an altogether different panorama of universal history. In the beginning God created heaven and earth, and man as a part of this creation. There was a beginning, and what begins must move toward some end. Consequently, history had a direction; it did not repeat itself, as the Greeks thought, in endless cycles. With Christianity, this direction of history took on an even more definite cast. History began with the fall of man, when Adam and Eve sinned in the garden of Eden, and moves forward to its ultimate end in the Last Judgment when the damned will be consigned to hell and the elect be established in the heavenly city. And here once again the Enlightenment of the eighteenth century proceeded to secularize an orginally Christian idea: social progress took the place of spiritual redemption, the heavenly city of the saints was replaced by the utopian society of the future; the elect were the social progressives and the damned (to be consigned in this case to the hell of liquidation) were those who resisted this forward march of History. The future would not repeat the follies of the past but succeed at last in redeeming mankind from barbarism, superstition, and irrationality. Hence the present in which we live is unique and irreplaceable because it is the arena in which decisions that could alter the whole life of mankind in the future may be made. It therefore provides the writer with the most compelling material he could possibly treat.

In fact, most of the great writers in the century that followed the Enlightenment were either suspicious of or downright hostile to the idea of progress. Still, its prevalence did transform the general consciousness and provided the background against which they wrote. Even those most pessimistic about modernity wrote with a sense of vast commotions of the human spirit going on, of rumblings in the depths that, however ominous in their drift, must become an essential part of the novelist's subject matter. Even on its negative side, the uniqueness of the present provided a striking theme: if the time were stale and unprofitable, there was the conflict and tragedy of the hero who dared to struggle against it.

That was Stendhal's theme in *The Red and the Black*, and it was a landmark in the history of the novel when he added the subtitle to it, "Chronicle of the Year 1830." The subtitle indicates that the characters and their actions in the novel are not fully intelligible apart from the historical conditions of France at that time. Stendhal the realist was not seeking to portray reality generally but the reality of 1830. We can hardly imagine a novelist doing this a century earlier. Fielding's *Tom Jones*, for example, is also the story of a young man who is an outsider seeking to win a place for himself in society. (In other respects, of course, Tom Jones and Julien Sorel are miles apart in temperament.) But Fielding could not have added a subtitle "Chronicle of the Year 1749" without going against his own artistic intention, which was to depict not the actual conditions of his own age but pervasive comic types that could just as well be located in any other historical milieu or moment. It took almost another hundred years before the novelist felt himself so existentially rooted in his own time that his art sought to become the mirror of its uniqueness.

The foregoing has been hardly more than a condensation of Auerbach's history, with some philosophical interpolations of my own. Henceforth we begin to diverge from Auerbach.

After so much history the realistic novel had at last arrived. The novelist took upon himself the task of descending into the depths of his own time to become the subtlest and profoundest recorder of contemporary life. The novel became history more revealing than actual history—ah, but precisely because it was fiction. In their aesthetic theory the realists never solved this paradox. They presented imaginary characters more real than actual personages in the news; and their readers understood themselves and the life of their time more deeply through these men and women in novels that they might imagine themselves to be than through the factual reports they scanned in journals and periodicals. How could this be reconciled with a literary theory that remained chained to stark actuality? How is it that man becomes more revealed to himself through the forms of his imagination than through the reportage of facts?

The theory did not count for much among the English and Russians, in whom other motives were at work. Realism as a self-conscious theory played an important role only among the French, who in their tidy way do not like to launch a literary movement without its appropriate manifesto. Practice may depart quite a bit from it, but the program must be there. It gives such reassurance of one's clarity. In this case it did make clear the climate in which realism was born—a climate dominated in France by positivism and the spirit of science. In his introduction to the *Comédie Humaine* Balzac tells us that this vast series of novels is intended to be a "natural history" of French society of the time, carried out in the same dispassionate spirit as the natural histories that scientists produce of the animal world. This was a dreadful confusion of the purposes of science and art, and of course the artist could not remain within that framework. Balzac is full of exaggerated and grotesque effects, touches of mysticism, and even magical demonism that link him up with the Romantics. Nor could any of the other great realists adhere entirely to their credo. Stendhal, the social chronicler, was always haunted by his own romantic dream of an Italy that never really existed as he imagined it. In Flaubert this division becomes anguish. In *Madame Bovary*, probably the most perfect example of the realistic novel, he dissects mercilessly the romantic illusions of a wretched woman, but he could not kill the Madame Bovary in himself. From that petty material reality which he had depicted with such scrupulous fidelity his spirit had to escape into another age when saints once were real *(St. Julian the Hospitaler)* and into the dream of barbaric splendor in ancient Carthage *(Salammbô).*

The pull between romanticism and realism in these writers

was, philosophically speaking, a case of the perennial tension between imagination and actuality. In theory realism never resolved this opposition; but in practice the great realistic novelists rode roughshod, as life always does, over contradictions in theory and triumphed as artists. In their works the realistic novel reached its pinnacle in the nineteenth century.

But it could not stay there. Reality never stays still; and when our reality changes our modes of representing it must alter. The world has become more complex and fragmentary to us, and the consequent changes in artistic form have often been shocking to readers used to more traditional patterns. In the novel these innovations fall under two main headings: (1) the fragmentation of time and (2) the fragmentation of character.

1. In the traditional plot time is a straightforward sequence of events from earlier to later. Imagine it as a straight line along which we move from past through present into the future. All the parts of the line are external each to each. This is the time in which we are good public citizens, keep our appointments and pay our bills punctually, and reckon each day in the calendar as identical with another. In short, it is an accurate picture of time so far as it is an impersonal and public affair. Where time becomes an intimate and personal reality, the line bears little resemblance to the concrete reality. Yesterday came before today, certainly; but yesterday can also be present and potent in the reality of today. And tomorrow, which has not arrived, may already poison or redeem today. The novelist may therefore abandon the straight line of chronological plot in order to represent past, present, and future as layers that underlie each other. And even that spatial metaphor will not do, for the layers do not lie under but penetrate each other. Proust thought there was a special connection between memory and the sense of smell. And with good reason. An aroma may penetrate a room, impalpable and diffuse but overwhelmingly present, like the unpicturable reality of time itself. It is the nearest image we can find in the sensory world for the pecularly pervasive but bodi-

less presence of time. Was Proust consumed by memories because as an asthmatic he trembled at the slightest odor?

Even worse: time does not have the simple homogeneity of space. Dense and concentrated here, rarefied and vacuous there, the parts of time are not indifferently equal to one another. Our moments do not march past us like a procession of identical and faceless marionettes. Their unique qualities extend, distend, and leap over the continuum of time, if indeed it be a continuum at all. An event of ten years ago, charged with meaning, may be closer to me than last week's trivia. And, who knows, ten years from now some unpredictable cause may excavate those trivia and bring them closer than the bagatelles of that moment. Any experience may thus be located in a number of different temporal perspectives. Inevitably this will bring on comparison with the world of Einstein's physics. The comparison is permissible provided we understand that the artist's discovery is his own and independent of such ideological scavenging. The novelist may be compelled, sometimes to the bewilderment of his reader, to move backwards and forwards in his chronology in order to indicate this multidimensional order that the varied density of time imposes. In Auerbach's terms: the representation of time in the modern novel becomes "multi-layered, multi-dimensional, and multi-perspectival."

Time looms here like a monster with many heads. That is a heavy burden for consciousness to carry. It is easy to see why some writers would want to be free of it—to escape into the Now of the pure present, for example, like Ernest Hemingway. But that strategy too, as we shall see, also carries its own renunciations. Time disappears from the world of Kafka because his hero is impotent to enter the world of human time, blocked by an impossible calling and the cruel whim of the higher powers. The strategies may be varied. But behind them all lies that sense of time as problematical and baffling—multidimensional and multilayered—that was unexplored by the novelists of the nineteenth century.

2. As with time so with our human reality that is spun out within it. Character dissolves into a multitude of perspectives. A personality is not a hard outline given all at once and persisting in that constant form throughout the narrative. There are layers below layers, and at each level the psychological topography may show us a different map. The process may be carried so far that in some novels the character tends to disappear into these perspectives and layers altogether, as in the canvases of some abstract artists the figure is painted out. The hero becomes a problem without a solution because the terms of definition can never be stated. "I was never really there," Beckett's character exclaims over his absence from his own life.

These were not merely innovations in technique. True, they began as devices to extend the scope of realism. By means of the stream of consciousness and multiple perspectives the writer could bring the reader closer to the texture of actual experience. Our scholar guide Auerbach, for example, considers these newer developments as variations in the history of realism. But he knew only the forward wave of the modern movement, and he deals with it only as it fits into the general history of realism. These changes in our sense of time and human character are too fundamental to be stuffed back into the mold of realism. Of course all art does bring us before reality in some sense. But the realists had a much more exclusive sense of reality in mind than that. In retrospect we can see better than they could what their presuppositions were: reality was mainly external and physical; it presupposed a world stable within chronological time, the unbroken chain of cause and effect, and characters who had the definiteness of things or objects and were the products of that causal chain. Back of realism, in short, there lay the philosophy of scientific materialism; and this becomes explicit in France in the case of Zola and his followers. Very much a nineteenth-century philosophy, and in its way a very abstract and selective version of reality.

The realistic illusion is to forget the selective character of all art. (Of course I am talking again about the theory of the realists; their practice was and had to be quite different.) The realist cannot transcribe "a slice of life," to use that woeful slogan. Even in the writing of so-called realistic dialogue you cannot take down stenographically exactly what people say. To cite a realist close to home: John O'Hara is said to have a good ear, and he does; but read him carefully and you will see that the dialogue of his characters is as formal in its rhythms as the hexameters of Racine. All art is artifice, and realism became a great style only because it was as stylized and selective as any other convention in the history of art. Its reality, consequently, is only one among the various realities that art offers. Every form is the sum of its negations and inclusions. The narratives of myth and saga may lack the meticulous fidelity to external facts, but they lay hold of a truth about man and his cosmos that may be lost under the details of documentation.

Besides, when the house is about to come down, who is interested in counting the furniture? As time and human personality dissolve into perspectives, the meaning of existence itself becomes questionable. Nihilism becomes an increasingly prevalent theme. And perhaps not so much theme as threat; for the subject seems not so much chosen as lying unexpectedly in ambush, ready to assault the writer's imagination with a vision of a world without meaning. Beside this prospect that man and his world may be emptied of their value the details of realistic accuracy seem beside the point. We are thrown back upon ultimate questions, and the imagination must cast about for more primal and elemental forms in which to find sustenance. Thus what began as experiments in the novel to bring it closer to the fluid texture of reality became in the end a drive to get beyond realism itself, to recapture if possible the pristine reality of myth that was available to the ancient storytellers.

That may be the key to all modern art: the need to return to the source of art itself. The innovations in the novel have to be understood along with parallel dislocations in form in the other arts, in painting, sculpture, and music. The same *Zeitgeist*, after all, is at work in all of them. The imagination has had to free itself from the tedium of reportage. Much destruction has ensued on the way. Indeed, an observer from outside might very well say of our art of the last fifty years that there seems let loose in it a rage to destroy, as if the culture itself were bent on working toward conclusions that destroy its own premises. Yes, but in this rage to destroy may be present the birthpangs of a new reality struggling for expression. That is the reality through which all of us are now living, though it becomes clear only at moments in the imaginative utterance of a few. And it is there that we must look for the history that is taking place behind our backs.

Part I

The World Without Meaning

2. Nihilism and Lucidity

To live with what I know—and only that.

January 4, 1960; end of a midwinter vacation; two men in an automobile driving back to Paris from the South of France. The trip seems in every way ordinary. But on the way to Paris it begins to rain. Not too heavily, but enough to make the road slippery. Suddenly the car skids, spins off the road, and crashes. The driver is only shaken up. His passenger, beside him, is instantly killed.

This kind of accident, happening to person or persons unknown, is reported every day in the papers. It has become part of the banality of our modern environment. When the man killed is Albert Camus, a famous writer still young and at the height of his powers, we call this death absurd. Perhaps there is no greater absurdity in the one case than in the other. From the point of view of chance, which dispenses our mortality so casually, one death is an indifferent fact like any other. Yet we persist in counting one man's death as different from another. "I call this death shameful," Sartre wrote in a eulogy the next day, thus surrendering, despite what he had said elsewhere in his philosophy, to our invincible human urge to internalize death within a life, to give it the stamp of the dead man's person. He had been a close friend of Camus, then an intellectual antagonist; but he buried past differences to deliver a moving assessment of what Camus had come to mean to his time. He was one of the very few in our day, Sartre said, who seemed to be seeing a light at the end of the tunnel. After all that toil of the spirit, to be coming near the end of the fetid tunnel, and

27

then to be snuffed out—absurd! Camus might have replied that that is precisely the absurdity of our condition: that we go on demanding that our human meanings (in this case, to get to the end of the tunnel) ought to escape the indifference of fate.

Shameful or not, the accident seems almost like an illustration lifted from some of his early pages on the absurd. Life, when it imitates art, is usually singularly uninventive. On the other hand, for a man who had lucidly faced the question whether human life was meaningless, this was an appropriate death. The irony became a little grimmer when later an unused railway ticket was found in Camus' pocket. He had been planning to take the train, but at the last moment his friend and publisher Gallimard (the driver) had persuaded him that it would be a pleasanter trip by car.

At the time of his death Camus had become more than a writer to his many readers; he was a moral conscience for thousands of young people in Europe and the United States, as he is still today. He was the model of a committed writer; he had been through everything to gain his ticket to modernity: the Communist party and his break with it, the encounter with Existentialism, a Nihilism that still permitted him to speak with exaltation of the human lot, the dangerous life of the Resistance, a crusade for justice that seemed to lift him above the battle of conflicting political ideologies. Yet with all these credentials of involvement, he is a rather paradoxical figure with which to begin an exploration of modernism in art and literature. From the experimentation in form and language that has been one of the hallmarks of modern literature, Camus remained aloof, deliberately pursuing a kind of classicism that takes us back, beyond the realistic novel of the nineteenth, to the *récit*, the short moralizing tale, of the eighteenth century. More and more, toward the end, he began to feel uncomfortable with much of the art of our time, and he even expressed condemnation of its artistic aims. His most explicit attack is in a late essay, "Helen's Exile," which seems to me not to have been noticed enough by his commentators. Helen is the ancient symbol of human beauty, and modern artists, in Camus' view, have exiled her from our midst to pursue an art of tortured expressionism. Are we really incapable of those antique and sumptuous images of beauty? Imprisoned in our gray northern cities, we relegate the feast of the senses to the southern sunlit civilizations.

In retrospect, with all his work laid open before us, Camus quite clearly never gave up his North African heritage; and for him that meant the heritage of the Mediterranean and the ancient Greeks. In temperament he remained something of a provincial, a *colon*, an Algerian Frenchman. Even in politics, despite his radical beginnings, there was a streak of conservatism in his nature—though this conservatism can be easily misunderstood and was in fact deliberately misrepresented by his left-wing opponents. In France, where the whole culture is so overwhelmingly centralized in Paris, the provincial writer is apt to resist this Parisian atmosphere by insisting on a kind of peasant identity and therefore tends to run in a conservative mold. Though it may seem at first strange to say so, there is a certain kinship between Camus and writers like Maurice Barrès and Charles Maurras. Not for their reactionary politics certainly, for that side of them would have been abhorrent to Camus. But then, that is because both Barrès and Maurras chose to be ideologists, and since they were not of the Left, their ideology had to be of the Right. Camus' politics cannot be systematized; he avoided ideology, and toward the end his political utterances revolved around particular social questions and the complex problem of justice in dealing with each issue on its own terms. But of course, this insistence on the limitation and sobriety of political discourse must nowadays strike many as very conservative indeed.

Yet, we may well begin with Camus, for he poses with a thematic clarity the problems that have haunted our century. So far as Nihilism is concerned, there have been more drastic and powerful expressions of this attitude in contemporary letters. To confine ourselves just to the French: Céline's *Journey to the End of Night*, with its convulsive disgust, is a more explosive blast against the human race and its varied sordidness; Samuel Beckett has gone further in reducing the nihilistic equation to the ultimate terms that $0 = 0$; and Jean Genêt has attacked the values of society with a more baroque and shocking violence. But Camus has something these writers lack: the balance and grace of classicism. We feel, consequently, with him that we are facing the nihilistic issues themselves rather than some obscure individual malady or misfortune that is not the lot of everyman. "The Cartesian of the Absurd," Sartre called him, meaning that even in this murky atmosphere where ordinary human standards become clouded Camus is nevertheless compelled, like the great Descartes, to pursue clear and distinct ideas. This clarity assists us in getting our bearings, although, as we shall see, it is often deceptive and ambiguous.

There is also the further advantage in taking off from Camus that his writings fall into a rather neat and symmetrical pattern. There are two principal periods, each of them marked by the parallel, or almost parallel, publication of a novel and a book of essays that "explain" the novel. Thus one speaks, with a certain pedagogical simplification, of Camus I and Camus II. In the first phase we have the novel *The Stranger* and its companion volume of essays, *The Myth of Sisyphus*. This is the Camus of alienation, exploring the solitary ego in its confrontation of the absurdities of human existence. He says "I," but he has not yet learned to say "We." In the second phase (a decade later) we have the essays of *The Rebel* and, finally, his last novel, *The Fall*. Here attention has shifted from the individual outside society to human brotherhood. The question of suicide which haunts the individual in his self-confrontation gives way to the question of murder and its justification, if ever, as an action by the group. Camus has here learned to way "We." Between these two stages of his development there occurs the novel *The Plague*, which makes clear how the transition is made from the "I" to the "We": under the threat of the plague, which can kill any of us, we learn that we are all bound to one another under the same sentence of death.

A very neat and symmetrical development indeed! But the reader must be warned, even as we make use of it, that pedagogical schemes like this have at best only a provisional and approximate truth. A writer cannot be cut up into such tidy packages. It is a measure of his talent that he comes to us as a whole being in anything that he writes, and the same being even though his points of view may shift. Camus' earliest writings—sketches of Algerian life for a local newspaper—already sound the keynote which provides the resolving chords for his last works: that in the end we are saved through the body and its tie to the earth, which bring with them the wisdom of knowing our limitations. Camus' development is real and deep enough, and one of the most instructive amid the choppy intellectual crosscurrents of our time; but it is a development that returns him more and more to what he was to begin with.

With such admonitions out of the way, we begin with the period of his experiment with nihilism: fictionally incarnate in the novel *The Stranger* and accompanied by the philosophical exploration of *The Myth of Sisyphus*.

I

Meursault, the hero of *The Stranger*, is an obscure clerk, a nobody pushed along passively by the stream of life. He has no trait that would single him out except a certain honesty about his own feelings. (In this respect he embodies Camus' own injunction that one should learn to live lucidly and without self-deception.) When his mother, who has been living in an old people's home, dies, Meursault does not weep; he has no particular feelings at the funeral—his own and his mother's life have gone separate paths—except a sense of fatigue and heat. He has a brief affair with a girl; and while he enjoys swimming and making love with her, he cannot say that he loves her. When she asks him if he does, he replies, "That has no meaning"— though he is willing to marry her if she wants him to.

This indifferent compliance is quite astonishing. Having no extraordinary claim upon life, he is willing to go along with other people so as not to raise any trouble. His neighbor across the hall, Raymond, not a particularly attractive type, forces friendship upon him. Meursault is not especially eager, but he lets it happen. "Ça m'est égal"—it's all the same to me—is his persistent response to life.

Raymond becomes involved in a scuffle with some Arabs, and Meursault, through a series of trivial accidents, kills one of them. He cannot say why he has done it. The Arab had drawn a knife, but Meursault had only to walk away for the encounter to end. Perhaps he has done it because of the heat; at any rate, the scorching air over the Algerian beach made it impossible for him to think. It is an "absurd" murder—as meaningless as most of the other links in the chain of Meursault's life. His is a passive destiny, and the murder itself is something that comes over him passively. A few minutes earlier, he had thought: "And just then it had crossed my mind that one might fire, or not fire—and it would come to absolutely the same thing." All things—including the pulling of a trigger or not pulling it—are of equal value. Such is the lucid indifference of the absurd man.

The second part of the novel deals with Meursault's trial and conviction. The sense of absurdity now shifts to the whole apparatus of justice. Lawyers, judges, and jury appear to dance in a weird *ballet mécanique*, a rigid parody of human justice, as they proceed to take the life of another judicial victim in a way that has little to do with the individual truth of the condemned man himself. Later Camus was to become one of the most prominent spokesmen against capital punishment, and this stand is already implicit in his first novel. Witnesses from the old people's home are introduced to testify that Meursault did not cry at his mother's funeral, implying thereby that he was not a man of good will. In this absurd world a man is condemned to death because he did not weep at his mother's funeral.

Through the procedures of the trial Meursault remains with the detached attitude of the spectator. Still the outsider, he is isolated from other human beings and the senseless machinery of society. But in prison the climax of the novel occurs, and Meursault, galvanized at last into revolt, acquires a human identity. A priest visits him in his cell and talks to him about God and the next world. Suddenly, Meursault has had enough; and in an outburst of passion—the first he shows in this book—he declares that he is loyal to this earth, and that all the religious abstractions of the priest are not worth one strand of a woman's hair. Left alone again, after the priest has gone, Meursault confronts his death with a somber exaltation. It is in the face of death that he has risen to human authenticity. All men are under this same sentence of death, and the few brief moments of life that are left them make them all privileged. In his revolt, he hopes only that on the day of his execution there will be an immense crowd of spectators who will greet him with howls of execration.

However significant the change in Camus' later attitudes, he nevertheless preserves a basic continuity on the matter of rebellion. It is in rebelling that Meursault, like the man of the later work *The Rebel*, achieves the only authenticity that is possible for him—when he draws a line and says in effect, "So far you have gone, but no further; take my life, but do not try to dupe me; leave me with my own lucidity and my own truth." The difference is that Meursault remains solitary in his revolt; he cannot say, like the man of *The Rebel*, "I rebel, therefore we (my brothers under the yoke of injustice) exist"—that is, are drawn together in a common cause. Meursault, in his rebellion, is still the stranger, the outsider to the rest of mankind; they are the Others, and his enemy.

Meursault is a curious kind of outsider beside the varieties of alienated figures thrown up by the literature of the nineteenth century. Only by placing him alongside them do we gain an

idea of the distinct historical coloration of Nihilism in our time
—of the odd and deceptive shapes this specter now assumes a
hundred years after it burst, like the Underground Man of Dostoevsky, out of the European cellar.

II

In Balzac's *Comédie Humaine*, Rastignac, as a young man on
the make, is a historically new kind of character. Gazing out
over Paris, he shakes his fist at the swarming city as at a mortal
enemy and declares: "I will conquer you." Rastignac is an outsider—but in a much less alienated sense than Meursault. He is
outside his society because he is not yet on the inside command-
ing it. What he lacks is merely social and economic position.
There is no metaphysical dimension to Rastignac's alienation.
The society itself, in which he wishes to come to the top, is not
placed fundamentally in question. Stendhal's Julien Sorel, in
The Red and the Black, experiences a similar kind of alienation,
though his rejection of his society goes deeper than Rastignac's.
Julien finds his society mediocre and boring, and therefore
would like to see it changed more completely; though there is
always the prospect that, if he can get to the top, he can make
things a little livelier, or at least they will seem more lively from
that vantage point. Neither Rastignac nor Sorel has been
touched by the withering finger of nihilism. Their values are
never in doubt, and they are driven by a Napoleonic will in
pursuit of these values. In comparison with them, Meursault is
an outsider even to ambitions. Those in society who do nourish
ambition are to him the "others"—beings to whom he is
remote. He is content to drift so long as he can just keep his
head above water. Life for him is, as James Joyce put it, many
days, day after day.

It is with the nineteenth-century Russians that the figure of
the outsider acquires an ultimately philosophical depth. Russia
is the land where nihilism first appears as a dedicated and orga-

nized movement of destruction. A representative nihilist of the 1850s is found in Bazarov of Turgenev's *Fathers and Sons;* and later Dostoevsky was to portray the same kind of nihilist in the throes of a religious and metaphysical convulsion. Turgenev's Bazarov is intent on destroying the existing order. What he would replace it with is not so clear, for the Russian nihilists had not yet made contact with the doctrine of Marx—a historic encounter that would come with Lenin. So far, Bazarov's revolt has, it would seem, only social and political dimensions. He is alienated not from existence itself—or at least he expresses no such alienation—but from the specific kind of social order that surrounds him. Yet the passion of his estrangement is so intense that it has metaphysical implications. Bazarov is pledged to science and the rational corrosion of all values that rest on anything other than science. He is young; and in the short-sightedness of youth, he does not have the imagination—which would later trouble Dostoevsky and Nietzsche—to see that the destruction of religion with its transcendent values, and the absolute reign of reason in the form of the physical sciences, would beget some fearful problems of their own in the due course of history. His hatred of the existing order is so intense that it is a religious fanaticism. In its grip, he has no question at all about the meaning of life. That meaning is guaranteed him by his single and unwavering passion for destruction.

In Dostoevsky, however, the nihilist is thrown open to the most probing kind of self-questioning, and in some cases he even initiates the process of tormented self-inquisition himself. The question of nihilism, for Dostoevsky, does not involve re-forming the social order; it demands the ultimate decision for or against God; and if the latter option be taken, then every-thing is permitted—all values are equal—and the engineer Kirillov (in *The Possessed*), convinced that there is no God, kills himself in order to assert his own freedom. Even when the outsider, as in *Notes from Underground*, is indicated to be a social phenomenon—a creature regularly and inevitably produced in the bureaucratic operations of modern society—his fulminations have an ultimately metaphysical content, as he rages against materialistic philosophy.

Camus' hero is altogether different from these predecessors, and the degree of this difference is a revelation of how far and fast history has moved since the nineteenth century. Meursault does not want society changed. The social mechanism is so incomprehensible and absurd in his eyes that he could not even begin to imagine at what point it might be changed; and even if it were changed, he would find the new order just about the same. As for the ultimate philosophical questions, Meursault is totally unaware of them. The question "What meaning does life have?" would itself be meaningless to him—at least as he is when we meet him at the beginning of the book. He has not risen yet to the level of any such question. Moreover, this hero, who is supposed to be so bleak a nihilist, is a likable person. Something of Camus himself—a fond identification with his own creature—has rubbed off on his character. Whereas the Russian writers of the nineteenth century presented their heroes as monstrous warnings to society, the nihilist of Camus is the silent fellow next door, though just a little more honest in his feelings and without the sentimental slogans of the common man. If Meursault is any evidence, mankind has had no trouble surviving the death of God, which nineteenth-century writers—whether believers or atheists—looked on with so much apprehension. God is so very much dead that for Meursault the word itself has lost any meaning; and when the priest who visits him in his cell exhorts him to turn his thoughts that way, Meursault cannot understand why this man should direct any passion in that direction.

Seen in this historical perspective, Meursault emerges, not so much an outsider, but very much an insider in the world of today. Camus later observed dryly of his character, "He does not ask questions." Millions of human beings now live in his estrangement from the ultimate questions—or what were thought to be ultimate questions in the last century. He is a perfectly ordinary fellow, a waif of society, an insignificant clerk without distinction or ambitions. There must be millions like him. However, most lack Meursault's stubborn honesty that will not be beguiled by machine-made sentimentalities, mass slogans, or empty abstractions. This is the one respect in which Camus lifts his character out of the rut of the mass man and makes him a vehicle suitable for his own ideas. Meursault retains the dogged courage of his honesty, and he is true to his own sensations of the physical world. He likes the girl Marie because he enjoys with her the pleasures of the flesh—swimming and making love—but that is all. When she asks him if he loves her, this question too is another abstraction that has no meaning for him. The absurd man remains loyal to the earth and to the truth of his own sensations. Quite obviously, among his other predecessors, he also inherits Hemingway's ideal of the virile and masculine hero.

The Myth of Sisyphus, as a philosophical essay, is not to be taken as the "explanation" of *The Stranger* as a novel. The latter stands on its own two feet as a work of art. A novel may be as philosophical as you please; but if it is to succeed as a novel, it must so embody its ideas that no exposition in the way of philosophy is required for its comprehension. Nevertheless, the two works are companion pieces; they were published in the same year, 1942, and they give us two different facets of Camus' feelings about life at that time. Despite his effort to make the essays of *Sisyphus* appear like pieces of a detached and objective chain of reasoning, there is a highly personal mood that reverberates throughout; and from other sources we know what personal disaster turned his thoughts in this direction. Camus had had a brush with death: a young man in love with the Mediterranean sea and sky, fond of athletics, he had suddenly been discovered to be tubercular. This closeness to death brought a shock of recognition that no chain of reasoning could ever induce. How absurd was this splendid gift of life if it could be taken away so arbitrarily by death! (Notice that the discovery of the Absurd in this case does not come out of world-weariness or flagging energy, but out of high-hearted youth and its joy in life when these are threatened by death.) And, consequently, how vain and useless all human efforts must be, since they are doomed to ultimate extinction. He was therefore ready to find a congenial figure in Sisyphus, the mythical hero whom the gods condemned in the lower world to roll a rock up a hillside from which it would always slip back. Sisyphus is the hero who exemplifies useless and ceaseless toil. The absurd man must face the same prospect: all his desperate struggles may come to nothing, yet he goes on, like this Greek hero, pursuing his chosen task, ceaselessly pushing his rock up the hill.

"Does life have meaning?" Camus asks; "and if not, why go on living?" The fundamental philosophical problem thus becomes the question of suicide: the absurd hero—he who judges that life is absurd and has no meaning—nevertheless goes on living within this condition of absurdity. Why? Because, says Camus, by destroying him the act of suicide would abolish that state of tension between himself (with all his intellectual and spiritual claims) and the universe (in all its vast indifference to those claims)—the tension in which his being vibrates and which gives him his strictly human identity.

This logic is not altogether convincing. To begin with, the question itself—What meaning does life have?—is also somewhat elusive. Christian theology once provided an answer definite enough to make, as it seemed, the question itself definite. Man exists to serve God in this world, and to be happy with Him in the next. Here—as the Existentialists have rightly pointed out—man is considered as an object whose end is preassigned to him; he does not create his own meaning. But, worse than this, the terms of the old formula, apparently so tidy and conclusive, turn out when examined to lead us into unimaginable mystery. The Divine Nature, whose ends we are to serve, is absolutely incomprehensible, as the believers themselves admit, to our human minds. But this effort by religion to explain the universe is not any more pitiably feeble than that of science or philosophy. Scientific explanation dissolves the network of familiar meanings that make up our world in order to replace them by some system of meanings of a different, and allegedly more comprehensive, order; but this system in turn is inconclusive and reposes on a base that is itself inexplicable. Wherever we turn, we find existence in the end, as in the beginning, a mystery that resists our efforts to comprehend it.

None of this is new. Men have gone through the motions of these arguments, in one shape or another, for the last two centuries. What is different with Camus is that he proposes we give up the question whether life has a meaning, which can lead only to bewilderment, and instead proceed on the assumption that it has no meaning. What then? All that we know—and if we are not to dupe ourselves we must remain with what we know—is the condition of our finitude and mortality. Any leap beyond the world as it is given—a leap to God, the supernatural, the transcendent—is the result of a desperate cry of the heart in its impossible demand that the world and man have a meaning; but that leap, noble as it may be in some cases, is also a betrayal of that lucidity of mind that would remain stubbornly only with what it knows, and will not surrender the truth of its perceptions for a fantasy about what lies beyond them. Hence the point of what Camus calls "lucid indifference." One has to remain indifferent to the absurdity of the world in order not to surrender this earth to those who would seek its meaning in some earthly heaven of the future for which what we have in the present must be destroyed. This absurdity of the world occurs on two levels: (1) the inability to explain the universe, since explanation only pushes the mystery one step further back; (2) the senseless spectacle of human life in the society around us with its oppression, injustice, and the impersonal routines that grind people down. The absurd man—which means merely the man who has learned to live with absurdity

—can keep his balance only by a certain indifference, heartless as this may sound to some. After all, he knows that his own values, however passionately he gives himself to them, are a matter of indifference to the universe. Like Sisyphus, we cannot be sure that the rock will not roll back; that the efforts of today will bear fruit tomorrow; or if they do succeed, that they will continue into the far future. In 10,000 years mankind may not exist in a universe gone dark; or the culture which we have prized so much—the works of a Shakespeare or a Goethe—may be lost, forgotten, or no longer comprehensible to whatever creatures still exist. Time and mortality are the twin conditions that embrace not only the individual man but the whole race.

Sartre wrote a long and memorable review of *The Stranger* and *The Myth of Sisyphus*. At the time he and Camus were friends, and both were rising stars in the literary firmament of the 1940s. In addition, Sartre was the leader of the then burgeoning movement of Existentialism, at once its high priest and superb publicist. Camus was also publicly regarded as belonging to the group, partly because he was personally close to Sartre, partly because of the somber tone of his thought, though he himself insisted, as always, on his independence. It is interesting to note that Sartre, in his review, takes Camus to task for not always understanding the Existentialist thinkers to whom he refers. The confrontation of the two men on this point is revealing. Though their names have been and still are persistently linked (at one time in the United States the names Sartre-Camus were parroted almost like a brand name for Existentialism), the two men were, as individuals, altogether antithetical personalities. Sartre is the urban intellectual, brilliant and cerebral. Camus, the provincial, with the dust of the earth still clinging to his feet, was always a little uncomfortable in the Parisian intellectual circles. (The two personalities were destined to quarrel and break even if there had not been political issues to foment it.) On certain academic philosophical matters, Sartre is indeed right: Camus does misunderstand some of the

Existentialist thinkers. But what of Sartre himself and his own use of other Existentialist thinkers? Here the shoe is on the other foot. Sartre aimed to take over the thought of Heidegger and build on it, but the apparent appropriation was in fact a misunderstanding. Heidegger's quest for Being as the open region between subject and object, between Self and the Other, was transformed by Sartre into a subjective humanism in which consciousness is divided from objects and the ego irreparably divided from the Other. Sartre was the professor of philosophy, but Camus had shrewder philosophic instincts. He had read only some fragments of Heidegger, but his temperament and insight brought him closer to one essential theme of the German thinker. For Camus, as for Heidegger, finitude and mortality remain at the very center of the human condition, and it is within the horizon of these limitations that the resolute struggle to live goes on. On the title page of *The Myth of Sisyphus* Camus quotes from the Greek poet Pindar, and the quotation might have come equally well from Heidegger: "Do not aspire after immortal life, but exhaust the field of the possible."

III

Both *The Stranger* and *The Myth of Sisyphus* were written about the time of the fall of France before Hitler's armies in 1940. When they were published in 1942, Camus was already working with the Resistance, a brotherhood of rebels bound together under the sentence of death, if caught, at the hands of the German Gestapo. There was thus a rather startling contradiction between the activities of this young author and the mood of his books: while he was bound together in heroic and dangerous intimacy with others in the Resistance, his writing explored the loneliness and isolation of the absurd hero. The experience of comradeship under the threat of death forced Camus' thinking to take a new turn. For one thing, suicide could not be the only philosophical problem when murder seemed to have become the rule within the violent history of this century. As a leader in the Resistance, Camus himself had to participate in decisions about killing other men, informers in the ranks or collaborators with the Nazis who might threaten the lives of his own men. To be cast in the role of judge—and a judge over life and death, at that—was not an easy one for him; and he later recoiled from it to become, in his own expression, a "judge penitent." Throughout the rest of his life, his mind was to become haunted by the question: Under what conditions can a man be justified in taking another man's life? These experiences were the background out of which emerged two books with a very different kind of emphasis, *The Plague* (1947) and *The Rebel* (1951)—once again a novel balanced against a book of essays, almost as if the author wished deliberately to preserve a symmetry with the two works of his earlier period.

In *The Plague* Camus once again seeks his model in a work earlier than nineteenth-century realism. This time, however, it is not the classical short novel of eighteenth-century France but Defoe's *Journal of the Plague Year*. But the parallel with this older author is in fact slight. Defoe had hit upon the trick of writing an imaginary journal describing the events in a city under plague, but presented in such a way that the reader was to take it as an account of real happenings. It is thus a supreme hoax of imaginary journalism, capturing its readers by the sheer weight of frightening physical details. Camus does go to considerable length at times to convey the actual medical details of bubonic plague, but this is only incidental to his main purpose, which is to pose the moral problem of how man should act in the face of death. He is, first and last, a moralist, in the classic French sense of that word. The physical plague as such becomes symbolic of another kind of pestilence that lurks in the heart of man and may spring up at any time. Significantly, when Camus returns to this theme—a city of men under sentence of death —in his play *State of Siege* a year later (1948), he makes the plague in question that of a totalitarian regime that has imposed its terror on the Spanish city of Seville. Biological pestilence has given way to a thoroughly man-made terror.

The Existentialist philosophers had spoken of "extreme situations" as the point of no return where the comforting routines of daily life and the intricate self-deceptions behind which we hide collapse, and where or not at all a man must create a Self. Camus' novel seems to come up with rather a different judgment: under the threat of death, people carry on more or less in line with their habitual characters. The religious turn to their religion, actors become more melodramatic, lovers continue to fornicate—and some doctors go methodically about their business of trying to save lives. When the plague lifts, one has the feeling that life will go on as it once did, and the unfortunate pestilence will gradually fade away from memory like a forgotten nightmare.

But not altogether. On one man, the hero Dr. Rieux, the lesson of the plague is not lost. At the end we discover that he is in fact the narrator—the author of this plague journal—and it is to his voice that we have been listening throughout. Germain Brée has correctly said that in each of Camus' novels we hear the different voices of their different narrators and that the tone of the voice speaking tells us as much as the events narrated. Dr. Rieux's tone is calm, matter-of-fact, scrupulous, modest—like the man himself. He is, in fact, so colorless or gray to the casual eye that in any circumstances other than the tense situation of the plague, he might be considered a bore. It is a difficult thing for a writer to present a person who is really good; as Blake remarked of *Paradise Lost*, Milton could not help making Lucifer far more interesting than God. Camus just succeeds in making Dr. Rieux interesting only through the deep philosophical message of which the doctor is a modest incarnation.

Dr. Rieux, quiet and modest and limited as he is, is an example of the mystery of the ordinary man who keeps mankind from slipping back into the jungle. Throughout the plague he wears himself to the bone trying to save people's lives. Why does he do it? He cannot say. His project, like that of any man, remains ultimately unjustifiable. In this, but only in this, he remains one with the Absurd Hero of Camus' earlier phase: the reason for living, as the reason for doing what one considers one's duty, must remain ultimately unspoken. Is life worth living? *Solvitur ambulando:* the answer does not come from reason but from the activity of life in the course of which the question itself, still unanswered, disappears. Dr. Rieux does not seek to give reasons for his medical dedication; he is not a philosopher, not a man given to abstractions, and in this acknowledgment he is acknowledging once again his own limits. He does what he does without ultimate justification but without striking any heroic stance. He is altogether free from some of the histrionics which surround some of Camus' earlier instances of the Absurd Hero—the Don Juan, the actor, the conqueror. Indeed, he shies away from intellectual arguments with other characters who harbor different ideals of life, conceding easily that there may be other goals—like the love of a woman—for which a man might give his life. Thus, above all, he is a man of moderation and limits; he does not seek to absolutize his own ideal of life and impose it tyrannically upon others, even though the events of the plague place him for a while in an almost dictatorial role of restricting the comings and goings of others. Here in this extraordinary ordinary man, who accepts modestly but unfalteringly the limits of his human condition, Camus had found a character to embody his new philosophical outlook.

This new viewpoint is expounded at length in *The Rebel*, the book that made final his break with Sartre and Sartre's circle. Their friendship had already been broken off over questions of politics. At the time French intellectuals were inclined to be fellow travelers of Stalinism, either evading the facts or leaning over backward to find some historical rationalization of the evils of life in the Soviet Union. Camus felt that justice must be impartial, that oppression is still oppression whether it be of the

Left or the Right, and that Soviet slave-labor camps were not to be passed over because the Nazis had had their concentration camps. Sartre and his circle felt that such criticism of the Soviet Union inevitably played into the hands of the bourgeois reactionaries in France. This quarrel had hardly been kept private, but with the publication of *The Rebel* it became explosively public. The book was denounced in a review in Sartre's magazine *Les Temps Modernes* by Francis Jeanson; Camus responded with a letter of protest, purposely not addressing Sartre by name but as "Monsieur le Directeur"; in turn, Sartre replied with a long passionate invective against his former friend, accusing him by turns of pretentious philosophical ignorance and of selling out his earlier revolutionary attitudes for the more comfortable one of bourgeois "moderation" (another name, in his view, for conservatism). The whole squabble generated much fire and smoke, with occasional bright sparks of insight, but hardly any steady illumination.

In retrospect, Camus' book was indeed very vulnerable. He was not professionally equipped to handle the vast spread of material, the innumerable figures in modern intellectual history, that he sought to draw within his net. At times, the book is rambling and diffuse; at other times, repetitious like a record stuck in its groove and grinding out the same refrain over and over. But despite these flaws, the book remains a major intellectual document of our times. Camus may have lacked the requisite learning (as Sartre repeatedly insisted against him), but he had the shrewdness and stubbornness of instinct to see the human center around which the confusions of modern history turn.

And his theme is really quite simple. Camus wished to defend what might be called "ordinary values"—the values by which so many unpretentious people like Dr. Rieux live—but he found himself in an intellectual situation dominated by two schools that rejected those values: on the one hand, Existentialism (in its Sartrian version) and on the other, Marxism (in its monolithic

Stalinist form). An incidental irony in this situation was that Sartre, his former friend, seemed to want to belong to both schools at once.

Consider Existentialism first. The Existentialists had emphasized the contingency and fragility of the safeguards we put up against anxiety. "We move over seventy fathoms," Kierkegaard had said, indicating thus that the insecurity of ordinary life is such that we can at any moment plummet below the surface into the depths below. All human order, all human structures, are safeguards that man has erected against the void. At best, they are always precarious, and often, instead of being merely protective, they become modes of evasion. Such had been the message of Tolstoy's *Death of Ivan Ilyich*, the story that had become central to the Existentialist canon: the whole structure of bourgeois values crumbles when Ivan Ilyich has to confront his own death in fear and trembling. This existentialist protest is valid against those who would seek to sit smugly within their day-to-day routines as if these were absolute and inviolable. But what Camus wished to insist upon is that only within the finite and ordinary—within those moments, transient and scattered though they may be, when banality seems to be transfigured and to redeem itself—shall we find values to live by if we are to find them at all. Nietzsche has said somewhere that we should beware of looking at monsters too long lest we ourselves become monstrous, and by gazing into the abyss too long we may become abysmal. The abyss is certainly there, and not to be evaded; but need we go on staring at it forever? In any case, however deeply we may have looked into the depths, we have to go on living within the realm of the day-to-day and the commonplace.

(That Camus does not do full justice to the Existentialists cannot be denied. He seems unaware of the fact that at the very beginning of this movement, Kierkegaard spoke of the necessity of the "double leap": the first that takes us beyond the confining horizons of the banal, the second which reinserts us into the occasions of daily life. Kierkegaard's hero—the Knight of Faith, as he calls him—knows that the daily round hovers over the void, but he lives as solidly in this round "as a butcher or a tax collector." But that Camus may be unfair to the Existentialists is beside the point; we are concerned with what he has to say, and how he says it against the background of the Existentialist movement, *as he understood the latter.*)

Marxism, however, is the more threatening antagonist for Camus. Here is an ideology that not only can capture the minds of Western intellectuals but possesses all the instruments of temporal power at the disposition of the ruling group in the Soviet Union. Beware of an idea that has come to power. It can, if its partisans have no sense of limits, seek to make life itself subservient to it. In the name of the idea of economic justice, an admirable one, Marxism was willing to sacrifice a whole generation, millions of human beings, in Soviet Russia. All the values of ordinary life—including decency, friendship, honesty —are to be abandoned, if need be, to achieve the one absolute goal of History: establishment of the classless society. Modern totalitarian regimes, as Camus sees them, originated in a certain intellectual totalitarianism that had been germinating in Western civilization since the French Revolution. Intellectual fanaticism consists in taking an idea or set of ideas as absolute; then imposing them without any sense of limits, boundaries, qualifications, upon all the irregular and complex contingencies of our ordinary world. The limbs that do not fit the bed of Procrustes are to be lopped off.

The strategy of Camus, and a clever one, is to present this argument for moderation and limits within the context of rebellion. Usually a plea for moderation is received by guffaws on the Left as a disguised apology for the status quo. No doubt it very often is, but it need not be. And why should we allow the ideologists of Revolution to rob us of the original sense of rebellion, which arose out of a certain sense of limits? The rebel is, first of all, not an ideologist but a man, a concrete creature of flesh and blood. He has been the victim of oppression and injustice; for a time, perhaps even a very long time, he submits; but there comes a moment when he reaches the breaking point and can bend no longer without ceasing to be a man. In effect, the rebel draws a line, and says "So far, but no farther; if oppression goes past that limit, I could no longer believe myself a man." His rebellion thus arises out of his setting a limit beyond which he will endure oppression no longer. Past that point, he declares "I rebel; therefore we exist," with this gesture drawing together all his brothers in rebellion. Camus, in this description of the act of revolt, is thus attempting to resolve three of his problems at once: (1) if rebellion arises out of this establishment of limits, then it can never forget that its own aims at certain points cannot be total but must be subject to limitation; (2) the earlier solitary ego of Sisyphus is now dissolved in the brotherhood of rebels; the ultimate source of community is the revolt of men that binds them together against their human degradation; (3) having laid their own lives on the line, the rebels can answer the question that haunts modern history: When can murder be justified, if at all? Their answer: One can kill only when one's own life is also at stake.

What Camus seeks to describe here is the human core of revolt, what makes it an affirmation of man that takes us beyond any form of Nihilism. But such has hardly been the way of modern revolutions. These have taken place under the leadership of a disciplined corps of revolutionaries, ideologically motivated and capturing for their own programs the unrest of the masses. Now, there would be nothing wrong with the professional revolutionary as such; the oppressed, after all, are worn down by their oppression, and may require the energies of leadership. But the trouble is that the professional revolutionary is apt to become the servitor of his ideas rather than their master; and consequently he is led to set his abstractions above the processes of life itself, and in their name to murder, if need be, millions of people. We first observe this process in the

French Revolution, with which Camus' historical exposition begins. In the holy cause of establishing justice for the poor and wretched, leaders like St. Just were willing to let heads roll on the guillotine. The truth of his ideas—so he fanatically believes—cannot permit the leader of a revolution to temper justice with mercy. That would be human, all too human, an acknowledgment that he must somewhere draw a limit to the validity of these ideas. Camus is speaking here from his own troubled conscience. He had been something of a St. Just of the Resistance himself, having to mete out judgment of life and death on collaborators, and the uneasiness of guilt and doubt about the justification for murder did not leave him for the rest of his life. This is the torment of conscience that, as we shall see, lies behind the fulminations of his last novel, *The Fall*.

But Camus' message is not confined to the political sphere alone. The whole of modern culture, as he sees it, is infected with a Faustian lust for the unlimited. We are the civilization that revels in the gigantic, the colossal, and indeed the super-colossal. The words "moderation," "balance," "limits," evoke only the associations of tepid conformity among us. For the ancient Greeks these were exalting words that signified the glory of their civilization over that of the barbarians. A central episode in Greek mythology is the struggle between the giants and the gods. The giants are monsters of darkness, enormous and formless, full of destructive frenzy; the gods are the shining Olympians, each one definite within his own Being, reigning within the boundaries of his own appointed sphere. The gods triumph; and for the Greeks this was a victory of light over darkness, of the formed over the formless, of the human over the monstrous. This revulsion against lack of measure and proportion runs throughout the great period of Greek art. It is the motif that is woven through their great tragedies, where the transgression against limits upsets the balance of nature and brings about the downfall of the tragic protagonist. It is almost impossible to exaggerate the value which the word *peras,* limit,

had for the Greek mind: the exhilaration at once of self-con-
quest and of self-liberation that it symbolized. We moderns, on
the other hand, are partisans of the giants. The more gigantic
(however unnecessary) our buildings the more we boast of
them; the more formless our art the more expressive we find it;
the more absolute and sweeping our ideologies the more dog-
matically we hold them.

Camus ends by invoking another Greek hero to set beside his
earlier figure of Sisyphus: the storm-tossed and prudent man,
Odysseus, who after much wandering comes home to his native
Ithaca to till its sparse fields in stubborn and loving persever-
ence. The political aspect of Camus' message could be read as
a plea for a Third Force: ancient Europe, caught between the
two giants of the Soviet Union and the United States, must turn
to cultivating its own garden, pursuing its own limited goals,
which alone will restore it to its proper place in the world
community. Beyond politics, attacking the *hubris* of modern
culture, the arrogant claims for the absoluteness of any man-
made ideology, Camus is once again recommending that man
learn to live within the limits of his finite and mortal condition.
This seems to be *Sisyphus* once again. True; but not quite. The
writer, like the voyager Odysseus, takes a long time to come
around to home, to find himself, to find what he was groping for
in the first words he wrote. He returns, but to himself, not to
what he was. The long voyage has taken Camus through many
crucial areas of modern experience, much confused turmoil of
this century's history, and the message has become both transformed and enriched. For one thing, the specter of Nihilism
seems to have been laid to rest at last.

Or has it? His last novel, *The Fall*, hardly suggests that the
author had come to peace with himself. It is one of Camus' most
deliberately ambiguous books, at once mocking and self-mock-
ing in tone, dark and baleful in its atmosphere. In each of
Camus' three novels, to recall Germain Brée's remark, there is
a single voice speaking, and we have to listen to the tone of its

voice, not merely what it says, if we are to grasp the author's full intention. Here the voice speaking is oratorical and smooth, as befits an advocate at the bar, but also reverberating and hollow—a voice speaking out of some dehumanized emptiness.

The narrator-protagonist is Jean-Baptiste Clamence. John the Baptist, *clamans in deserto!* Symbolism as explicit and pat as this is rare in Camus. Yet its explicitness vanishes the moment we try to pin down what Clamence can possibly be prophesying that would evoke a parallel with the saint who baptized Jesus. The symbolism of the character's name turns out thus to be only one more ironic touch in a work piled high with ironies. Clamence begins his story in a seamy dockside bar in Amsterdam. Through the heart of this Dutch city runs a system of circular canals, resembling one of the levels of Dante's hell. This setting conveys the atmosphere of the tale, which is infernal and satanic, as well as the character of Clamence, who at the end, though grotesque and absurd, has become as baleful as a devil out of the *Inferno*.

As a lawyer in Paris, Clamence had been successful in every way: in the courts, with women, and in winning the admiration of his colleagues. The subsequent story has to do mainly with the course of events by which Clamence's image of himself becomes pictured in his own eyes. The fall referred to in the title is not the fall from grace, as it would have been in a more theological period, but a contemporary man's fall from his own self-conceit. One night while walking across the Pont Royal he sees a young girl standing in the shadow; a little later after he passes her, he hears a splash that may be the girl hurling herself into the Seine. He does not go back to find out or to help her. He keeps himself from becoming involved in the possible death of another human being. Nothing happens immediately; but gradually this small incident eats away at his good opinion of himself. Small annoyances begin to make him look ridiculous in the eyes of others. He becomes eccentric in the courts, and his colleagues begin to be wary of him so that his practice falls off.

The idea of guilt, which had begun over an incident for which he could not be held legally responsible (it is even possible the splash in the water was not that of a suicide), now becomes towering and absolute and claims his life. "Each man is guilty to each for everything," Dostoevsky's Father Zossima had said. Clamence chooses these words as his destiny, but out of malice and vindictiveness rather than in the spirit of Christian charity Dostoevsky had intended. His mission is to haunt the Amsterdam Bar and tell his tale to any guest there who will listen (he invokes here the unquiet ghost of Coleridge's Ancient Mariner, who is also driven to tell about his own fall), and by so doing awaken the listener's own guilts and make him squirm.

What did Camus intend by this odd tale? He offers us a prefatory quotation from Lermontov that tells a good deal:

> Some were dreadfully insulted, and quite seriously, to have held up as a model such an immoral character as *A Hero of Our Time*; others shrewdly noted that the author had portrayed himself and his acquaintances. . . . *A Hero of Our Time*, gentlemen, is in fact a portrait, but not of an individual; it is the aggregate of the vices of our whole generation in their fullest expression.

One could play the game of gossip that sometimes passes as literary criticism and try to ferret out references to Camus himself, or to Sartre, or Jean Genêt, or others. But Camus' is not a work of tittle-tattle realism; Clamence is a genuine creation of the imagination, a composite portrait of a whole generation —though, in truth, only of its darker side. The vice indicted here is the same that Camus had sought to dissect analytically in *The Rebel*: the absence of a sense of limits within contemporary thought. Excess turns into its opposite; and here, in *The Fall*, the excess of guilt turns into irresponsibility. Clamence revels and glories in the sense of his own rottenness (and, consequently, of all other human beings too), but this intoxicated self-loathing has not brought him a responsible conscience in the ordinary human sense of this phrase. He tells us that he has passed from the role of a judge to a judge-penitent, and in trying to make others repent he assumes the dual role of both judge and judge-penitent. But now as a judge-penitent he is harsher in his condemnation of other human beings than he ever was when he had a hand in the glib decisions on justice that are made in the law courts. In *The Rebel* Camus had named, as an important part of the sense of limits, the need to develop the conception of "a limited culpability." One takes upon oneself a restricted number of things for which one can be charged guilty or not. The man who chooses to be responsible for everything ends up by being responsible for nothing. Clamence is an irresponsible buffoon; but, like the buffoons in Dostoevsky, he is menacing and destructive.

But there is another message in *The Fall* beside this picture of guilt that has become perverted and meaningless through its own excess. Clamence is also the victim of his own fine language —indeed of language itself. The more intricate the patterns of rhetoric he spins, the further he is carried away from reality. As a composite picture of the time, Clamence represents our contemporaries as trapped in words, caught up in abstractions that distort rather than reveal, that—in the oldest words of Greek philosophy—create Seeming rather than Being. The philosopher Heidegger has described the history of the West as the gradual estrangement from Being. (I am not sure that there was any explicit influence here upon Camus, but the parallel is imposing.) According to Heidegger, this estrangement takes place despite, in fact because of, all the sophistications of modern consciousness, and all the technological intricacies of our culture. Our technical mastery over nature sets us at a distance from it; we set objects over Being; caught in our cities, our fabricated mazes, we can no longer surrender ourselves—as Camus puts it in *The Rebel*—to those elemental things which are the stuff of all art and poetry: "The sea, the sand, the sun and the stars." Clamence is a special, but also very pointed, illustration of this loss of Being. We have spoken of a certain emptiness to him. In the end, he has become almost a vacuum —a creature of words without Being. If Clamence were a little less clever, he might touch reality a little more.

Has Camus been unfair to his generation in this scathing portrait of Clamence? Behind Camus' novel lie the memories of the fervor and verbiage of Parisian literary circles in the years after World War II. That was a time when rhetoric flourished, and all manner of literary, moral, and political stances were struck on the less authentic fringes of the Existentialist movement. Again and again one could read in the pages of the French reviews articles about the universality of guilt, the compliance of victim and executioner, while all kinds of injustice close at hand were passed in silence. It was as if the awful shades of Dachau and Buchenwald could be invoked to plunge readers into a feeling of abysmal guilt over the human species as a whole so that the prosaic and limited responsibility for matters within one's compass might seem too paltry a thing to engage a sensitive soul. A dilettante is always a suspect figure; and a dilettante in guilt is unmanly. Clamence is therefore anathema to Camus, who—as both artist and thinker—was in search of a virile ideal.

That search he had taken over from Hemingway and Malraux, among others. But how different the emphasis has become! The swaggering sportsman and outdoorsman of Hemingway, the high-strung adventurer of Malraux, have become quiet, modest, bound by limits—a Dr. Rieux in fact. "Virile ideal" is sometimes misunderstood as implying mere vulgar masculinity. More deeply, it is simply our conception of a man whose response to life is in fact his answer to the question of values. The novelist does not refute Nihilism by abstract arguments but by creating a character in whom the value of life is redeemed. The question "Does life have a meaning?" is answered, in the only way that ultimately matters, by individuals who have meaning. Rieux and Clamence are the two opposite poles of Camus' world; the first, a man living within his own limitations, quietly ready always to listen to others; the second, the oratorical ideologist who can listen only to his own voice and with whom dialogue is impossible. They are also, in Camus' view, the two poles between which the modern world will have to choose.

IV

There is also another debt Camus owes to Hemingway in the matter of style. True, the influence is in only one work, the first part of *The Stranger*, but those are pages that, stylistically speaking, have been influential on other French writers.

When asked in a newspaper interview how he had been influenced by the American novel, Camus replied rather brusquely that his real literary models were the French classics. The answer was not altogether an evasion; in all his writing he labored to assimilate himself to an older classicism, and in the judgment of posterity, I believe, his works will stand as classics beside Mme. de La Fayette and the Abbé Prévost. Yet his work, even apart from the contemporary quality of its themes, belongs in its language and tone unmistakably to our age. Indeed, what makes *The Stranger* stylistically fascinating is just the effort to absorb the innovations of Hemingway and the American novel into the mold of French classicism. And the odd thing is that this dubious marriage works.

It is curious that this question of style is so little discussed in a writer like Camus, who worried much over such matters and labored so hard to write well. (Sartre's circle, at the time of the blow-up over *The Rebel*, ridiculed Camus for straining too much after "fine writing.") Camus is so much the artist in the public arena that his works are a battleground of contemporary ideologies. His interpreters are therefore drawn mainly into the discussion of his ideas, almost as if his works were wholly and solely thematic—intellectual skeletons and nothing else. But the qualities of style and form in a work may be just as philosophically revealing as a writer's ideas, and sometimes more so.

If it were otherwise, we would not here be attempting to sketch the spiritual physiognomy of our period through its art; it would be sufficient merely to review the various philosophies and ideologies that have run their course during the first half of this century. Confucius is reported to have said in one of his more audacious moments: "I care not who writes the laws of a country so long as I am able to write its songs." The ancient sage was not expressing here any latter-day aestheticism. He meant that the actual life of a people transpires less at the relatively abstract level of its social structures than within the felt texture of experience, in the moods and emotions that bind or divide us in the daily round of life. That is why art, which is so much a matter of texture and style, reaches a stratum of historical reality deeper than that of ideas.

The French discovery of the American novel, in the years between 1929 and 1939, was an explosive event for young writers like Camus and Sartre. The excitement was not always purely literary in nature. There was also the joy of discovering the exotic in a whole style of life, of which they had already become aware through American jazz and movies. The French tradition tends to be a very inbred one; their writers perpetually return to a few classics, whose themes they re-create and enrich, so that their literature seems perpetually in the process of refining itself. The discovery of the American novel was like the opening of a window in an elegantly furnished but closed room. These American works seemed always to bring with them in one way or another the presence of the frontier, of wide and unenclosed spaces, of life on the open road, all of which was fascinating to young people who had grown up within the settled and clearly marked boundaries of the French way of life. Here was a literature less polished, often brutal and sometimes crude, but with all its violence in more direct and immediate contact with the violent tenor of modern life. Naturally too, there were also the usual ironies of misunderstanding that attend the diffusion of one culture into another. It sometimes seemed as if the French, in their intoxication with this American literature, did not distinguish carefully among the writers they imported, bestowing as much attention and adulation on the thrillers of James M. Cain as on the novels of Hemingway and Faulkner.

But if the French surrender themselves, as Sartre remarked apropos of this American influence, they do so only partly, a little at a time, and only to find themselves again. They found themselves in this case by contriving a very good philosophic rationale for their American craze; they could adopt the techniques of American fiction only by assimilating these devices to their own intellectual and artistic ends. The American style seemed to offer a way out of the impasse in which the so-called psychological novel found itself. In France, this latter had reached its culmination in the imposing and intricate labyrinth created by Proust. One could go no further in that direction, the younger French writers felt, without becoming wound in a cocoon of subjectivism that shut one off from the external actualities of the contemporary world. By contrast, the technique of the American novel is one of sharp and staccato externalization. The style here is often close to that of the reporter. Facts, events, happenings are set forth in their abruptness without any attempt at psychological analysis or explanation. We do not try to get inside, but deliberately stay outside, the facts. In Hemingway, particularly, this style seeks a deliberate flatness, which is appropriate to represent a world that stands flat and opaque over against the individual, a world where fact has become brute fact, external and contingent, for the observer who stands coolly at a distance from it and refuses to be taken in by what he sees. Not to be taken in is not to be a part of it, and therefore an outsider. The American imitators of Hemingway produced innumerable parodies in the manner of "tough guy" literature. The French, on the other hand, whose response was more intellectual than populist, saw in the Hemingway style an expression of the only viable philosophic attitude amid the lies and confusions of a brutal and alien world: the desire, as Camus puts it, "not to be a dupe," and to retain no matter what happens one's "lucidity" of mind.

This was the vehicle Camus found at hand for his own artistic encounter with Nihilism. However the question of Nihilism may present itself to the philosopher, for the writer it takes a different turn; he has to depict, directly and without comment, the world as an absurd and meaningless spectacle surrounding his character. How shall he proceed? Observe Camus at work in the opening pages of *The Stranger*: "Today Mother died. Or maybe yesterday. I'm not sure. I received a telegram from the Home: 'Mother passed away. Burial tomorrow. Deepest condolences.' That doesn't say. Maybe it was yesterday." The short jerky statements of fact succeed each other like disconnected atoms. Meursault catches the bus to go to the old people's home. It is hot in the bus. He is sleepy. At the home he is taken to see his mother's body. He does not look at it. They leave it covered. He sits beside the body all night. Some of the old inmates come in to hold the wake beside him. He has little to say to them. He dozes, wakes again, dozes. The chair is uncomfortable. Then daylight, and they proceed to the burial. And so on, and so forth.

What, after all, does the whole of philosophy have to tell us about meaning other than that it is a matter of connectedness? An object means something to us when we are able to situate it within some pattern of relations. It becomes meaningless when we cannot connect it with other things, when it is torn out of context, disconnected. Camus tells his story in sharp staccato sentences, each reporting an external impression without any psychological analysis, and each impression external to the succeeding one. The connecting thread that would supply meaning to the succession of discrete facts is abolished. The American technique of externalizing the narrative has been pushed here to the point where the observer himself almost vanishes. Meursault's subjectivity is emptied into the objects around him; but these do not give him back another and more glorified image of himself; they stand distant and disconnected—a world that is so external to him that it can never be *his*. Sartre gives a very apt image to explain the effect of this technique: imagine a man observed talking in a glass telephone booth; we observe the changing expressions of his face, the gestures of his hands, and they seem absurd to us because we are unable to hear the conversation that binds these isolated facts together. A completely externalized narrative has just the same effect; an action is seen wholly from the outside, and its inner meaning is lacking.

The question remains whether some of the more ordinary and traditional values of fiction do not disappear when this technique is pushed to an extreme. Camus seeks to salvage some of those values as his story unfolds. Meursault's language, in the latter parts of the novel where he is humanly redeemed through his revolt, becomes charged rather than inert. The flatness of style gives way to a rather splendid if tight-lipped eloquence.

However, younger French novelists have pushed the technique to a point where Camus, the traditionalist, would disapprove. Among this "New Wave" within the French novel the best-known in this country is probably Alain Robbe-Grillet, author of *The Voyeur* and scenarist for the extraordinary film *Last Year at Marienbad*. Robbe-Grillet has also written brilliantly on his theories of fiction so that we are left in no doubt how far he wants to go in recasting the form of the novel. In his view, the narrative is to be so externalized, so absorbed into the surface of things, that he would not even permit metaphor itself into the description of a landscape or an interior, since all such metaphor seeks to make the object described into part of an inner human world. We cannot say, "The village slept in the curve of the valley," for that is already an attempt to assimilate an external physical fact into our human world of waking and sleeping. The village happens only to be located in the valley. That is the bald physical fact, to which we are to hold if we are to evade illusion. When asked what influence had led him to these audaciously experimental views of fiction, his answer was: "The first thirty pages of *The Stranger*."

True; but this original influence has been stretched to a point where the resemblance to Camus is hardly discernible. The narrative becomes so purely external that it dissolves into a shifting sequence of images as if a camera were roving over a landscape, freezing at certain moments on any item it chose. Here at last the novel has surrendered to the cinema. In fact, Robbe-Grillet's novels can be read without any distortion simply as preparatory outlines for scenarios. When he first met the director Alain Resnais to discuss their possible collaboration, the latter remarked that he thought any of Robbe-Grillet's novels would do for a film without their having to work out a new script. Robbe-Grillet is being entirely consistent in wanting the novel to surrender to cinema. For if the novel is to be reduced to a sequence of purely objective images, then the novel must take second place to the cinema, which has in the camera a much more powerful and immediate visual instrument.

But much—and indeed very much—is lost in this push toward absolute immediacy of the image. (And what happens here with the novel is true for other experiments in modern art that have sought to convey the impact of pure and uninterpreted sensation.) In Robbe-Grillet the externalization of the narrative becomes fragmentation. The technique, which should have been a means, becomes an end in itself. The hero of *The Voyeur* is Mathias, a traveling salesman who returns to his native island (unidentified) in order to sell some watches. The images flicker past like a bizarre newsreel: the boat leaving, a piece of string on the deck, the quay, Mathias knocking at door after door trying to sell his watches; then we seem to be involved in a terrible crime—the rape and murder of a young girl—and it dawns on us that this Mathias is a homicidal maniac. But perhaps not; we are left uncertain; the images of murder may be only projections of his own fantasy.

On first reading the novel is gripping; we are carried along with the kaleidoscopic shifting of images, the roller-coaster whirl of objective sensations, and the detective-story puzzle about what exactly is going on. But when this excitement wanes, the novel is curiously disappointing and empty. It leaves one with nothing. Mathias does not exist; he has disappeared among the shards and fragments of sensory fact. He is a bore, except possibly as a vehicle for Robbe-Grillet's own sensations. The film *Last Year at Marienbad*—elegant and gorgeously stylish as it is —had the same lack of substance. A film can compensate by the seductions of camera technique, spectacle, sound track and music, while the more austere form of the novel cannot get by with such sensory blandishments. Even then, when *Marienbad* is over, we are left with empty and meaningless lives caught up in the fragile suggestion of a plot that is really, when one forgets the lovely gowns of the star, quite trite.

Camus, the man of limits and moderation, keeps away from such technical excesses. He is too bound to the question of Nihilism—he feels its presence too menacing to be made light of—to hurl himself over the abyss where art becomes the arbitrary whirling of a kaleidoscope. Meursault's disconnected world still bears with it the anguish for a meaning that has departed. Without that anguish the question of Nihilism disappears, for we would already be Nihilists. Robbe-Grillet's fiction not only accepts but revels in the fragments it creates. To a more classical temperament like Camus it would therefore be a nihilistic art. Robbe-Grillet was trained as an engineer and scientist, and in his essays (which in some ways are the most interesting things he has written) he shows the cool intelligence that goes with these professions. For engineering or science the fragmentation of experience is not a matter of human anguish but simply the powerful analytic tool by which objective problems are ground down piecemeal and solved. The anguish at the fragments has hitherto been left to philosophers and artists. In the future, if Robbe-Grillet's theories were to prevail, the artist may join the scientist in the cultivation of pure dispassion.

This brief excursion on Robbe-Grillet has not been pointless. The younger writer in his borrowing casts a light on the author from whom he borrowed. In comparison with the New Wave of French novelists, Camus already looks dreadfully old-fashioned. Indeed he is; his ties with tradition—in art as in politics —are too strong to let him become a thoroughgoing "modernist," though just for that reason he provides a good key to the more sensitive parts of this age. Only where there is still an anguished attachment to what has been can there be a sense of the peculiar malaise of transition that disturbs our period. "This age and its adolescent furies," Camus exclaimed in one of his more vitriolic moments. But we have also to remember what the psychologists tell us is the meaning of youthful storm and stress: that adolescence is the period of confusion in which we struggle for an identity and sometimes establish it. Camus is a good witness to the need of this time of need. His world opens backward on earlier writers of this century, at whom we must now look.

In particular, he sends us back to reread Hemingway, in whom retrospectively we shall be surprised to find some unexpected things. Sartre remarked apropos of *The Stranger* that Camus brought to the Hemingway style a philosophic rationale that the American writer lacked. True, Camus is a novelist of ideas in a way that Hemingway is not. But ideas are not the only, and perhaps not the most important, way that philosophy enters a work of art. On the level of style, the philosophical problem that occupies us in this section—the encounter with Nihilism in some of its contemporary versions—turns about the widespread use and fascination of a certain fictional technique. In Hemingway we can see this technique not as a matter of intellectual contrivance or literary borrowing, but as it is born in the struggle of language to stand close to things themselves.

And nothing is more truly philosophical about art than a style as it comes to be within that open clearing between man and the things that engage him, where he has to draw breath again and rediscover, if he can, whether he means anything or nothing.

3. Winner Take Nothing

A nothing that he knew too well.

We are currently being flooded by biographical revelations about Ernest Hemingway. Since his death, the memoirists and biographers have been very busy. All the sealed drawers and cupboards of his life are being jimmied open, scoured, and emptied. The disclosures are not always flattering, at times indeed they are painful and grim. Nor do the biographers always show as much good sense or tact in making use of their discoveries as we might wish. That final night in Idaho, ending in the bright sunlight of a Sunday morning when Hemingway took his life with a shotgun blast, seems to tilt the balance toward the morbid side. There is enough darkness that haunts the edges of his work without our obscuring it melodramatically with the gruesome manner of his death. What is very clear from all the evidence is that he was a very, very sick man in his last years. But anybody who has expended himself so fiercely on life has almost earned the right to be sick in old age; and in any case this final sickness is not necessarily the point of view from which to judge him or his work.

Nevertheless, the facts about his life are useful because they remind us that Hemingway was an exceedingly complex man. And his was a complexity he could not conceal from others despite his poses of the simple outdoorsman. Morley Callaghan, who knew him before he was famous when they both worked as reporters on the Toronto *Star*, tells us that even in those days there was something obscurely strange and different about him. If Hemingway entered a room, Callaghan says, people would immediately begin to wonder about him without his having said or done anything unusual. He had only to walk down the street in a trench coat in order to attract attention and set people asking if he were on some mysterious and secret mission. The quality was indefinable, but it was there and not to be missed. It is against this complexity of the man that we have to understand the peculiar simplicity of the style he labored so hard to achieve. We speak of certain writers as "stylists" in the sense that they cultivate very agreeable effects in language; but this purely "aesthetic" sense falls far short of what style meant for Hemingway. For him style was a moral act, a desperate struggle for moral probity amid the confusions of the world and the slippery complexities of one's own nature. To set things down simple and right is to hold a standard of rightness against a deceiving world. This style is so far from being a merely "literary" phenomenon that Hemingway in fact set a pattern of life for a whole generation. Young men turned up in New York or Paris trying to walk, talk, and gesture in the Hemingway manner.

But at the center of all these varieties of style—in sport, hunting, warfare—there is the style one carries off with language. The philosopher will recognize and accept this extraordinary claim for language. Since the Greeks, language has been acknowledged as lying at the center of man's being. If style is what ultimately confers value on life, it is only within language that these values can find their ultimate expression. Style is not a literary confection, but a matter of balance, rhythm, and simplicity; and these are the qualities that hold a man together in his actions in the world. In comparison with some of the greatest novelists, undoubtedly, Hemingway falls short in richness of characterization (his characters tend to be flat), in the depth of psychological insight (his range here is narrow), and in fertility at creating situations (his plots are usually uninventive). No matter; language will carry the day and make do for all of these.

For in language man comes to the truth of being that is both appropriate and possible for him.

This matter of Hemingway's style will therefore be worth philosophical exploration.

The opening pages of *A Farewell to Arms* are probably as well known as any in modern letters. Quotation of them seems gratuitous, but for the purpose of close scrutiny it is well to have them, almost as visual as a painting, before our eyes:

In the late summer of that year we lived in a house in a village that looked across the river and the plain to the mountains. In the bed of the river there were pebbles and boulders, dry and white in the sun, and the water was clear and swiftly moving and blue in the channels. Troops went by the house and down the road and the dust they raised powdered the leaves of the trees. The trunks of the trees too were dusty and the leaves fell early that year and we saw the troops marching along the road and the dust rising and leaves, stirred by the breeze, falling and the soldiers marching and afterward the road bare and white except for the leaves.

The plain was rich with crops; there were many orchards of fruit trees and beyond the plain the mountains were brown and bare. There was fighting in the mountains and at night we could see the flashes from the artillery. In the dark it was like summer lightning, but the nights were cool and there was not the feeling of a storm coming.

Sometimes in the dark we heard the troops marching under the window and guns going past pulled by motor-tractors. There was much traffic at night and many mules on the roads with boxes of ammunition on each side of their pack-saddles and gray motor-trucks that carried men, and other trucks with loads covered with canvas that moved slower in the traffic. There were big guns too that passed in the day drawn by tractors, the long barrels of the guns covered with green branches and green leafy branches and vines laid over the tractors. To the north we could look across a valley and see a forest of chestnut trees and behind it another mountain on this side of the river. There was fighting for that mountain too, but it was not successful, and in the fall when the rains came the leaves all fell from the chestnut trees and the branches were bare and the trunks black with rain. The vineyards were thin and bare-branched too and all the country wet and brown and dead with the autumn. There were mists over the river and clouds on the mountain and the trucks splashed mud on the road and the troops were muddy and wet in their capes; their rifles were wet and under their capes the two leather cartridge-boxes on the front of the belts, gray leather boxes heavy with the packs of clips of thin, long 6.5 mm. cartridges, bulged forward under the capes so that the men, passing on the road, marched as though they were six months gone with child.

There were small gray motor-cars that passed going very fast; usually there was an officer on the seat with the driver and more officers in the back seat. They splashed more mud than the camions even and if one of the officers in the back was very small and sitting between two generals, he himself so small that you could not see his face but only the top of his cap and his narrow back, and if the car went especially fast it was probably the King. He lived in Udine and came out in this way nearly every day to see how things were going, and things went very badly.

At the start of the winter came the permanent rain and with the rain came the cholera. But it was checked and in the end only seven thousand died of it in the army.

The influences that helped to form Hemingway's style have been discussed and cataloged as if they were so many ingredients in a recipe. But no really creative act ever takes place through the mechanical addition of parts. After the new work or the style has happened, we may of course decompose it into all the strands of influence that went into its making. Its creative richness in fact may sometimes lie in this multitude of antecedents that it has gathered into itself—and transcended—but it could not have been predicted from those antecedents unless we ourselves were to go through the ardor and toil of creating it. As a young writer Hemingway toiled hard; he was also a very alert young man, all eyes and ears to pick up what he needed to forge a style that would be, in spite of all the borrowing, his own and uniquely his own. The influences closest at hand were those of Gertrude Stein and Ezra Pound. It is a rather remarkable experience, if you have not read it for some time, to pick up Gertrude Stein's *Three Lives* and feel how close it seems to Hemingway. But then you realize you are reading her with ears that have been attuned by the rhythms of Hemingway. Through Pound Hemingway was brought into contact with the goals of Imagist poetry—particularly of focusing on sharp, clear-cut images. And of this aspect of Hemingway's prose Ford Madox Ford has remarked that reading it is like looking through a perfectly transparent brook with all the boulders and pebbles clearly outlined through the water. But beyond these more immediate influences, Hemingway as a very self-conscious artist knew that he himself and his material had to stick deeper in the mainstream of American literature, and he therefore reached back for his primal source in Mark Twain's *Huckleberry Finn*. He himself has written that *Huckleberry Finn* was at the center of all that was best about American literature. Open the book to the earlier chapters about the river, and we seem to be in that lucid world of Hemingway. Mark Twain's language, cutting through abstractions, lets things appear and be what they are. But here again, the general point holds: the genuinely new work of art does not repeat but re-creates the past, or at least puts it in fresh focus. We are able to hear Mark Twain's rhythms more sensitively because we have been taught by Hemingway to hear them.

The questions of influences aside, it is more significant to ask to what end this style is being used. What is the vision it communicates?

The situation, of course, is World War I, and the action is taking place on the Italian front. The reader is not told this, but knows it only indirectly; the one geographical identification is the name of a particular town, Udine. One can imagine another kind of narrative in which a general sketch of the war, the location of the opposing armies, or the line-up of the various powers might be given first, and then the author would proceed to the tale of his individual characters. One would begin thus with a general framework within which a certain number of individual destinies are played out. That way of telling his story would be too abstract for Hemingway. What, after all, is "the war"? An abstraction in the mind of generals and statesmen. The men know marching, the smell of the guns, the dust in the roads, the sound of firing far off. The abstraction, called by orators "the war," decomposes itself into a number of atomic sensations with only a questionable relation among them. All facts—so long as they are facts for the senses—have the same value. The abstraction, the universal under which the sensory particulars are to be subsumed, has become meaningless. The honest observer is left only with those sensory fragments.

Accordingly, the syntax itself has a minimum of grammatical subordinating structures (paratactic rather than hypotactic, as the grammarians would put it). Everything in this world must be placed on the same level, and any trace of hierarchical order, even in language, must be abolished. Every phrase, like every fact, has equal value with any other. There is very sparing use of commas, since these would break the rhythm of the prose. The rhythm itself suggests the movement of marching feet— not the stamp, stamp, stamp of orderly regimental drill but the looser rolling or dragging movement of men coming and going monotonously. Commas suggest relation, order, structure; here what needs to be brought out is the brute facts themselves, and they must be left as unstructured as possible. The narrator is jealously on guard against being the dupe of any kind of abstractions. He can survive only by carefully protecting that small corner of his vision that makes up his own truth and that the powers of the world cannot take away from him.

Hemingway's hero is an outsider, not to the ordinary world at large like Camus' Meursault, but to a special situation, the war. Since the carnage of the war is senseless and incomprehensible, his rebellion and sarcasm are directed at it as a particular historical event, and at the lies of the various establishments that support it; but his nihilism is not extended to men and women generally. In fact, the insanity of the war is made into the background of a very touching and highly romantic love affair, to the illusion of which a character like Meursault could never give himself. The love affair between Lieutenant Henry and the nurse Catherine Barkley, which thrilled young readers during the twenties, does not wear quite so well today; or, rather, it wears like a beautiful episode from a great old movie that touches us because it has the quality of its period and, though beautiful, does not seem altogether real now. The young couple talk a little too much as if they were trying to convince themselves they are not lying about their love. It is all somewhat hoked-up, even if beautifully so. There are fewer than twenty years between Lieutenant Henry and Meursault; yet if they are to be taken as standards, the century has moved very fast in that time toward the loss of its values. One thing Hemingway, true American that he was, never became a nihilist about was the dream of romantic love.

Yet if Hemingway's rebellion is directed specifically against the historical event of the war, it is not a case of mere antiwar protest. The First World War was not an isolated disaster that fell upon European civilization from outside, like an earthquake or a tidal wave. It erupted from inside this civilization, and for that very reason was the turning point in the history of this century. Not only did the war transform governments, social systems, and national boundaries; the very quality of life itself was never to be the same as in the years before 1914. Two remarkable testimonies to the sweeping nature of this change are to be found in Robert Graves's autobiographical work *Goodbye to All That* and Ford Madox Ford's monumental tetralogy of novels, *No More Parades*, which is just beginning at this late date to win the recognition it deserves. Both Graves and Ford had gone through the war as soldiers, and in the course of that ordeal had learned that the Europe they had known would never return. It was easier for Hemingway—a young American, hardly more than a stripling—to find himself an alien to this war. It was, after all, *their* war—something fomented by the Europeans themselves, even though the Americans were later to enter it. The Europeans, however, and particularly those Europeans who had come to maturity before 1914 and had enjoyed the fruits of bourgeois civilization in its flower, could not push the war off on anyone else. If they were honest, they were bound to recognize that, by and large, it had begun with popular approval; at its outbreak vast and enthusiastic crowds had marched through all the capitals of Europe, ready for the cleansing self-sacrifice of patriotism. After all the banners and parades, when the fighting had slumped down into the filth, blood, and grinding monotony of the trenches, the exaltation turned into a shock of recognition. Since the war was no external accident, but came out of European civilization itself, this civilization had to be questioned more profoundly than it had ever been before. Hence the dissident, quizzical, and profoundly problematic quality of all European culture—in literature, music, the plastic arts, philosophy—in the 1920s.

This was the climate within which Hemingway began to write. Much as he strove in those early stories in *In Our Time* to capture the wonder of the Michigan woods as he remembered it from boyhood, he was living in Paris in the midst of a Europe that, in the words of Paul Valéry, "knew that it too was mortal." Henceforth he will never be able to recapture that innocence that the war has stolen from him. It is this cry of the heart for the stolen birthright of his innocence that we hear in the famous passage in *A Farewell to Arms*:

I was always embarrassed by the words sacred, glorious, and sacrifice and the expression in vain. We had heard them, sometimes standing in the rain almost out of earshot, so that only the shouted words came through, and had read them, on proclamations that were slapped up by billposters over other proclamations, now for a long time, and I had seen nothing sacred, and the things that were glorious had no glory and the sacrifices were like the stockyards at Chicago if nothing were done with the meat except to bury it. There were many words that you could not stand to hear and finally only the names of places had dignity. Certain numbers were the same way and certain dates and these with the names of the places were all you could say and have them mean anything. Abstract words such as glory, honor, courage, or hallow were obscene beside the concrete names of villages, the numbers of roads, the names of rivers, the numbers of regiments and the dates.

For a whole generation of youth this was the classic statement of protest against the butchery of World War I. But a work of art can never remain limited in its horizons by the particular historical circumstances that engendered it. To be a masterpiece it must always be able to re-create itself with fresh meanings for new and different situations. No protest novel ever succeeds in being great literature if it remains only a protest novel. Hemingway's book is no mere propaganda tract against the war. His revulsion against the war turns him positively in the direction in which at least some truth may be gleaned. If his innocence has been stripped from him, if he can never return to that wonder of the world when, as he says of the young Nick Adams, "In the early morning on the lake sitting in the stern of the boat with his father rowing, he felt quite sure that he would never die," nevertheless there is left a man's stalwart persistence in remaining true to those things that can be regained because perhaps they were never lost. To be true to the concrete rather than the abstract! To the names of rivers, of villages, to the numbers of regiments! To the things themselves!

I do not find it at all far-fetched to invoke the name of Edmund Husserl here and his phenomenological movement in philosophy. Of course, the two men "have nothing to do with each other"—in the usual sense of these words. Hemingway had no particular interest in philosophical ideas, but his choice of a certain mode of truth to be *his* truth was an existential commitment that only a pedant would deny to have genuine philosophical significance. For his part, Husserl also was intent on cutting through abstractions in order to find some terra firma beneath the clamorous battle of words that went on among the modern philosophic schools. It was also one more struggle in our rather frightening century to stand fast amid the turmoil of words. According to Husserl, our thinking had become saddled with ready-made prefabricated abstractions that did not reveal but obscured the look of things. In order to think better we would have to learn to look better; and that meant we would have to learn to see things in ways we had forgotten. Husserl therefore coined the slogan "Zu den Sachen selbst!" (To the things themselves!) as a rallying cry to bring philosophers closer to experience. Phenomenology has since become rather heavily academicized; but its primal motive was an effort toward a great humility of mind. Philosophy could no longer aim, as in the past, to build sweeping speculative systems that would hold together all of reality *sub specie aeternitatis.* Instead, it must content itself with holding fast, and remaining true to the gift of experience and what is given in that gift. After so much *hubris* of thought, philosophy must learn a modest and earthbound sobriety. As Husserl's follower Heidegger puts it, "Thinking must learn again to descend into the poverty of its materials." The ancient Greek sage Heraclitus, found by visitors sitting in his kitchen beside the warm stove, declared, "Enter; here too there are gods." And if the warmth of a kitchen stove may sometimes recall us to the truth of being better than the loftiest abstractions of reason, why not also the remembrance of certain names of rivers, of villages, streets, or the numbers of particular houses and regiments?

There is one theme and one theme only that philosophy has had to deal with since its beginning among the Greeks, and that is the everlasting struggle between Being and Seeming. Philosophy was born among the Greeks as the witness to this struggle. They, perhaps more than any other ancient people, had been shocked by the presence of illusion in human life. What we took to be solid, crumbles; what we took to be radiant truth turns into glossy image; what we took to be forthright turns into a trick of words. As soon as man begins to think, he is haunted by the need to find something stable amid this flux. This ancient duality between Being and Seeming is always there, hidden behind even the most technical and apparently arid disputes of philosophers. It emerges whenever the most formal of positivists is trying to show that the position of his adversaries is illusion and not reality. And it is in the light of this ancient struggle between the two that we have to read the passage from Hemingway quoted earlier, if we are going to read him philosophically at all. Against the semblances that are blared out in public places Hemingway must hold to that small circle of things in whose closeness he finds truth and being.

In the Western Indo-European languages there are two separate, but not necessarily unrelated, aspects of the idea of truth. One is contained in our English word "true": to be true to something is to hold fast to that thing and to persevere with it in patience. The German word for true, *wahr*, is connected with the word *bewahren*, to guard or preserve. It is the same root that appears in our English word "wary"; and significantly Hemingway uses often the image of the hunter, who must be wary out in the field as the writer Hemingway must warily guard those things that ultimately have meaning for him. (The same root appears in the Latin *verum*, meaning true.)

The second aspect of truth that the ancient languages have preserved in themselves comes to us from the Greek *aletheia*, usually translated as truth but which literally means "unhiddenness." Truth happens when a thing comes forth from the hidden into the open, from the darkness into the light, and is revealed as what it is. And we ourselves are capable of truth to the degree that we can let the thing be what it is so that it can shine before us as it is, while the veil of abstractions—woven either by our routines or by other people's empty phrases—falls away. Then we see it, as it were, for the first time. "I know" in ancient Greek is *oida*, literally "I have seen." Both these senses of truth are present in Hemingway's struggle "to put down what really happened in action" rather than "what you were supposed to feel, and had been taught to feel."

In fact, these two ancient senses of truth explain the two aspects of the Hemingway style that we previously noted. Style for him, we said, was a matter not of belles-lettres but of a style of life. Style provided a moral gauge or standard to which we must hold fast, which we must guard and preserve that it might also guard and preserve us. "It is what we have in place of religion," says Lady Brett Ashley in *The Sun Also Rises* after she decides to stick to her code and not play the bitch by ruining the young bullfighter Pedro Romero. But this morality of style is possible only through that other dimension of truth: the right style is one that lets us see things as they are. Only if language opens up some clearing, some open space in which we can lay hold of them, can we come close to and hold fast to the things that matter. In the language of Heidegger: truth as the rightness of a human act or attitude presupposes truth as *aletheia*, unhiddenness. We have to see truly in order to act rightly.

But these virtues of style, like everything else in human life, exact their price. To maintain a style requires discipline, toil, a kind of Spartan asceticism against the flabbier and easier thing to do. It is a mistake that some critics have made to think that Hemingway preaches a "cult of sensation" as if he were presenting us with some gluttonous or childish epicureanism. Yes, his characters—at least the ones that count for him—do seek to live in the present. Robert Jordan, in *For Whom the Bell Tolls*, as he is about to die, thinks: *"Now,* it has a funny sound to be a whole world and your life." But the "Now" can mean so much only if the disciplined courage of a whole life goes into the encounter with that moment. Exacting as the demands of this style are, it is only natural that the writer should slip at times. Hemingway does many times; he has written things, when the well was a little dry, that sound like parodies of himself. But even where the writing goes well, this style—as formal and stylized as Racine—imposes limitations inherent in itself. As a style of Spartan spareness, it exists by a constant process of excision, elimination, and rejection. Hence there is much left unsaid in Hemingway that is said by other novelists.

In his less pugnacious moments Hemingway would have admitted this. He understood that everything in life costs us something. There is nobody undefeated—despite that title to one of his stories—because success is paid for by a defeat somewhere along the line. In philosophical language, for us humans there is no Being without Nonbeing. Hemingway also understood that, and in one very short story, as we shall shortly see, he said it better than any other writer in this century. His tragic vision —if we can call it that—is altogether implicit in his style. Every mode of vision, which is what a style is, by its very nature must exclude things from its field. To focus a camera is to scan out other objects, other shades and lights, other ranges of possibility. All that we can rightfully ask is that when the camera is focused, and the shutter clicks, the image will come out sharp and clear and so fresh that we are really seeing it for the first time just because it was always there before our eyes though we were not able to look.

I

Of course, Hemingway's popularity depended on more than the famous style. He was also the writer of adventure stories, with all the excitements of physical action that can hold less intellectual readers. The contests of war, of hunting and fishing, bullfighting and boxing—these are subjects that can engage a popular audience even when they may be vehicles of more recondite and quite unpopular meanings. There is one important sense in which Hemingway may be said to be the most successful of modern writers: bestriding the chasm between highbrow and lowbrow, he was celebrated by both camps. This split between "the two audiences," which began in the nineteenth century with the universal spread of literacy, has been taken as the inescapable burden of all modern culture since. Hemingway manages to escape its restrictions. A whole generation of journalists and popular fictionists produced parodies of him in the well-known "tough guy" style while at the same time elaborate analyses of his books were being printed in the scholarly literary quarterlies. No other writer managed to speak to both cultures.

The vigor and excitement of the action, combined with the freshness of sensory perception, place much of Hemingway's work in the category of what might be called "boys' books." There is no denigration at all in this label. The genre includes some great works that we find it impossible to forget as adults. One obvious example of course, which Hemingway perpetually reread and studied, was *Huck Finn*, at once an enchanting boys' book and a monument of the American language. We discover Hemingway in our youth, and between him and us as readers there is always this secret covenant of youth. His first novel, *The Sun Also Rises*, was taken as the definitive lament for "the lost generation" of World War I; yet when we read it now, it has a freshness and exhilaration of youth that have disappeared from most writing today. These young people who proclaim their disillusion so readily are really having a high old time discovering Europe in the twenties and "travelling on the dollar," as Malcolm Cowley put it in a rather revealing memoir of the period and its atmosphere. To fish in the Basque country, watch the running of the bulls in Pamplona, or haunt the cafés of Paris —all these are exciting parts of the archetypical American experience of discovering another continent, though the terrain this time is that of an older civilization and not of the wilderness.

Hemingway is here solidly in the American grain. He finds himself there not merely by natural temperament but also by his deliberate and self-conscious attempt to place himself within that tradition, as shown by his penetrating reflections on American writing and writers in *Green Hills of Africa*. His postwar characters in Europe are a reincarnation of *Innocents*

Abroad, but since they have known the disillusion of the war they must guard against their innocence by being wary. Hemingway, the trained hunter, stalking down the Boule Mich' in Paris is as watchful of sights and sounds as Fenimore Cooper's Natty Bumppo on the prowl through the primeval forest listening for any menacing snap of a twig. Innocence and adventure —they are always present in Hemingway even when the tone and message of his stories border on the far edge of nihilism.

This innocence is part of the dream of an idyllic wilderness, as in the story "Big Two-Hearted River." Nick Adams is going fishing for trout in the Michigan woods. Here the style is more staccato than usual, yet it does not convey meaningless absurdity but magical enchantment. Fact after fact, each is outlined with marvelous clarity in the dew-wet morning where things seem to come to birth in the light for the first time. There is the water brown over the pebbles. There are the trout holding themselves steady with moving fins. Nick's shoes are squelchy as he walks in the cold stream. Step by step he gets his fishing gear ready. The grasshoppers jump in the wet grass; he catches some in a bottle for bait and then threads one of them with the hook: "Nick took him by the head and held him while he threaded the slim hook under his chin, down through his thorax and into the last segments of his abdomen. The grasshopper took hold of the hook with his front feet, spitting tobacco juice upon it." How can the same technique of style achieve two opposite effects—absurdity and meaninglessness in one place, and here enchantment and magic?

The same short staccato sentences report their disconnected facts, but now there is a thread of meaning, like an invisible string through the pearls of a necklace that holds the facts together. Fishing has meaning. But this meaning does not come through the human cleverness or contrivance that may go into the activity. Nick Adams has found this meaning only because for a moment he has escaped from the absurdities of human civilization. This meaning is not man-made; it descends upon man only because here for a brief while he lets the things of the earth be as they are and lets himself belong to them. "There was the meadow, the river and the swamp. There were birch trees in the green of the swamp on the other side of the river." These things of the earth are simply there; they do not answer any questions or tell us about any meanings of an abstract or general kind, but man himself acquires a meaning as he lets himself be there along with them. The earth gathers and holds all things, man included, together in the dew-wet morning. Step by step, Hemingway brings us back through the imagination of a boys' story to that morning of the world where we have at last discovered paradise lost. This dream of the unspoiled wilderness where all are redeemed haunts the American imagination, and perhaps secretly tarnishes our innocence at its source by a guilt for the virgin continent our civilization has raped and plundered. Hemingway's story methodically documents the same vision that Fitzgerald put at the end of *The Great Gatsby*, speaking of New World as it first appeared to the Dutch sailors under Henry Hudson: ". . . a fresh green breast of the new world. . . . for a transitory enchanted moment man must have held his breath in the presence of this continent, compelled into an aesthetic contemplation he neither understood nor desired, face to face for the last time in history with something commensurate to his capacity for wonder."

It would be possible thus to construct a very simple picture of Hemingway's career as the story of a Midwestern youth whose imagination would have been content with the lovely adventures in the Michigan woods except that the First World War tore him away, spoiled his innocence, and left him disillusioned. Simple, but not quite true. It would be the kind of biography that assigns everything to external events and nothing to the destiny that a man creates for himself out of his inborn temperament. The fact is that the dark shadows haunt even this boyhood paradise of the Michigan woods. In "Indian Camp," Nick goes with his father, who is a doctor, to help deliver a squaw who is having a hard time in childbirth. The woman's husband lies covered over with a blanket in the bunk overhead. When the child is finally delivered, Nick's father lifts off the blanket to see how the husband is doing. The Indian, unable to bear his wife's sufferings, has cut his throat from ear to ear. Death is never far away in the world of Hemingway, not even in the unspoiled woods of Michigan. He would have gone in search of the somber and violent in life even if the war had not thrust those facts upon him. In arranging his stories, he inserted short paragraphs between them dealing with some kind of violent action—either from the Greco-Turkish war that he had covered as a correspondent or bloody scenes from the bullring. It is as if these inserts were to place the more idyllic stories against their proper historical background, to set them as relatively peaceful interludes in the continuing condition of this century, which is that of permanent violence.

Here again, Hemingway is perfectly in the American grain. Violence, someone has said, is as American as apple pie. How much this cultivation of violence is connected with our famed American innocence would be a tempting subject to explore. I venture to think they are not unconnected. The innocent are very often more brutal than the worldly. An older and more worldly-wise person may do you harm, but it is more likely to be within the rules of the game that society prescribes. In any case, Hemingway's pursuit of the theme of violence is more than a matter of being in the native American grain; he sees that the violent is woven into the structure of life itself. Life is a contest, an *agon* as the ancient Greeks understood it, in which we are all, variously, prot*agon*ists and ant*agon*ists. Hence, the violence in Hemingway is stylized, since it is always played, even in nature, perhaps above all in nature, according to some form. The violence erupts within the patterns of war or the patterns of the bullring. Hence there is little of that random and sensationalistic violence that cheaper writers, falsely patterning themselves after him, throw in for fireworks. Of course, he does lapse on occasion, and when invention is lagging there is always the temptation to throw in the fireworks for filler. Near the opening of *To Have and Have Not,* for two pages shots are sprayed in all directions in an episode that is pointless except perhaps in suggesting the atmosphere of random violence in which the rest of the story will be played out. The passage is too long and not worth quoting anyway, but the last sentences convey the tone:

> He shot twice over the nigger's head, coming on, and once low.
>
> He hit a tire on the car because I saw dust blowing in a spurt on the street as the air came out, and at ten feet the nigger shot him in the belly with the Tommy gun, with what must have been the last shot in it because I saw him throw it down, and old Pancho sat down hard and went over forwards. He was trying to come up, still holding onto the Luger, only he couldn't get his head up, when the nigger took the shotgun that was lying against the wheel of the car by the chauffeur and blew the side of his head off. Some nigger.

The cynicism is a little forced, as much in this novel is forced, because Hemingway was laboring against the onset of Marxism in the thirties, a climate in which—for reasons we shall see later —he could not be very comfortable, and at this stage he was momentarily scraping the bottom of the barrel. Much more significant is the quiet and menacing violence of "The Killers." It is only natural that as violence has been the stuff of history in our century, so it has become a staple in the entertainment of the masses. But all those countless reels of movies, and droning hours and half-hours on television, filled with the noises of shootings, screeching automobile tires, and assorted mayhem, never capture the inner essence of violence as it is disclosed in this simple and quiet story. Here the violence is so stylized that it never explodes in action: Nick Adams and the Negro cook are tied up by the gangsters, but later released unharmed, and that is all. But the threat and the menace are in the air, and that is enough to establish the quiet vibrating presence of violence.

Philosophically speaking, the violent and menacing go hand in hand. Violence is woven into the warp and woof of life because the menacing is always lurking beneath the surface of things. This stylization of violence reaches its acme in the bullring, and that is why this form of contest captured Hemingway's imagination. The bullfight turns violence into pure ritual. The liberal imagination of the 1930s sneered at Hemingway's passion for bullfighting as childish and silly. Perhaps it was; but whatever the moralities involved, whether or not Hemingway was being a nonhumanitarian, his imagination required this cleansing rite. The modern world was formed by the rationalism of the Enlightenment and of the French Revolution. Spain escaped these things, and that was one reason why it became Hemingway's adopted country. While the French during their revolution were enthroning the goddess of Reason in the cathedral of Notre Dame, the Spaniards went on with their bullfights. This ritual of death in the afternoon, which can be traced back to Neolithic times, brings us back to an older and deeper stratum in human nature.

Though so much in Hemingway is solidly in the American grain, there is one rather startling exception: these "boys' books," these fresh and open adventure stories, always end in the defeat of the hero. America is the country, William Dean Howells once said, that wants a tragedy with a happy ending. It is a mark of Hemingway's extraordinary success as a writer that he managed to be vastly popular with the general public even though he lacked the upbeat ending. The solitary hero, alone at the end, has to reckon upon defeat. This is the prevailing pattern in Hemingway, and it almost never varies. Jake Barnes (in *The Sun Also Rises*) remains as he was, but all the gaiety of those expatriate lives has flickered out like so many ghosts only to leave him alone in his own void of impotence. Frederic Henry (in *A Farewell to Arms*) has fled the war and lost his beloved in death. Robert Jordan (in *For Whom the Bell Tolls*) is killed in the Spanish Civil War. The old fisherman (in *The Old*

Man and the Sea) is defeated by the sea, or because "he went out too far," like a hero of Greek tragedy who has exceeded the due limits fixed for man. It always looks as if the defeat followed from some specific situation within the field of contest where the action takes place. It is defeat by the war, by the bulls, or by the monstrous sharks of the deep. But the specific situation is only a pretext. Any field of activity will do just as well to illustrate the inevitability of defeat. For this defeat is not just the occasional mishap or failure in some field of action but is woven into the fabric of human existence itself. Life is the contest in which even the winner will take nothing.

It is easy to see then why courage should become for Hemingway the indispensable virtue. What is the menace that lurks in Hemingway's world? What is it really that we have to fear? It is that at some moment when we do not expect it our courage will fail us. Driven by this fear, Hemingway went out of his way to test his own courage—in war, the hunting of big game, deep-sea fishing. But all these ordeals by fire were no guarantee that courage might not desert him that dark night in Idaho when he was led to take his own life. In life there is never any guarantee. What is the fear behind this fear that courage can always desert us? It is the presence of the void to which, however we hide from it, we are always exposed. Courage is therefore not the special and gaudy virtue of the man of action; it is the act of life itself as we endure from one moment to the next. Courage is to know quietly and surely that the void is always there, ready to spring, even though sometimes by going off to the wars or hunting big game we may actually be running away from its presence. Hemingway did not run away from it as an artist; in one very short story, only eight pages, "A Clean Well-Lighted Place," he has delivered this message of the void behind our fears without any fanfare of violent action; and delivered it almost with the crispness of a definition, as if he were producing a summation of the real question and the real challenge that always had lurked behind the external tests of war or hunting.

II

The story first appeared in the volume *Winner Take Nothing* (1930)—a title deliberately and carefully chosen to strike the philosophical tone of the whole collection. The scene is a café in a Spanish city, probably Madrid, late at night. An old man sits drinking alone, while two waiters hover at the rear of the café until he finishes and they can lock up. The younger waiter is impatient to get home to his wife; the older waiter, who understands why the old man does not want to go home, explains: " 'I am of those who like to stay late at the café. With all those who do not want to go to bed. With all those who need a light for the night.' " The younger waiter, who belongs to another breed, cannot understand. At last, he gets the old man out, and leaves the older waiter to lock up; and at this point, in the soliloquy of the older waiter, occurs one of the most remarkable passages in all of Hemingway:

> Turning off the electric light he continued the conversation with himself. It is the light of course but it is necessary that the place be clean and pleasant. You do not want music. Certainly you do not want music. Nor can you stand beside a bar with dignity although that is all that is provided for these hours. What did he fear? It was not fear or dread. It was a nothing that he knew too well. It was all a nothing and a man was a nothing too. It was only that and light was all it needed and a certain cleanness and order. Some lived in it and never felt it but he knew it was nada y pues nada y nada y pues nada. Our nada who art in nada, nada be thy name thy kingdom nada thy will be nada in nada as it is in nada. Give us this nada our daily nada and nada us our nada as we nada our nadas and nada us not into nada but deliver us from nada; pues nada. Hail nothing full of nothing, nothing is with thee.

This antiphonal repetition of "nada," the Spanish word for nothing, and the blasphemous transformation of two traditional Christian prayers into invocations to this Nothing may make some readers gag. But Hemingway, who always considered himself a believer though slightly in arrears, was never flippant about Catholicism; and he is not likely to have taken blasphemy upon himself lightly. Nor is there any gratuitous seeking for the sensational here; in rhythm and tone this passage fits in perfectly with the whole story. This soliloquy only names what the story as a whole work of art reveals—the presence of Nothing. The atmosphere is sketched in with a few slight but perfect strokes: the shadow of the leaves against the electric light, the terrace, the empty tables, the laconic chatter of the waiters. And through and around all these, and just as real, circulates the presence of this Nothing.

Our ordinary response to any experience like this is to dismiss it as "a mere mood." To talk about Nothing is nonsensical. Yet if we take Hemingway at his word here (and he uses words carefully), he has already forestalled such a response. "It was not fear or dread," he tells us. "it was a nothing that he knew too well." Fear and dread are moods; but what is in question for the waiter here is not a mood but a presence that he knows and knows all too well. So far as the mood of Hemingway's story is concerned, it is in no way morbid, despairing, or deranged. Rather, its tone is one of somber and lucid courage. Here he dares name the presence that had circulated, unnamed and unconfronted, through and behind much of his earlier writing.

As a matter of fact, human moods and reactions to the encounter with Nothingness vary considerably from person to person, and from culture to culture. The Chinese Taoists found the Great Void tranquilizing, peaceful, even joyful. For the Buddhists in India, the idea of Nothing evoked a feeling of universal compassion for all creatures caught in the toils of an existence that is ultimately groundless. In the traditional culture of Japan the idea of Nothingness pervades the exquisite modes of aesthetic feeling displayed in painting, architecture, and even the ceremonial rituals of daily life. Yet Western man, up to his neck in *things*, objects, gadgets, and the business of mastering them, recoils with anxiety from any encounter with Nothingness and labels any talk of it as merely "nihilistic" (in the pejorative sense of this word, as implying some kind of moral delinquency or slackness). On the question of Nihilism we seem to shuttle back and forth between rhetoric on the one side or on the other. But how can we possibly understand what is really at issue in this question unless we are able to think soberly about the "nihil," the nothing, that lies at the heart of this word? Hemingway's story, so spare and sober in itself, invites us to a corresponding sobriety of thought.

The story was published in 1930. If we assume that it was in the works a little earlier, then we can say that it was being created at just about the same time that a German professor, Martin Heidegger, delivered the lecture inaugurating him in the chair of philosophy at Freiburg University, entitled "What Is Metaphysics?" the subject of which was Nothingness. (The reader will again, I hope, smile tolerantly at this rather literal-minded use of temporal correspondences. A respect for the synchronous dimension of time is one of my private superstitions, which I nevertheless strive to moderate with a judicial irony. An appreciation for the synchronicity of temporal events is one of the marked characteristics of primitive thought, and I like wherever possible to keep my peace with the thinking of primitives, which by the way we find more and more to have a validity that we had not suspected.) At the conclusion of that lecture, which subsequently became very famous and, for some philosophers, infamous, Heidegger declared that Nothingness lies at the heart of Being because in fact Being and Nothingness are one and the same.

Being and Nothingness, Being and Nonbeing, are identical! The assertion struck, and still strikes, many philosophers as scandalous nonsense. Of course, what was intended was not that bare identity that prevails within the world of objects, where everything is simply and vacuously identical with itself. The morning star is identical with the evening star. Here we have two different descriptions that happen to name one and the same thing. This is the kind of identity that holds within the world of objects. But Being is not an object or thing, for Heidegger; and certainly Nothingness would even be less so. The identity that holds between them is not the identity between two different names that name the same object. They are identical because they belong to and with each other, because they are revealed in experience as uniquely and inextricably meshed with each other. But even with these qualifications, the assertion that Being and Nothingness belong to each other will seem a puzzling and arbitrary paradox to many people. What does this "belonging together" mean? In justice to the simple but pure vision of Hemingway's story we must push our thinking further.

Consider that strange reality which we call time. We find it impossible to think of time as a thing; it is a non-thing, a no-thing. Perhaps because they could not thingify time, many philosophers were led to conclude that time was not real, that it belonged to the world of appearance rather than reality. That may well be; but if time is not ultimately real, nevertheless it is within this unreality that we humans are born, live out our days on earth, and die. For us mortals time is a sovereign, perhaps the sovereign, reality. But what is real in time, we say, is the present. Yesterday is gone, tomorrow is yet to come; today is here, and to be here is to be present. Yesterday, which is *no* longer, and tomorrow, which is *not* yet, belong to the negative realm of nonbeing. But consider today, which we say is present and therefore real. Half of it is already gone, and is therefore *no* longer; half of it has *not yet* arrived. This present reality is thus made up of negatives. Suppose we shorten the length of time to this present hour. Here too, part of this hour is *no* longer, part is *not* yet. No matter how far we go in shortening the interval we find always a finite duration in which past-present-future are joined together. Time, so sovereignly real for us mortals, is thus compounded of Nonbeing.

More significant even than this divisibility of time is the fact that the present has its identity only through past and future. The present cannot be experienced except as the juncture between past and future. Today is today only because it separates —and joins—yesterday and tomorrow. We never experience the present as a solid self-contained reality; it opens backward on the past and forward on the future. What we experience is not the separate tenses of time, but the three together: past-PRESENT-future. The past, to repeat, is *no* longer, the future *not* yet. But without the nonbeing of the past and future, time would not be real. We mortals exist between the immense stretch of the past that is no more and of the future that is not yet. Creatures of time, we are creatures of non-Being. The language may sound rather high-flown, but it merely reports the most pervasive and ordinary reality of life as we toil in that flickering region between past and future. Struggling today to connect yesterday with tomorrow, our lives are a continual traffic with nonbeing. We are such stuff as dreams are made on, said Shakespeare. Probably. But certainly, and in a very literal sense, nonbeing is the stuff of which our lives are woven.

This philosophic excursion may seem very remote from Hemingway's simple little story. No doubt, Hemingway never went through any chain of reasoning like the above. He did not need to; the artist in the simplicity of his vision has seen and therefore knows (in the Greek sense of *oida*, "I know, I have seen") without the halting steps of analysis. Philosophic interpretations of works of art are only the pedantic steps of a schoolboy tracing this vision in order to dismember it and see how it works.

We have labored at length on the exegesis of so short a work because this little story seems to us to provide the key to Hemingway, to mark out the center from which we must read backward to all the earlier and forward to all the later writings. To say what he had to say here Hemingway needed neither heroic nor violent action. In tone it is one of the quietest things he ever wrote. All the derring-do, all the explosions of violent action, are so many gaudy fireworks that flicker against the void that is always quietly and persistently there. It is persistently there, in Heidegger's phrase, as the silent power of the possible. Possibility, Heidegger says further, is a prior and more basic reality in human existence than is actuality. The actualities of violence gather their meaning as the Menacing through the possibility of Nothingness that lurks behind them. In the light of this story we can also understand the obsession with death that looms everywhere through Hemingway's writings. Dying may come in many ways—in warfare, the bullring, by random gunshot. The actual modes vary, but the possibility that lurks is one and the same, and its meaning is this: I die, and become Nothing, and the world becomes Nothing for me.

There is no morbidity in these observations. Nothingness, as a possibility, is simply an inevitable part of the human condition. No more but no less. Even those for whom religious faith still provides the hope of heaven do not escape this lurking question. For faith is faith and not certainty, as Kierkegaard pointed out, and therefore can never dispel, but must always live in vital tension with, the doubt that menaces it: "Lord, I believe; help thou my unbelief." The essence of faith is the inner contest with its antithesis, which is the possibility of Nothingness. There are also other and more external ways of waging this contest. Against the ravages of time with its menace of Nonbeing mankind has sought to erect a buttress of stability in social institutions, traditional values, and religious rituals. We need all of these; but in philosophical honesty we have to recognize that they are only methods of coping with a condition of mortal life that can never be eradicated. One is not an irresponsible nihilist in pointing this out.

Hemingway also says: ". . . and a man was nothing too." This statement could be facilely misunderstood as a depreciation of human existence as petty and worthless. In the context of Hemingway's story, however, these words have just the opposite meaning: they indicate the region of Being within and against which men rise to authentic grandeur. Man, so far as we know, is the only animal who is conscious of his own death. He is therefore the only animal who projects and sustains his being within nonbeing. He did not have to wait for modern Nihilism in order to find this out. It is the discovery in which almost at the dawn of history he begins to be the strange creature that he is. The most moving hymn ever sung to man and his works is the choral ode of Sophocles in *Antigone*. There are many strange and awesome things, the poet tells us, but the most awesome is man himself. He drives his ships over the stormy sea; he tills the earth remorselessly with his plows; with his cunning snares he captures the birds of the air, the beasts of the field, the fish of the deep, he masters the wild horse and the mountain bull and puts the yoke upon their necks. And, most of all, he has speech, in which he can fix his shifting thoughts and so found cities and civilization. There seem to be no limits to his audacity and his skills. But with all these powers, "He comes upon Nothing." He seems able to devise an escape from everything, but he has no contrivance against death. *Ep' erchetai ouden*, "He comes upon Nothing"—these are the simple and straightforward words of the ancient poet. Clearly, the Nothing is not an invention of the high-strung sensibility of our period. Nobody has ever accused Sophocles of being a sick soul.

We are now (through this little story of Hemingway) able to take a more penetrating view of modern Nihilism, as well as of the discrepant attitudes that stem from it. Part of it is an authentic discovery, or rediscovery, of an ancient, inexpungeable, and very prosaic truth: man is the being whose Being is always open to the menace of Nonbeing. So long as Christianity worked, faith could provide a means of holding oneself steady within this condition. The rediscovery of this condition, in the midst of a secular civilization, was too strong for some tender souls, who crumble under its burden. Hence the cynical "nihilism" that abandons all values. On the other hand, the discovery that man and all his works are mortal is too disturbing for a technical and industrial civilization, which today, as at its inception in the eighteenth century, is founded upon the idea of progress. The shadow must be banished from the glittering metallic surface of our technological wonders. Hence, the thought about Nothingness is banned as something "morbid," a socially undesirable and reprehensible state of mind. Both attitudes—the indifferent relapse into or the smug and extravert flight from the Nothing—are inauthentic. Hemingway's story, on the contrary, teaches us that there is a more truthful, manly, and sober way of facing this Nothingness.

But one cannot gaze at this pure possibility forever. We humans are driven to turn our eyes away from it to facts, events, things. Hemingway's vision is so accurate that he records this impulse too. The older waiter, at the close of the story, thinks to himself: "Now, without thinking further, he would go home to his room. He would lie in bed and finally, with daylight, he would go to sleep. After all, he said to himself, it is probably only insomnia. Many must have it." "It is only insomnia"—with a sudden and quiet click the camera has changed its focus. The interior possibility is banished, and we are returned to the external world where insomnia is merely one among many statistical facts. "Many must have it"—these "many" are the other people, never ourselves, the others who are faceless and anonymous items on a list of statistics. We need such a public and routine world to shore us up from the other vision.

But insomnia is perhaps a more privileged philosophical state than the old waiter thinks. Each night, in those moments before we go off to sleep, we are alone, sundered from others and their world, passing into the shadow that is a simulacrum of death, ready to sink into the ancient waters of the unconscious. It is a situation that easily begets anxiety, and the old prayer records it: "Now I lay me down to sleep. I pray the Lord my soul to keep. If I should die before I wake, I pray the Lord my soul to take." Hemingway suffered from insomnia nearly all of his adult life, and he knew the subtlety of its ways. In "The Gambler, the Nun, and the Radio," the action takes place against the background of the writer's insomnia. This story belongs to the same period as "A Clean Well-Lighted Place," and because it is so similar in mood and deals, in the last analysis, with the same reality, it illuminates some of the things implicit in the other. In any case, it can do well as a summation of Hemingway, since it marks out clearly the three points in the spiritual compass between which he was always hovering.

Mr. Frazer, a writer who can be taken as Hemingway himself, is in the hospital at Hailey, Montana, having broken his leg in a fall from a horse. He has already become impatient and bored at the long period of recuperation. Two men, a Russian and a Mexican, have been shot and are brought into the hospital ward. The Russian, a beet worker, has been wounded in the thigh, and keeps the hospital awake all night with his screams; the Mexican gambler, Cayetano, far more seriously wounded, keeps stoically quiet. A detective sergeant tries to get him to tell who his assailant was, but Cayetano remains true to his own code, and will not talk even though he believes he is going to die. Mr. Frazer, acting as interpreter, tells him there is no dishonor under these circumstances for naming the man who shot him: "One can, with honor, denounce one's assailant." But the Mexican's code calls for silence, and even if these are his last moments, he must live nonchalantly and gracefully with the code that he has chosen, absurd as his silence might seem to others.

There is also a young nun, Sister Cecilia, who serves as nurse in the ward and also visits Mr. Frazer in his private room. She is an altogether engaging person, and Hemingway has completely succeeded in presenting her as a convincing and attractive example of genuine religious faith—not a very easy thing for a writer to bring off. Part of the success is due to the good humor with which she abounds. Mr. Frazer, who has a radio, invites her to listen to a broadcast of a Notre Dame football game, but she refuses:

> "Oh, no. I couldn't do it. The world series nearly finished me. When the Athletics were at bat I was praying right out loud: 'Oh, Lord, direct their batting eyes! Oh, Lord, may he hit one! Oh, Lord, may he hit safely!' Then when they filled the bases in the third game, you remember, it was too much for me. 'Oh, Lord may he hit it out of the lot! Oh, Lord, may he drive it clean over the fence!' Then you know when the Cardinals would come to bat it was simply dreadful. 'Oh, Lord may they not see it! Oh, Lord, may they fan!' And this game is even worse. It's Notre Dame. Our Lady. No, I'll be in the chapel."

Religious faith is more convincing when it permits itself a sense of humor. Hemingway respects her, and if he himself is not a believer, he nevertheless has complete belief in *her* faith. The faith of Catholicism, as a faith, is always honored in his writings. Amid all the bawdy army talk of *Farewell to Arms*, the priest, who is present, is always respected as a man of God by the young Frederic Henry. The blasphemous prayer in "A Clean Well-Lighted Place" thus gathers more meaning when we reflect that it comes from a man who did not take such blasphemy lightly.

Three Mexicans, who have come to visit the gambler, call on Mr. Frazer. They are identified sparsely as the big one, the small one, and the thin one. The last will not take a drink; it mounts to his head, he explains. He is also the somber atheist of the group. "I was acolyte," he says proudly. "Now I believe in nothing. Neither do I go to mass. . . . Religion is the opium of the poor." Hemingway-Frazer obviously does not like this thin and solemn atheist who cannot take a drink. Later, Mr. Frazer, hovering on the void before sleep, ruminates on the opium theme: " 'Religion is the opium of the people. He believed that, that dyspeptic little joint-keeper. Yes, and music is the opium of the people. Old mount-to-the-head hadn't thought of that. And now economics is the opium of the people; along with patriotism the opium of the people in Italy and Germany.' "

The passage is revealing on the subject of Hemingway and Marxism. On the whole, Hemingway was uncomfortable with the Marxism of the 1930s. Though he had sympathies with poor and ordinary folk, the abstractions of the Left went against his grain. For the Marxist, as the orthodox party-liner Georg Lukacs has put it, "the developmental tendencies of history partake of a higher reality than the 'facts' of mere experience." Unfortunately, History (with the big H) can become an abstraction in the name of which millions of people are slaughtered as millions were slaughtered for the abstractions of nationalism in the First World War. And against such abstractions Hemingway the artist would take shelter, like his character Frederic Henry, in the concrete names of rivers and towns and streets. Hemingway finally did give way to the *Zeitgeist* in his big novel about the Spanish Civil War, *For Whom the Bell Tolls*; but the capitulation is only partial since its hero, Robert Jordan, fights out of a sense of identity with the Spanish people and is only an indifferent Marxist. And the book is marred by a certain oratorical tone in parts, which is due, I think, to the solemn pieties of that decade.

In any case, in the present story Hemingway clearly rejects the atheist-Marxist in the person of the thin Mexican. Mr. Frazer's sympathies move between the opposite poles of the nun and the gambler. She is a woman of simple and unshakable faith, whose love and cheerfulness nothing can daunt. Cayetano, on the other hand, is the absurd hero who carries out his code, even if it is only the code of a cheap gambler, defiantly and gracefully against the Void. It is what is left him in place of religion. Hemingway never makes any bones about his belief that this code is a replacement of religion. In *The Sun Also Rises*, Lady Brett Ashley deserts the young matador Pedro Romero because she feels her dissoluteness will corrupt him. "You know, it makes one feel good deciding not to be a bitch," she explains. "It's sort of what we have instead of God."

And Frazer-Hemingway? What is left for him? As a man of action, he can give himself to the ritual that is absorbing enough to make one forget the Void. But the writer is in another boat; he is an observer who must keep a wakeful eye on the uncanny presence behind all human actions. So Mr. Frazer has his insomnia. He is condemned to be the sleepless consciousness recollecting the actions of the day and mindful of the darkness into which they may all pass. It is a lonely vigil, a solitude in which all beings recede to a distance. But Mr. Frazer also has his radio. He can tune in on Minneapolis and Seattle and hear distant voices speaking to him through the darkness. He also has imagination, and in his mind's eye he can see the people getting up in Minneapolis or riding in the white taxicabs of Seattle. In the great Void people are at once very far off and painfully close. He does not have the faith of the nun, and the code of the gambler is available to him only intermittently in his pursuit of style, whether in language or in action. He hovers between them both in the lucid wakefulness that has made its peace with Nothingness. It may not seem much perhaps, but it is something. Besides, there is always the possibility of sleep before morning.

4.Backward Toward the Earth

... it's not even time until it was.

The face of Medusa was supposed to turn men into stone. Painted by the artist, however, it may amuse, delight, or enchant the viewer. There is always a risk in a work of art that would present us with a meaningless world. The artist may be frozen by the Medusa face, find himself and his art without meaning, and become speechless or incoherent. On the other hand, if he succeeds, he may so enthrall us that we take his vision too lightly. The rhetoric of Nihilism may even become fashionable. A generation of young people struck the stance of the early Hemingway characters without even imagining what the disillusion of World War I must have been like. Today students can throw around the words of Sisyphus and Meursault as if the experience of an absurd world were an adventure of high-hearted youth. When we come, however, to Faulkner and a novel like *The Sound and the Fury*, the terror is so plainly there that it becomes difficult to see how anyone could take it lightly.

Our argument so far—to look backward for just a moment—has turned chiefly around a certain question of style: the use and meaning of a technique that appeared for the first time in history in the fiction of this century. This technique requires the dissolving of experience into small and sometimes random moments, the severing of the more abstract threads of custom, convention, or belief that usually hold these moments together so that we are presented with a world that lacks the meanings necessary to bind its fragments together. Though a splendid contrivance of art, this device was also a child of historical necessity. It seemed the only means by which the writer could bring to expression that desolate prospect of a world becoming more and more meaningless in our time. Properly presented, this fragmented world might even have its own seductive rhythms and graces.

In Camus this style has already acquired the restraint and measure of French classicism; indeed, the technique had almost become classic in the modern repertoire, since a decade and a half of Hemingway imitations, good, bad, and indifferent, lay behind Camus' use of it. In Hemingway, one of the progenitors, the staccato prose that reduces everything to its sensory components can also be suffused by a magical lyricism, since in pulverizing the abstractions of social man we are permitted to regain the sensory wonders open to natural man. In Faulkner's *The Sound and the Fury*, the technique is carried to much bolder lengths of experimentation and more shocking effects of horror, beside which Camus and Hemingway pale into almost half-hearted nihilists. At the same time, though it carries the disconnecting and dismembering of experience very much further, this novel—such is its superb and paradoxical triumph as a work of art—is a far more intricately and internally organized whole than anything done by Camus or Hemingway. *The Sound and the Fury*, for all I know, may be the most powerful statement of the absurdity of human existence ever written. Accordingly, it should carry us a long step forward in our effort to understand this modern specter.

I

Like nearly all of Faulkner, this novel cannot be read apart from the rest of his work. We understand it—in the most literal sense of grasping the situations and the characters of the Compson family with which it deals—through many facts that we learn through other parts of the Faulkner saga. All his writings together build one larger work, a single imaginary world, and the references of his imagination crisscross back from one book to the other. In the deeper sense too, we understand this novel only as it is in tension with the other side of Faulkner, the folk poet and folk humorist, who eventually emerges and must emerge to compensate for the vision of absurdity. Faulkner himself remarked that *The Sound and the Fury* was the favorite of his novels, in the way in which a mother may favor the most delicate of her children. This is the most high-strung, avant-garde, and anguished of his works; the healing and reconciling element had to come from an older and riper Faulkner. Nevertheless, we must make the effort to take it up alone, to read it just as it is, if only to recapture that initial shock of recognition with which it first flayed our nerves. It is one of the earliest of his works, written before *Sartoris* (which appeared the spring of 1929), though not published until later that year. In any case, it is the novel from which we may well begin to read Faulkner.

The book is divided into four sections, labeled only by dates: April 7, 1928; June 2, 1910; April 6, 1928; April 8, 1928. At first glance, this looks like an altogether arbitrary shuffling of the time order. In fact, this nonsequential sequence is very carefully planned. While Hemingway and Camus disconnect experience into atoms, they both preserve the ordinary temporal sequence. Faulkner goes further and dislocates the order of time itself, since chronology is just one more prop by which man tries to assure himself that his existence has order and meaning. Actually, the flashback to the second section, eighteen years earlier, is artistically in place, for on that day Quentin Compson, a student at Harvard, commits suicide and thereby destroys forever the future hopes of the Compson family and consigns them henceforth to their own tight circle of doom. The section thus holds together and explains the three other parts, though this structure becomes clear to us only when we have worked through the whole. Faulkner's imagination is as dense and cryptic as life itself, which divulges only scraps and hints of information as we move forward in darkness in order to look backward with some glimmer of understanding.

But even if we grant the author the familiar prerogative of a flashback, why the scrambled order of the April dates—7, 6, and 8—instead of the usual order? We will have much to say later on Faulkner's treatment of time, which is one of the most profound among the many modern literary experiments with this baffling category. Suffice it for the moment to observe what is simply and directly implied by this cutting and reshuffling of the temporal order. Nothing less than that time itself has no intrinsic order but is a kind of homogeneous stuff into which we can cut where we will, and transpose where we will, always finding the same viscous substance congealed around people and events. In a homogeneous substance you can move backward or forward indifferently. Earlier or later you will always find the Compsons exactly where they were.

If we inquire further about the significance of these three dates, we are in for a greater shock. In the Year of Our Lord 1928 Easter Sunday fell on April 8. Thus the three dates—April 6, 7, and 8—were, respectively, Good Friday, Holy Saturday, and Easter Sunday. These are the three holiest days in the Christian calendar, commemorating the death of God on the cross, his burial in the tomb and descent into hell, and his resurrection on Easter morning. How far does Faulkner intend the parallel with the sacred mystery of Christianity? We know from other works that his imagination was intermittently haunted by the Christian drama, and we have no reason not to take seriously the fact that he has very carefully dated these three particular days of the year. But if we are to follow the parallel seriously, we have immediately to ask: Who then is Christ in this horrendous tale of the Compsons? The only answer would seem to be Benjy, the feeble-minded youngest son, who is repeatedly mentioned to be thirty-three years old, the age, according to tradition, at which Jesus was crucified. This identification of a slobbering idiot as a Christ figure must strike many readers as coarse and unfeeling even when they are not literal believers. Dostoevsky, in *The Idiot*, had created a Christ-like figure in the character Prince Myshkin, who is afflicted with epilepsy, "the sacred disease," and finally goes mad. But Myshkin is lucid throughout most of the story, and he has a remarkable effect upon some of the people he encounters. He fails, of course, as such a character is bound to, with the neurotics to whom he draws closest, and finally passes into the night of madness. But en route he has made us believe in his sanctity, and to the extent that we do we are still believing in the viability of the Christian view. Benjy, on the other hand, remains locked within the closed circle of his wailing and blubbering idiocy throughout.

Yes, one cannot deny it, there is a certain brutal and unfeeling streak that runs through Faulkner's temperament. The violence of his imagination does not flinch from such things as rape, murder, insanity, sodomy: and sometimes he seems intent on thrusting these themes aggressively before the reader's attention. In Jason, the youngest Compson son, he has created one of the coldest and meanest men in literature, and yet one detects a certain enjoyment on the author's part as if he were releasing a certain mean streak in himself. But a brutal image may enable the writer to say what he has to say in the most blunt and unmistakable way. Sometimes he may have to follow the admonition of Yeats and

> Cast a cold eye
> On life, on death,

however offensive this cold and cruel gaze may seem to the sentimental.

Half a century separates Dostoevsky's Myshkin and Faulkner's Benjy, and in that time the chances of Christianity, to which Dostoevsky himself could hold only by the skin of his teeth, had hardly improved. Faulkner in 1929, however his feelings may have been tempered later, tells us by this Christ-Benjy parallel: Look and see, do not deceive yourselves by sentimentality, here is the hopeless and dead end at which your Christian tradition arrives. Christ was the victim of man's sins who died in order to bring the hope of redemption. Benjy is simply a victim through the brute contingency that he was born at all. Faulkner's vision goes back beyond Christian hope to the oldest and starkest pessimism of the Greeks: "Better never to have been born."

All of the foregoing, however, are facts *about* the book. We have yet to begin to read it, and read it as we should, as if for the first time. We turn to the first page:

> Through the fence, between the curling flower spaces, I could see them hitting. They were coming toward where the flag was and I went along the fence. Luster was hunting in the grass by the flower tree. They took the flag out, and they were hitting. Then they put the flag back and they went to the table, and he hit and the other hit. Then they went on, and I went along the fence. Luster came away from the flower tree and we went along the fence and they stopped and we stopped and I looked through the fence while Luster was hunting in the grass.

What is happening here? Every word is simple and understandable, but the sense of this whole—at first reading, anyway—is opaque. The first words of the next paragraph supply the clue: "Here, caddie," one of the men cries. They are playing golf. Why does the author not write simply: "Through the fence I watched them playing golf"? That would imply that what they are doing has some meaning; the game of golf would be a structure that binds together the discrete fragments of action —"he hit and the other hit." Hemingway's hero (in the passage analyzed earlier) had come to disbelieve in the abstraction "the war," and he was able to see it only as the shambling march of men along a dusty road. But war is a very high-level and complex abstraction, and its unity as a single phenomenon—the

War of 1914–18, for example—exists only in the minds of generals and historians. The game of golf is a much simpler structure, yet even this elementary universal disintegrates here into its minute particulars, and we are immediately aware that we have descended to a much more abysmal level of fragmentation than we encountered in Hemingway. Who is this "I" speaking? Shortly, we piece together through the density of the text that it is none other than Benjy, and that at the very outset we are inside the mind of an idiot and looking out on a world more opaque, flat, and alien than any character of Hemingway or Camus could ever confront.

Can a character of such feeble intelligence be self-conscious enough to say "I" at all, to distinguish between self and the blank data of sense and memory that flicker across his empty gaze? Probably not. Yet we are willing to concede its use as a literary device, a convention as formal in its way as the use of blank verse for dramatic speech. It is a mistake to think that the stream-of-consciousness technique ever gives us the total and literal contents of a character's mind, for that enormous flood could never be captured and represented by art. Wherever the stream of consciousness succeeds—in Faulkner, Joyce, Virginia Woolf—it requires some very strict convention on the writer's part to screen the welter of data. This "I" of Benjy—perhaps psychiatrically impossible—is the feeble and minimal glow needed to light up the darkness of his agony.

His consciousness flickers back and forth between the present, in which he is led around helplessly by the Negro boy Luster, and the past of his childhood when, though just as helpless, he could still play with his brothers Quentin and Jason and his sister Candace (Caddy). But here we are not dealing with normal memory in its passage from one plane of time to another. Here the planes of time collapse into one and cease to be distinguishable. Present and past blur into one indistinguishable substance. To heighten this effect Faulkner employs some puzzling ambiguities. Quentin, for example, is the name of the son who has killed himself at Harvard, but it is also the name of the niece, Caddy's daughter, who is now living with the Compson family; and the reader may sometimes momentarily confuse one Quentin with the other as the narrative pulses between past and present. The Compson father is named Jason, but so also is the youngest son; and at times we are unsure whether we are dealing with one generation or the other. Benjy was originally christened Maury, and is still so called by his mother, sometimes making us uncertain for a moment that she may not be referring to an uncle Maury, who is still about the premises. One generation passeth away; and the next . . . shall be confused with it. The past annexes the present to itself.

Faulkner's, of course, is not the first experiment with time in the novel of this century. But however much he may be carrying forward the innovations of his predecessors, he is really moving in a different and radical direction of his own. In the novels of Proust and Virginia Woolf we are presented—to use the phrase of Erich Auerbach—with a "multi-layered version" of time. The more cultured and high-strung their characters the more sensitive they are to those different layers of time. One almost feels that the fragility of their characters in time has become an excessively civilized neurosis. Faulkner, however, is after different game. Time for him is not an affair of delicate and cultivated sensibilities because he is driven to break through to something more primordial. From the first, though he was not fully aware of it, his imagination is not to be confined to the realistic novel, however complex its modern techniques have become, but is propelled toward the mythic. The time he is concerned with in *The Sound and the Fury* is the time that is proper to doom; the time of breakdown, and that means the breakdown of time. The plane of the future has disappeared from this closed world, and the other planes of time, however on the surface we appear to flicker from the past to present, have collapsed into one plane for the Compson destinies, as they have so collapsed in the mind of Benjy. We have fallen into this timeless time as if into some primeval ooze, and however our footsteps seek to move, they always sink in and remain stuck. Faulkner's characters—in this novel and elsewhere—often run around in frantic chase or flight, but they always turn out to be running in a circle.

Why this destruction of time? Curiously enough, time is not altogether abolished in the world of Faulkner. Its reality—to speak dialectically—is established through its absence. The more hopeless the character's situation becomes, the more time has closed in upon him, even become meaningless to him—the more he grasps at some external vestige of time, not out of a will to be consoled, for he knows that he is damned, but out of some archaic instinct he cannot resist.

We see this happen on the day eighteen years earlier when Quentin Compson committed suicide at Harvard. Having accidentally broken his watch, he proceeds to twist off the damaged hands. The watch has lost its indicators, but it will still go on ticking. Faulkner has here a perfect image for the time that encloses Quentin. Time has lost its direction (there are no pointers on the dial), but it goes on ticking statically as if marking time for a duration that goes nowhere. Time has ceased for Quentin, but he must carry that watch all day and hear it ticking away in his pocket. More than this: Quentin is compelled by some obscure impulse to enter a clock repairer's shop, full of the ticking of many timepieces, and ask whether any of the numerous clocks has the right time. To compound the absurdity, he does not want to be told what the right time is but just if any of the clocks is set right. Absurdly again, he leaves the shop before the jeweler can tell him what time it is. He does not need to know, it is in fact meaningless for him to know, but he has been compelled to make this absurd gesture as a parting ritual to that kind of time that in a matter of a few hours will have disgorged him.

(Another outcast of time, Joe Christmas in *Light in August*, makes a similar absurd gesture. Christmas has killed a woman, and for days he has been in flight from a posse. Dazed, half crazy with hunger and exhaustion, desperate, he is hiding in the woods when he sees a man on the road. At the risk of his life he goes out to ask, "What day is this?" It is pointless for him to know, since time has already closed its accounts with him and he is foredoomed to be caught. But he has to ask, if only out of an absurd and uncontrollable compulsion to restore contact with that invisible sequence of time that confers order and meaning upon human life.)

The technique of presenting the meaningless—as we are exploring it in these chapters—consists in letting the universal disintegrate into random particulars. Faulkner employs this device as unflinchingly with Quentin, who is sane, as with Benjy the idiot. At first reading, we do not know what Quentin has set himself to do; we feel only some surge of intensity that marks out this day from others. The abstraction "A man is going to commit suicide" is never expressed; instead, the universal is dissolved into a flow of contingent and absurd details beside which the word "suicide" seems empty and remote. On repeated reading, everything coheres; and the small clues of what the day is about crop out with a grim and Sophoclean irony. For example, there is a brief reference to some flatirons that Quentin has bought. What are they for? They seem a curious item to be mentioned. Then, in the dense flow of Quentin's thought, he has a brief fantasy of himself rising at the Last Judgment, and he wonders in passing whether the flatirons will rise with him. It flashes upon us that the flatirons are to be used to weigh him down when he drowns himself.

Meanwhile, as he walks along the river, his thoughts keep turning about his sister Caddy and her wronged honor, and this tormented monologue flows in and out of all the small external events of this day. As one of the last of the Compsons, Quentin is a reincarnation of the old Scotch Presbyterian conscience that the founders of the clan had carried with them to the New World. But while this conscience had once maintained his forebears in their struggle with the harshness of life in the wilderness, it has now become a morbid and self-destructive relic. Quentin is so obsessed with the lost virginity of his sister that, without his committing the physical act, he is emotionally guilty of incest. And incest, physical or emotional, is the final overdelicate flower of inbreeding. It is part of Quentin's extravagant romanticism that he should feel himself dishonored by his sister's dishonor. But is he not also secretly a spurned lover taking his own life in despair at rejection?

Meanwhile, the casual events of the day flow on. By the river he watches some boys fishing. As he walks, he is suddenly and absurdly followed by a little girl, foreign and probably Italian, who does not speak at all but whom he addresses, again with that stab of Sophoclean irony, as "Sister." He cannot shake her and he cannot find out where she lives. Abruptly, a man—the girl's brother—and a policeman run at him, and he is charged with attempted abduction of the child. In view of what Quentin has in mind for this day, the irony could not be more absurd.

Before the justice of the peace, where he is led, some Harvard friends turn up and rescue him. Now their light banter flows in and out of his somber soliloquy. Finally, he has had a fistfight with one classmate, Gerald, because the latter has made some cynical remark about the frailty of women. But again, Faulkner does not present this fight as a matter of straightforward chronology; he works backward to the present incident through Quentin's tortured monologue about the past. Years before, as a boy, Quentin had fought with one of Caddy's illicit lovers, and of course had been hopelessly outclassed. Afterward, he and Caddy, in guilt and in love, intended to die together, but when he felt the beating of her blood in the vein at her neck he could not use the knife. He wakes up now to the flow of his own blood from a cut he has had in the present fight, and we realize that this climactic spasm of memory has occurred while he was lying unconscious from Gerald's blows. The two fights are the same fight. Once again, the present flows backward into the past to become indistinguishable from it.

So incident follows upon incident, but underneath all this flow of random and absurd details, there is another beat like the slow silent surge of an underground river moving into the sea, and carrying forward a man, who himself can only look backward, toward his own death. Quentin moves toward his suicide, as Sartre has observed, like a man walking backward toward a wall.

People talk a good deal about the absurd, but usually without reflecting on the "surd" that is concealed in this word. For the ancient mathematicians a surd was a quantity that could not be expressed in rational numbers. Hence, by extension, the surd in life is what resists expression in rational terms. It is the element in existence that is recalcitrant to abstraction. A nineteenth-century novelist—or a more old-fashioned novelist of our time —might have written: "On this day Quentin committed suicide." An expression of this kind would suffice for a certain kind of realistic novelist for whom reality was still contained within the habitual structures of everyday social life. Why does Faulkner proceed otherwise? Why is his text so baffling and opaque at first reading? He does not write this way out of arbitrary whim or to show his technical dexterity. Here, as everywhere in art, the manner of the telling—the style—is indistinguishable from the matter of the author's vision. Faulkner writes as he does because he is possessed, indeed obsessed, by another vision of reality than that of the traditional realist. The abstract word "suicide" does not reproduce the concrete reality of the day that Quentin lives. At the heart of reality there is the surd of existence itself. Ultimate reality is the surge of brute contingency that flows over and around and through us, and in which no day—even one in which we have not planned suicide —ever reproduces the abstract design we seek to impose upon it.

Quentin has twisted the broken hands off his watch. This

image, we have said, expresses perfectly his condition approaching death. But more than this: beyond Quentin's own situation, this image points in the direction in which the philosopher must search for a more primordial sense of time. It may seem odd to some readers that, among all the modern writers who have grappled with the reality of time, Faulkner should be the one who leads us to these ultimate depths on the question. Among American writers he had almost the least schooling. Hemingway at least finished high school, and in long residences abroad acquired a cosmopolitan sophistication. Faulkner, of course, read on his own a great deal more than he was willing to let on to when it suited him to claim he was not a literary man but only a "dirt farmer." Above all, we must avoid imputing thoughts to him that he did not hold. We do not know what such "thoughts" may be. Faulkner's speeches and essays are of the most fragmentary kind, significant biographically as a revelation of his attitudes toward some of the crucial social problems of the South. But we have the text of his novels, and that is the "thought" in him that counts. The imagination of the writer, tracing the contour and shape of his vision, achieves its own authentic thinking beside which the pedantry of any theory he may have borrowed will be only superficial. We must not impute to Faulkner thoughts that he did not hold; but we must try to think stubbornly through the matter that his fictions reveal. And Faulkner reveals the primordial essence of time because of all writers he has given us characters who have come closest to losing time altogether. This deepest reality of time is revealed to us humans through *anticipation.*

Let us pause for a few moments to dwell carefully on this point, for here the problem of time becomes inseparable from that of Nihilism. The watch is without hands, but there is still time. Reverse this image, and imagine a time not after but before there were watches. Man, after all, invented watches, clocks, hourglasses, calendars. What enabled him to construct such devices? How is it possible for him to measure time at all?

Because, in anticipation, time opens up before us, and in that open spread we can mark off the increments of duration necessary for our actions. There is a time for planting and a time for reaping. Early man could mark off a time for these actions because in anticipation time lay open before him. Time is, as Heidegger puts it, this region of the Open through which our mental act of anticipating is made possible to us. Time perpetually opens toward the future. Within this open region possibility dawns, and indeed possibility and Being become one. Man is the being whose Being is possibility because he is a being of the future. If this open horizon of time (through which and only through which the measurement of time is possible to us) happens to close for us, then the world also closes around us, opaque and meaningless. We are then back inside the mind of Benjy.

One need not be at the level of Benjy, however, to know the shadow of these moments when the world closes around one. Sometimes a glance around one's room suffices. These familiar objects become strange and opaque. One has only to persist in that probing and detached gaze with which certain modern painters might transfer these shapes onto a flat canvas. That door across the room, closed, has become a curious rectangle, not quite plumb, a white surface lined and soiled into off-white. Two darkish brown ellipses—a moment ago they were the knob —emerge crisscross from the white surface at one side. The door has ceased to be a door; it *means* nothing, it is merely itself, an object, inert and recalcitrant to my gaze. But the heavy moment passes, and with a click of the mind the meaning of that rectangle is restored; it can be opened, it leads beyond itself, it is a door. Anything in experience has meaning when it leads beyond itself to other things in some possible future experience; when, as we say, it is connected with other things and fits in alongside them within a world. But no object could lead us beyond itself if time did not open out toward a future. These three—time, possibility, and meaning—stand together as one reality. Time—as the emerging openness toward a future—is the condition that there can be any meanings at all.

Psychiatry offers us some remarkable exemplifications of this philosophical principle. The Existential psychiatrist Eugene Minkowski, in a book entitled appropriately enough *Lived Time (Le temps vécu)*, gives an extraordinary case study that, in its conclusions, could serve as a scientific parallel to what Faulkner reveals to us through art. The patient in this case was a man of sixty-six, intelligent and cultivated, but in the depths of a profound depression. He was also afflicted with monstrous and paranoid delusions, so extensive and varied that the psychiatrist could make no sense of them. Finally, Minkowski gave up the effort to add one symptom to another, like pieces of a jigsaw puzzle, but instead sought to penetrate past them into the inner world of the patient. And this meant, above all, asking what was his experience of time.

What exactly was our patient's experience of time, and how did it differ from ours? Monotonously and uniformly, he experienced the days following one another; he knew that time was passing and, whimpering, complained that "one more day was gone." . . . There was no action or desire which, emanating from the present, reached out to the future, spanning the dull similar days. As a result, each day kept an unusual independence, failing to be immersed in the perception of any life continuity; each day life began anew, like a solitary island in a gray sea of passing time. . . . What had been done, lived, and spoken no longer played the same role as in our life because there seemed to be no wish to go further.

No doubt, this is a highly morbid case. But a morbid state, after all, is one in which the human condition has gone wrong, and therefore can sometimes tell us about the things which go into the normal state which we usually do not perceive so long as we ourselves are healthy and take them for granted. So Minkowski continues:

Such was our patient's experience of time. How does it resemble ours and how does it differ? All of us may have similar feelings in moments of discouragement or dejection or when we believe that we are dying. Then the idea of death takes over and, blocking off the future, dominates our outlook on life. Our synthetic view of time disintegrates and we live, in a succession of similar days which follow one another with a boundless monotony and sadness. With most of us, however, these are only transient episodes. Life forces, our personal impetus, lift us and carry us over such a parade of miserable days toward a future which reopens its doors to us.

Normally we do not notice that the future is at the center of our awareness of time. Normally we do not notice that the temporal synthesis—the binding together of present and past—that we are constantly and mostly unconsciously performing is possible only because a future lies open to us. We think we exist at the moment and that the anticipatory dimension of time is only that passing occurrence of a moment when we happen to think of a particular task or pleasure that will be there for us tomorrow. It takes the abnormal case, as reported here by Minkowski, to instruct us otherwise.

A similar warning should be issued to those readers who would reject Faulkner out of hand because of the abnormality of his characters. These characters, indeed, exist at the extremities of the human situation—Benjy through the natural deficiency that casts him into the outer darkness, Quentin through the moral compulsion or distortion, whichever it be, that drives him toward suicide. But sometimes one must go to the boundaries of the human condition to see what that condition implies. A writer who is able to make the world disappear into that flat and opaque screen of moving lights and noises which is Benjy's portion of fate has already instructed us where we would have to look in order to reconstitute a human world. Our reflections upon Camus and Hemingway have prepared us for the conclusion to which he now leads us: Nihilism, at bottom, is man's encounter with the reality of time.

This encounter takes place on two levels. There is, first, the fact of sheer transience. Time sweeps us away and reduces us to nothing. We have only that fragile thread of the present to cling to, and few can do so with the conscious courage of Hemingway's Robert Jordan, who pronounces his and the author's Credo: "*Now*, it has a funny sound to be a whole world and your life." Transience is not only the individual's fate but the possible destiny of man and all his works. "In ten thousand years," Camus intones, "Shakespeare and Goethe will not be understood." The proudest triumphs of human culture will become meaningless. We fall then into the mood of the preacher of Ecclesiastes, in whom the transitoriness of all things begot one of the earliest voices of Nihilism: "Vanity of vanities, saith the Preacher; all is vanity."

But the encounter with time occurs also on another level, as we see in Faulkner. The monster of time is Janus-faced, looking in two directions, and indeed it can look backward meaningfully only where it is able to look forward. Time is not a succession of self-enclosed moments. The Now unfolds as the opening toward a future; and only within that open region of Being that time lavishes upon us can we think of establishing any order or meaning at all. If Nihilism is that condition in which the world ceases to have meaning for us, then the Nihilist quite literally, would have lost his roots in time altogether. Time would have closed in around him and thereby ceased. Anything less than this is a parody of the Nihilist's condition—the prattle of fashionable world-weariness or clever cynicism.

The third part of *The Sound and the Fury* brings us forward again to 1928, and to Good Friday, which chronologically is the first of the three days that make up the present time of the story. The I—the consciousness who speaks—is now Jason, youngest of the Compson sons, and the tone is altogether different from Quentin's. Jason is down-to-earth, rude, grasping, mean—the antithesis of his brother's sensitive and obsolete nobility. The murky atmosphere is now lifted a little. We learn many of the facts—Quentin's suicide and Caddy's marriage, for example—which give meaning to the earlier parts of the narrative. Here again, Faulkner's procedure is typical: the narrative must not stay external to the facts it reports but must unfold like the processes of life itself. "Life is lived forward, and understood backward," said Kierkegaard. These words of the great Existentialist describe exactly the experience of reading one's way through a Faulkner novel. It is a disturbing and baffling process on first reading, but it brings with it something of the dense quality of life itself; we know his characters intimately and intensely before we are able to piece together the facts that make their situation what it is.

Though the murkiness has lifted a bit, we are not by any means in open daylight. The tone of Jason's narrative is harsh, breathless, panting. He is forever on the move on this day: in and out of the hardware store where he clerks, in and out of the telegraph station where men have gathered to watch the stock-market figures, but mostly in pursuit of Quentin, the niece, toward whom he has assumed a parental role. She has inherited the amorous propensities of her mother, and Jason is hard put to keep her at this early age—seventeen—away from men. A circus has come to town, and she has taken up with one of its hands, a young man who is identified only by the bright red tie he wears. Jason pursues the pair into the countryside, but his pursuit is in vain. They trick him, let the air out of his tires, and he is stranded miles from town. He is always on the move, but going nowhere. An old Negro observes shrewdly of him: "A man what so smart he can't even keep up wid hisself." As always in Faulkner, the madder the chase the more it turns frantically upon itself in a circle. Jason, after all, is a Compson, and therefore locked within their closed world. Even in the only terms he would understand, money, he is a man without a future, as we learn from the next section, where the girl Quentin has run away from home with the money he had fraudulently acquired and which could have launched him on a new start in life.

The fourth and last part of the book hits us like a shock of chill air. The narrative changes from first to third person—a technical shift which is perfect, for now we see from the outside the characters whom we have already experienced from the inside, and all seem suddenly deflated in this cold gray morning. We watch the Compson family coming awake like so many shades assembling from a nether region. Quentin's flight and her theft (of money that in fact is rightly her own) are discovered. Jason flies off in pursuit. Meanwhile, Dilsey, the old Negro woman who has held the household together, and Luster, a young Negro boy, take Ben with them to church. It is Easter, but where in this cold dawn is there any sign of the Resurrection? Perhaps at the Negro church? But Faulkner presents the service as a grotesquery, and the visiting preacher as a weird monkey-like man. Nevertheless, Dilsey and the black congregation are moved, and who can say there is not the stirring of life in their feeling? The Negroes always lurk on the edges of Faulkner's world: they have survived, and in that survival there may be the seed of future life. In any case, this strange and unlikely service is the nearest we come in this novel to any hint of resurrection.

But Faulkner does not end his story on even this very faintly positive note. Jason has failed in his pursuits of Quentin and got only a very bad blow on the head for his pains. Frustrated and aching, he returns to the town square to find Ben and Luster in the carriage for their Sunday drive. Ben is howling—"Bellow on bellow, his voice mounted, with scarce interval for breath. There was more than astonishment in it, it was horror; shock; agony eyeless, tongueless. . . ." Luster has turned the carriage to the left, whereas Ben's accustomed order is the right turn. Jason leaps on the carriage and whips the horse around; and now as Ben hushes, we have the last appalling image of this appalling book: "The broken flower drooped over Ben's fist and his eyes were empty and blue and serene again as cornice and façade flowed smoothly once more from left to right; post and tree, window and doorway, and signboard, each in its ordered place." "Each in its ordered place"—these words are the last grotesque twist of Faulkner's irony. We too have turned around in a circle and come back to the beginning and are once again within the mind of Benjy. The final meaning and order conferred on the world of the Compsons is that which transpires before the flat and empty gaze of an idiot.

We are now able at last to grasp the full import of the book's title. It is borrowed, of course, from the lines of Shakespeare's *Macbeth*:

> Tomorrow, and tomorrow, and tomorrow,
> Creeps in this petty pace from day to day
> To the last syllable of recorded time;
> And all our yesterdays have lighted fools
> The way to dusty death. Out, out, brief candle!
> Life's but a walking shadow; a poor player
> That struts and frets his hour upon the stage
> And then is heard no more: it is a tale
> Told by an idiot, full of sound and fury,
> Signifying nothing.

Macbeth is here at the end of his rope, about to fight his last battle and be killed. All his tomorrows have collapsed into no tomorrow, and thereby vanished. He is in the condition of a Faulkner character for whom the future has been closed off. Are Shakespeare's words here no different from the voice of modern Nihilism?

If we look more closely, we shall find some very striking historical differences. For one thing, Macbeth's is a judgment *about* life; Faulkner does not want to talk *about*, but to present the thing itself: the sound and fury of life must vibrate through this novel, and by means of its peculiar technique, from opening to closing word. Moreover, Macbeth's is the judgment of one character spoken at a particular occasion within a play that is constructed in a traditional pattern that preserves chronological time, ascending through complication to climax and descending through denouement to a fitting end in which the moral order of the universe is also preserved, the evil perishing and the good—though after much bloodshed—triumphing. To convey a sense of the meaningless directly Faulkner must collapse chronological time, flatten out any semblance of climactic moments, and reduce the world finally to the flat façade before an idiot's gaze. Faulkner, we might say, has taken Shakespeare's words seriously and tried to produce a work of art whose very form would be the incarnation of Macbeth's judgment.

It is perhaps a paradoxical thing for a writer to attempt: to produce a work which shows us the meaninglessness of life but in which the author himself has not collapsed but still remains in firm control of his materials. Faulkner has succeeded, and that is what makes his novel unique and virtually inexhaustible for interpretation, both literary and philosophical.

The Polish writer Jan Kott a few years ago brought out an interesting and rather Existentialist interpretation of Shakespeare that sought to bring him closer to our own period. Like ours, Shakespeare's was an age of turmoil, confusion, and transition. Therefore we should be better able to understand him than did the relatively stable and settled nineteenth century. So far as the political plays are concerned, Kott has a good case. Through Shakespeare's lifetime England had gone through extraordinary upheavals, and even the Age of Elizabeth hovered long in a precarious balance, its political future uncertain as our own today. We can therefore no longer take the historical plays as mere costumed spectacles, empty processions of pomp and circumstance. On the contrary, they are charged with the most intense ingredients of drama—the conflict of desperate men over the realities of power. Certainly, having known Stalin, we find Richard III a convincing character in his grotesque evil and not a pasteboard villain out of melodrama, as he seemed to the critics of the last century.

But if the politics of that age were cruel and uncertain, theologically the life of England was still firmly anchored in the Middle Ages. Stormy as the times were, Divine Providence still ruled the world. However terrifying Shakespearean tragedy may be, the moral order of its world does not crumble. The good becomes tainted by evil, and succumbs, and that is the tragic possibility in life, but the evil itself perishes and is replaced by another good. Iago destroys Othello and Desdemona, but justice overtakes him. Hamlet perishes, but Fortinbras arrives to restore order in the unsettled state of Denmark. Even in the most horrendous of the tragedies, *King Lear*, where Shakespeare makes his darkest indictments of life as meaningless, Lear and Cordelia are killed but so also are the wicked sisters and the evil Edmund, while at the end good-natured old Kent and the virtuous Duke of Albany take over the shambles. However terrifying the things it had seen, the Elizabethan imagination was still Christian, and therefore ultimately optimistic.

What would some future historian of civilization make of this comparison of the lines of *Macbeth* with Faulkner's novel? What would he conclude from the fact that a major writer of our time is driven to far more extreme measures than the Elizabethan poet in portraying the sound and fury of life as closed and issueless? Do we suffer more than the Elizabethans that our art is required to take this extreme form? Probably not. The glittering age of Elizabeth was also filled with terrors: plagues and pestilence, tortures, and cruel oppressions—which we of a latter day would most likely be unable to bear. Two centuries of Enlightenment have not made us happy, but they have produced some humanitarian inhibitions that still glimmer here and there in the modern world. Besides, it does not make sense to speak of sufferings as neutral quantities that can be measured off one against another. Suffering varies, but each case is absolute for him who suffers. We suffer not more than but differently from the Elizabethan. Our suffering is more confused. We have so much more information and material power than that earlier age, and yet we still suffer. That too confuses us. The centuries of the Enlightenment had raised the expectation that some day suffering would be eliminated from the human condition; but suffering still persists, and among those too who are not in material want, and so we are again confused and uncertain about the goals which modern civilization had proposed for itself. Both his religion and his culture prepared Elizabethan man to encounter suffering. His religion told him to expect that life would be a vale of tears, and his culture instructed him that to everyone, no matter how lofty his station, a fall from fortune may come. When affliction falls upon the Western man of today, he is startled out of his wits as if something had gone wrong with the whole scheme of things, where nothing like that was ever supposed to happen, and so, again, he becomes more confused and uncertain of himself. To use a biological metaphor: we become almost like people who have been brought up in such a sterilized environment that we have lost our natural immunization and become defenseless against attacking bodies. So we suffer differently; and our suffering consequently demands a different kind of art in which to express itself.

An older parallel than Shakespeare also comes to mind. Faulkner's narrative turns around the three holy days of Easter. That is also the chronology of Dante's *Divine Comedy*. It is a fitting one too. Since Easter is the ritual of death and resurrection, the allegory of the lost soul that finds salvation is properly dated on those three days: on Good Friday it descends into hell, on Holy Saturday climbs Mount Purgatory shedding its sins, and on the Sunday of the Resurrection it soars into heaven. Dante's quest ends in the Beatific Vision—that vision in which we see the Divine Nature directly and are united and at one with it. Dante ends within the mind of God; in Faulkner's novel we begin and end within the mind of an idiot. What does so violent a contrast tell us about the six hundred years of Western civilization that lie between these two visions? That is a question worth pondering, and at some length.

II

Yet there is an opening in this closed world of Faulkner. A work of art that depicts a meaningless world is always in inner tension with itself. If it succeeds as art, it has introduced a meaningful act into a universe that it has judged to be empty and void. The work may fall a victim to its theme, as happens with so many ephemeral productions of our day, and sputter away without coherence or energy. From the concentrated power and the formal control of *The Sound and the Fury* we would guess that there must be some further spiritual fuel that feeds the flame. This novel seems to close all doors behind it, but some vision beyond it must sustain and contain a writer who can stare so unwaveringly at the blank face of idiocy and despair.

From this work we might *guess* this is so, but from it alone we could not tell what that saving vision might be. For that we have to turn to the whole body of his work, the rambling series of stories and novels that build and dovetail upon one another to make up a single work, the Faulkner Saga. The word "saga" is a little overworked nowadays, but it is exactly the right word here since it conveys the dimension of the legendary and the mythical into which Faulkner takes us beyond the petty niceties of realistic fiction. And here, to anticipate, we shall find that it is the power of myth that restores and sustains life beyond the closed world of Nihilism.

This saga seems to be as unplanned as life itself. It buds and grows organically from work to work, altering a character here and changing a perspective there, but always returning to the soil from which it grows. The unity of Faulkner's vision—the vision that takes us beyond the closed world of the Compsons —is the unity of this saga. But what is the unity of this vast and rambling body of stories? Its center is the land itself—the land that sustains and contains the destinies of all those odd souls that people Faulkner's imaginary kingdom of Yoknapatawpha County.

In the beginning was the land. Many years after *The Sound and the Fury*, which had gone out of print, Faulkner wrote a summary which was used as a brief introduction for a new edition. What he gives us is no neat clarificatory exposition which might assist the reader through the novel's tangled paths. Instead, Faulkner recasts the narrative from an older and riper perspective. He does not start his summary with the actions of 1928 or of 1910 that fill the foreground of the novel but with an event and a character not even mentioned in it: Ikkemotubbe, the Indian chieftain, and his original deeding of one square mile of land to a Compson forebear. The last part of this land was sold to send Quentin to Harvard and was turned into a modern golf course. The decay of the Compsons is their loss of the land, its passage into golf course and boardinghouse until it ends in the homogenized nightmare of modern urban civilization: "row after row of small crowded jerrybuilt individually owned demiurban bungalows." The history of the Compsons thus begins and ends with their relationship to the land. This fateful relationship holds also for the Sartorises, the Sutpens, and all the other would-be dynasts of the South—indeed, in Faulkner's view, for the South itself as a whole.

What we are observing here is not merely an external fact in social history. There is a well-known sociological interpretation of Faulkner—originally propounded by liberal Marxists—that takes up these same facts but does not go far enough. The South, so this interpretation runs, was an agrarian economy that contained within itself a fundamental contradiction in the form of slavery. It was therefore fated to be defeated in the Civil War. Its landed class, nourished on a gentleman's code of chivalry and honor, lingered on, but was doomed to perish. The Sartorises give way to the Snopeses, the tight-fisted and unprincipled peasants who have swarmed down from the hills to take over the towns and hamlets, and eventually the bank in Jefferson. A mechanized civilization gradually extends its tentacles over the land. Industrial capitalism captures and dominates the agrarian South. Faulkner, in this view, is the chronicler of the postbellum South—the historian of its decline and fall.

Unfortunately, this interpretation falls far short of the full sweep and power of Faulkner's mythic vision. To be sure, these historical facts do fall within the scope of the saga. Everything that has happened within the South is grist for the mill of Faulkner's imagination, which is as wide and embracing as the land itself. But the truth at which a saga, as poetry, aims, as Aristotle pointed out long ago, is more serious and "more philosophical" than that of history. And indeed Faulkner's vision is far more philosophically significant than social-minded critics realize. In the first place, his attitude toward the old Southern aristocracy is quite ambiguous. They were doomed, not through the impersonal forces of economics, but through the original sin of their relationship to the land. The first settlers sought to wrest family empires for themselves from the land. They set themselves up as conquerors of the wilderness. Usually we think of industrial civilization, with its mechanistic philosophy and its arsenal of machines, as the prime example of man's rape of nature. But Thomas Sutpen (in *Absalom, Absalom!*) is just as frenzied and Faustian in his passion to bestride the earth like a Colossus and build the biggest plantation in Mississippi out of the hundred miles of wilderness he inveigled from the Indians. The white man thought he could possess the earth but it was not his to possess. The wilderness recedes but does not vanish. If it were to vanish altogether, man would become an arrogant robot. Instead of laying claim to the land he must learn to let himself be claimed by it.

That is the message of "The Bear," Faulkner's longest and one of his finest stories. Old Ben, the bear, has eluded the hunters year after year until he seems unkillable—the incarnate spirit of the wilderness itself. The bear is the hunters' antagonist, against whom they must pit all their skill and cunning; but over the years he has also become a kind of kinsman, almost like a totem animal, a creature for whom they have learned to have awe and affection. The hunt has thus come to be a ritual, in the strict and sacred sense of a primitive ceremony, which links the hunters and the hunted together. But among all those taking part, only three, Faulkner tells us, were "taintless and incorruptible": Old Ben the bear; the mongrel dog named Lion who finally brings the bear to bay; and Sam Fathers, an old Indian, the son of a Chickasaw chief, who serves as guide to the hunters. They are "taintless and incorruptible" because they embody the primeval vitality of the wilderness that has not yet been conquered by the machinery of civilization. In the end, the bear is killed; but in the melee the dog, Lion, and old Sam Fathers also die. The three "taintless and incorruptible" creatures have perished, but their meaning survives in young Isaac McCaslin, through whose eyes we see the challenge, the ordeal, and the sacrament of the hunt.

Faulkner leaves no doubt about the ritual aspect of this hunt. At thirteen, when Isaac McCaslin had killed his first buck, Sam Fathers had anointed the boy's face with the blood of the quarry.

This ritual of initiation symbolically joins the huntsman and the hunted within the one circle of nature. It was in that "novitiate," McCaslin recalls, that he began to learn the meanings of the "humility" and "patience" that are the lessons of the wilderness. This humility is not Christian meekness, but reaches back into a more primordial past of mankind. The Indian once had this bond of humility with the land that nourished his life. The anthropologist R. F. Fortune tells us that the Indians, even when they picked the most common weeds for some use, lifted them as though they were sacred plants: "In the hole from which the root was withdrawn a pinch of tobacco was left. Often a knife or some money was left there also and the taker of the root uttered a brief prayer, 'I have taken what you have given, and I am leaving this here for you. I want to lead a long life and to have no harm strike me or my family.' " But the Indian lost this gift of humility, and thereby his bond to the earth, the moment he thought the land was his to possess: "On the instant when Ikkemotubbe discovered, realized, that he could sell it for money, on that instant it ceased ever to have been his forever." The primitive and holy life of the Indian ends at the point where the history of the White Man begins—in that Original Sin in which he dared to assume the arrogant Lordship over the land.

The land, be it understood, is no parcel of real estate. It is not a geographical or geological fact, nor even a matter of the total physical environment of which our ecologists speak. Nowadays, conservationists have made us aware of the vanishing wilderness, and the threat of universal pollution leads us to speak of restoring the balance of nature. The issue has become a popular one, even fashionable. We are told that the earth is a lonely spaceship on which we are all traveling and if we foul its environment we shall all perish. No doubt, this image of a spaceship is a forceful one for the practical purpose of warning people about the acuteness of the danger we face. But we shall never understand what Faulkner means by the land if we think of it as a spaceship. The notion of a spaceship brings us back into the technical world where man has assumed mastery over objects. But the land, as Faulkner understands it, is not an object, not a parcel of real estate, or of certain measurable square miles of geography; it is not so much a fact as a region of possibility—the region of Being in which man may learn once again the virtues of "humility and patience." In answering to this call of the land, man becomes—in the words of Heidegger—the shepherd of Being and not the master of beings.

The trouble with our current and laudable efforts in ecology is that we expect the problem of man's relationship to nature to be solved only as an affair of technical intelligence. Since technology has devastated the land, it is up to technology—or a more intelligent use of technology—to cure the mess. (Behind this is the covert assumption that "they"— the unnamed technical experts who at present rule our lives anyway—will come up with some new gadgets to save us.) But Faulkner is preaching no sermon for practical ecology, however much such sermons are needed at the present time. The vision of the artist is always more radical than the preachments of ideas. The wilderness of which Faulkner speaks is just that which is not manipulable by the calculations of man, and until we acknowledge it and submit to it we will continue to be the prisoners of our own *hubris*.

For only in that submission—and this is the culminating point of "The Bear"—does man achieve his true freedom. When the hunt is over and the bear killed, young McCaslin remembering it all sees Old Ben as the incarnate symbol of "liberty and freedom." And free even in his death—"Free on earth, free in earth." Analogously, man will find his freedom only in acquiescing to his finite and earth-bound nature.

From this longer perspective, we can see why it is a mistake to label Faulkner as essentially a chronicler of the postbellum South. We said earlier that there was an opening in Faulkner's world beyond that closed sphere in which the Compsons sit entombed. We do not understand this doomed family unless we see them as part of a larger whole, which is the history of the South and of the Civil War. But this circle of history does not measure the full sweep of Faulkner's vision. Human history opens backward toward the more primeval vista of the land. The Civil War and indeed the whole history of the South are in the end for Faulkner merely episodes in the enduring life of the land. The motifs of this history and of the Civil War are brought to a head in one climactic novel, *Absalom, Absalom!* in which Faulkner has produced his own strange and powerful version of the

Gothic romance. But here the war itself is a vague nightmare in the distance. The men go off to it, but it is never at the center of the stage. The central drama turns around a portion of the land—Sutpen's Hundred, the huge plantation that Thomas Sutpen had literally torn from the primeval soil. He speaks of this as his "design," the design that he is going to impose, whatever it may cost him and his, upon the wilderness. In this act of reckless will the subsequent doom of the family, with all its labyrinthine entanglements, is already sealed. But the whole history of the South is also contaminated at its source by the same violent will: so Negro slaves were torn from their own land and brought here in order to conquer the wilderness as rapidly as possible. Between the white man and the land there was thus interposed the shadow of the black man.

The blacks come to symbolize the qualities of spontaneity and naturalness which the Protestant conscience must uneasily banish from itself. As a regional writer, Faulkner was not only presented with the social drama of classes of men in conflict with each other but also the metaphysical drama of man in conflict with his own nature. The white man's fear of the black man is his fear of what he considers the darker side of his own nature. Hence the fear becomes pathological. At the climax Henry Sutpen kills his half-brother Charles Bon because the latter would marry Henry's sister (and therefore Bon's half-sister). Henry will accept the incest, but he cannot accept the fact that Bon, Thomas Sutpen's son by an octaroon girl in Haiti, is tainted by Negro blood. And Charles, who has lived among the Catholics and Creoles of New Orleans, understands this white man's Protestant soul and provokes him: "I'm the nigger that's going to sleep with your sister." The sickness of the South—social as well as psychological—arose out of man's will to impose his "design" upon the wilderness.

Faulkner's world opens backward behind historic time into

the immemorial time of the saga. He is fond of this word "immemorial," and sometimes indeed seems to overwork it; but its strict sense is appropriate here, since the immemorial is what is antecedent to historic dates.

It is not, however, the unremembered, though it is unrecorded; it is imprinted on the memory more indelibly than any dated record because it is the background we carry with us against which all specific dates are to be set. We come back thus to the question of time with which we started. No doubt, we shall have to come back to it again and again, since reality and time, for us mortals, are inseparable, and the novelist who would depict reality is necessarily caught up in some vision or other of time. For the ordinary novel, as for the purposes of ordinary life, time is the chronology of calendar and clock. That is the framework within which we give pattern to our life, establish some meaning for ourselves as we reckon up the past and portion out the future. The Compsons (in *The Sound and the Fury*) have lost their hold upon this kind of time; their world has become issueless, without future; time beats faintly but points nowhere, and therefore has effectively ceased. This was the appropriate view of time to convey the vision of a world that has become meaningless. But now that we move beyond such hopelessness as the Faulknerian saga buds from work to work and becomes as a whole more living than any of its parts, what is the sense of time that unfolds along with it?

Not, first of all, a return to the time of clocks and dates. These are devices of human calculation, and if man in the Faulknerian world is to find his meaning he must go back beyond them to that peculiar fullness of time that is found in myth. In "The Bear" the hunt took place at a certain definite time; but for young McCaslin remembering, and for Faulkner telling, it is transformed into the perpetual present of ritual. For the primitive, whenever the ritual is enacted, the god or the ancestor is alive through and within it. The ritual can be performed again at the proper needed time; it is recurrent like the processes of nature itself, like the cycles of day and night, of winter, spring, summer, and fall, in which time—moving forward but returning again—is felt in the fullness of its presence at every point. We can see now why Faulkner has surrounded his hunt with all the rituals of novitiate, initiation, and ritual.

This primeval sense of time is still preserved in the greatest saga of Western literature, the epics of Homer. We begin to understand the Homeric poems fully only when we try to imagine how they were originally experienced by their hearers. The audience knew the story in advance; it was only a question what episode they might desire to hear from the bard that night. The myth is thus perpetually present with them, renewed whenever the bard might appear to chant some episode from it. Historians can now conjecture a likely date for the fall of Troy; for the hearers of Homer's saga, that event could not be relegated away to a date, since it is perpetually present in the ritual of the bard's chant; the siege of Troy takes place again and again, and Achilles will pursue Hector around the walls of Troy forever. Interpreters have remarked on the leisurely and unhurried pace of the Homeric poems. The poet has no need to hurry, for everything in nature, the life of man included, takes place according to the unhurried "ordering of time," as the early philosopher Anaximander put it. Schiller, commenting on this unhurried pace, observed that "the Homeric narrative is present at every point." This is just the fullness of its presence that we find in nature itself.

The time of the saga, then, is the time of the land itself—of the rhythm of the seasons, death and renewal, sowing and reaping. Out of the gift of this time man once had meaning and was able to construct his clocks. Returning to this gift, he may once again acquire a meaning that the clocks of his civilization no longer provide him. Such is the sense of time that emerges from the Faulknerian saga. We need not confine ourselves to a story like "The Bear" where the material is explicitly ritual. Even when the subject is the odd and day-to-day gossip of a very small village, as in *The Hamlet*, the narrative unfolds with the unhurried and inexorable rhythm of the seasons. On the face of it, one finds it hard to call this book a novel or a collection of stories. It deals with incidents (including the love affair of an idiot with a cow, which incredibly enough Faulkner is able to bring off) in the life of the village of Frenchman's Bend, and the unifying thread of plot is the gradual infiltration of the Snopeses and their taking over of power. But the real and dominating unity of the book is the brooding rhythm of the seasons that encompasses the life of this little village. No other modern writer has embedded his characters so deeply within this enveloping presence of the earth.

According to the old Greek myth, the world was repopulated after the flood when Pyrrha and Deucalion threw the "bones of Mother Earth"—stones lying on the ground—over their shoulders and they sprang up as men and women. Faulkner's characters are so autochthonous that they seem to be exhaled from the earth itself. That is why there is always such volcanic energy to his creations. That is also why his more intellectual characters, the Benbows or Gavin Stevenses, pale beside his unkillable children of the soil—peasants, hillbillies, dirt farmers, Negroes. In the end, the answer to Nihilism is not intellectual but vital —as Nietzsche told us a century ago. Confronted by a world that has become meaningless, we cannot be convinced by rational arguments to find meaning in it. But if life-giving energy flows we are able to create values, and we can then find reasons enough to find the world meaningful. The gift of this energy is from the earth, from which the gift of life itself once came to the human race.

Humor is always a sign of vitality. So long as we can still laugh, we have not succumbed to despair. Faulkner's humor, which has a quality all its own, pervades most of his work, and yet has not been given enough attention by his critics. It would take a study as long as the present one to do it justice. It could very well be the starting point of another study of Faulkner, which, however, might come out with the same conclusions. For his is a humor of the grotesque and earthbound. It has a kinship—but only a faint one—with the frontier humor of Mark Twain, but goes further toward the grotesque. It is as if Faulkner's imagination, as fertile and encompassing as the earth itself, can look with equal tolerance on all its children—the violent and horrendous, and also the odd, eccentric, and ridiculous. He can even find humor, sardonic and extreme, in those monstrous forms of life, the Snopeses, who are spreading like a blight all through the South. No doubt, they appalled Faulkner the man, but as an artist he could not resist the impulse to make them funny.

POSTSCRIPT TO PART I:
BEHIND HISTORY'S BACK

In the years before his final breakdown Nietzsche set about preparing the great work that was to be the summation of all his thought. "What I am going to relate," he began, "is the history of the next two centuries. I shall describe what will happen, what must necessarily happen: *the triumph of Nihilism.*"

He did not live (though he continued in life) to complete the work: it was left a mass of fragments—notes, *aperçus,* outlines —to be collected by his sister after his death. The last eleven years of his life he spent a shuffling and slippered existence, his soul burned out and dead while his body lingered on. The philosopher of the will to power had become as helpless as a child. There were occasional moments of amiable and childlike lucidity; and a few times he burst into song, the firmness of his tone still preserving the marvelous clarity of his love for music. The historical march of Europe, which had consumed all the energy of his thought, rolled on and left him a pale specter in the wings, no longer able even to be a spectator of its illusions. He died in 1900—a fitting date, since it divides the two centuries that were his obsession. In all the capitals of Europe bells boomed, and parades were formed to celebrate the coming century that would surely continue the amazing progress of the one just ended. Amid the general excitement neither the populace nor its leaders paused to take note of the expiring ghost whose words had already placed a grave question over all their celebrations.

Prophecy is always an uncertain venture in dealing with human history, and we have not yet gone half the way into the two centuries that Nietzsche envisaged. Nihilism has not yet triumphed. There are still ordinary people like Camus' Dr. Rieux or Faulkner's Byron Bunch who carry on with a stubborn and patient and unrhetorical virtue. But if one diminished a bit the oracular sweep of his prophecy Nietzsche is not altogether off the mark. The history of our century could be written as the encounter with Nihilism. We have had state terror and organized murder, both of the Left and of the Right. These we know, and have no trouble recognizing; it is harder to spot the nihilistic phenomenon when it comes in more subtle modes. Nihilism now assumes guises and disguises which Nietzsche, bound to his own times, could not have foreseen in detail. There seems to be no limit to the ways in which human beings can practice self-deception. There is the Nihilism of Conformism, which no longer believes wholeheartedly in the routines that sustain it; but there is also the Nonconformism that may cast itself in the role of idealistic rebellion while in fact it harbors a nihilistic core and is driven secretly by an adolescent lust for destruction. And so on and so forth.

So far we have been toiling along the path of a single philosophical argument. Admittedly, it is an unusual kind of argument, for we have used as our premises not abstract and general statements, as philosophical arguments mostly do, but individual works of art. Still, if an argument in its widest sense is any procedure in which evidence is marshaled, then the artist must also be allowed to give his testimony. Of course we have to listen to him a little differently. When we hear the testimony of witnesses at law, we are intent simply on ascertaining the facts of the case. With the artist, we have to listen not only to what the witness says but how he says it: the intonation and rhythm of the voice are inseparable from the content of what is said. Style is not an external cosmetic laid on the surface but part of his essential deposition. And transformations in style in the case of a great art form like the novel are thus not mere external changes but extend deep down into the life of the artist and his period. That is why we made so much of questions of technique in fiction.

But an argument ought also to produce some conclusions. Have we reached any? I think so, and we may sort them out into two parts.

First: Whether the world (or human life) is meaningless is a real question. The power of these three writers is enough to establish its living reality. But equally clearly, it is not a question out of academic philosophy. These writers did not become entangled with it because they attended an evening course in philosophy or stumbled upon a book of metaphysics. The question assails all of us, or nearly all of us, at some moment or other in our lives. And to be there, to live in the question, is something very different from merely talking about it. I venture to think that those "healthy-minded" citizens who disclaim it must have been touched by it sometime or other though their principles forbade them giving it voice. Some endure in this question longer than others, and some all too long. Then there are the very few, the artists, who are able to give shape and texture to the question by producing their own individual vision of the void. And this vision—to judge from the three writers we have looked at—is quite different for our century than it was for the previous one.

The nineteenth century experienced the advent of Nihilism like the shock of an earthquake. Or rather, those few who were able to sense the advancing tremors of the earthquake knew the convulsions ahead. Dostoevsky may be taken as the most profound and revealing example. Certainly, no other novelist has presented us with more powerful figures of negation. Raskolnikov, Stavrogin, Kirillov, Verhovensky—they loom before us like infernal shades, streaked with smoke and flames, exhaled from the sulfurous furnace of the Dostoevskian imagination. But if we turn now to reflect upon these ominous figures from the vantage point of our contemporary writers, we are struck by a simple but extraordinary fact that establishes a world of difference between ourselves and the past century: these characters of Dostoevsky are always presented as unmistakably abnormal or deranged, and their nihilistic ideas—however brilliantly elaborated—are always represented as the poisonous web spun out of this derangement. The Russian novelist never fails to insist that those who find the ordinary world of human values without meaning are themselves sick and need to be cured.

To be sure, these characters have a fascination for him since they express a powerful side of his own nature; and he can involve us with such strange creatures more closely than any other novelist can. But though he has this power to plunge us immediately into the mind of a Raskolnikov and let us see the world as it takes shape for this character, we are never left in doubt that these are the wild and whirling thoughts of a feverish young man halfway between delirium and waking. The nihilist here is brought before us as the abnormal figure because he is seen within the framework of an accepted world. Among some writers of our century, on the other hand, it is the world itself— or at least some large segment of it—that appears unacceptable; and the art of the novelist is to capture the reader so within this negative vision that he will take it as the quite matter-of-fact way of seeing things. In Dostoevsky the Nihilist is a monstrous figure who erupts within the framework of ordinary life and would destroy its meaning; in our later writers this framework itself has become without meaning, and it is against the background of a meaningless world that the characters must struggle to find or lose themselves. Meursault and Frederic Henry secure whatever meaning for their life they can in revolt against the world. Raskolnikov, on the other hand, finds life meaningful only when, his derangement gone, he is restored in feeling to the common life of mankind. To be sure, we know that Faulkner's Benjy is abnormal: but his flat and idiotic gaze becomes—through the deliberate technical design of the author—the framework, from beginning to end, in which the history of the Compson family is unfolded. Which is as if to say that the world containing the individual Compsons is in its totality as idiotic as Benjy. With us, as compared with the previous century, Nihilism has become more total and therefore also more matter-of-fact. It has become an accepted style of our epoch.

Neither Camus nor Hemingway nor Faulkner is a "negative" writer. Quite the contrary: they have all, in one fashion or another, gone out of their way to reassure mankind of their good intentions, of their conviction of the worth and dignity of human life, and their hope for the future. In his Nobel prize address Faulkner seemed to be launching a cavalry charge of the old Confederate Army, bugles blowing and banners waving, in the cause that "man shall prevail." It is something to think about then that three such "positive" writers at some point or other in their careers, and prompted by quite different experiences, should have been so possessed by the vision of the world as meaningless that they bent all their energies to make this the core of convincing works of art. Of all his novels, Faulkner later told an interviewer, he had labored hardest over *The Sound and the Fury*, which happens also to be the most negative in its point of view.

No, we cannot accuse these individual writers of private willfulness or a bad digestion or an unfortunate childhood. Individually different as they are, they all share some part of a prevalent style, and a prevalent style speaks for a whole epoch. Instead of possibly blaming individual artists we have to ask what the motives of this style were. In 1919 Virginia Woolf wrote a memorable essay defending the methods of the newer novelists. These methods, she declared, aimed to bring the novel closer to life: to bring before us the myriad impressions that might cross an ordinary mind on some random occasion on some random day, and thereby to convey the vivid flow of life that slipped through the heavy net of the conventional novel. And these methods were affirmative, for it was an affirmation —was it not?—to show that the small occasions of life might harbor as much, and sometimes more, significance than the larger ones. At the time her mood was adventurous and brave, and she said nothing about the opposite power that these methods, as it turned out, had for the truths of the negative. What if in getting closer to life, the novelist found nothing there, or nothing much? If in disassembling experience into its atoms he found nothing to reunite them? In any case, as history turned out, our expectations about the novel began to alter. The neat climax, the carefully parceled-out progression of plot, the resolution in some major harmony—all of these very tuneful contrivances began to sound out of tune with reality. The melody that was flatted seemed to ring truer. Experience provided so many dissonances that we expected dissonant chords from our art. We began, in short, to be at home in the atonal world.

We shall have something to say later about atonal music. (Indeed, the main themes of this book could have been developed equally well, had we knowledge of that medium, from the art of music.) Younger composers today tell us that when they attempt the older tonal music their efforts seem to them mere pastiche, unconvincing and invalid, and they are driven into atonality and even stranger forms beyond that. Why is this? Our ears, which accept this newer music, are not physically different from those of our parents, which rejected it. But of course the ears and hearing are different things. The ears are natural objects, while hearing is a social and historical matter. That is how the anthropologist or psychologist might put it. The philosopher might put the same point differently: ears are physical objects, but hearing is a matter of our acoustical being. How then has our being changed that we hear so differently now?

Similar question for all the other arts.

The poet Hölderlin, whose insight could not save himself from the abyss, wrote:

> Where danger threatens
> The saving element wakens.

The danger that threatens should be obvious from our previous pages. Where are we to look for what may save us? We come now to the second, the positive part of our conclusions so far.

Camus, Hemingway, and Faulkner are writers with both a negative and a positive side: they reveal the threat of the meaningless, and they also provide a positive reaction to this ominous drift of our time. It is hard to compress what is common in this reaction into some tidy formula. Art exists in order to enable us to escape from the tyranny of formulas; the message of a work of art is the work itself—even when the work is cited, as it has been here, as part of a philosophical argument. Still, one does feel that these writers, if they are not saying the same thing, are at least pointing, or struggling to point, in the same direction —toward the same region of Being where they have found foothold, drawn breath, and managed to create.

Perhaps we can make clearer what this region is by indicating the directions in which they are *not* pointing. Does the saving element lie in the more intelligent application of science and technology? No, however desirable it would be to have a more intelligent use of technical intelligence. In the extension of social and economic justice? Again, the answer is no. In the extension of literacy, of the right to vote, in the emancipation of women, the spread of education, or the dissemination of more enlightened and rational attitudes generally? Again, no. The list could be expanded to include the goals of most liberals today—indeed to include all those ideals that the liberal and rational intelligence has set up for its goals, and therefore the goals of History, for the last two centuries. Not that these writers are opposed to these goals as such. Quite the contrary: all three spoke out forcefully at one time or another for humanitarian causes. (In his last years Faulkner was the recipient of threats and vilifications for taking a strong stand on behalf of the blacks in the South.) The achievement of such social goals would lie in the foreground of history, but the artist is involved with something deeper in the background. Presented with all the shining and estimable goals of the Enlightenment, he cries: Not there! Not there! Suppose all those goals achieved, what then? Where does a man breathe?

Humanism is an attitude which everybody is supposed to approve, though we cannot always be sure what is to be included in that approbation. Man is the measure of all things, runs one old humanist aphorism. But in fact men do not always like to assume this lonely and arrogant role of a measuring stick for all reality. Man is void and empty unless he finds something by which to measure his own Being. For Hemingway—behind all the wars and journeys and foreign cities—the measure of man lies in the memory of the Michigan woods in the morning of the world. Faulkner feels that in the Mississippi wilderness —banished but still lurking at the edges of the terrain that the human animal has already subdued—man finds his measure, finds himself and his freedom, because there he also finds himself bound. Camus, by contrast, seems a more urban type than these two, as a French writer perhaps cannot escape being, since the cultural life of that country is so fantastically centered on Paris. But among the Parisian literary circles he did feel himself something of an outsider and a provincial—a man of another climate. In some of his later essays, where he began to feel himself more and more a man of the Mediterranean and its sunlight, he became more scathing in his condemnation of the misty northern cities where men become caged in the gray labyrinths of their own making. In this connection one has to read very carefully and literally the sentence that occurs toward the end of *The Rebel:* "One can reject all history and yet accept the world of the sea and the stars."

Camus, of course, was addressing himself immediately to a kind of Marxism that locates the reality of man in the impersonal process of History (with a large H). But the force of his remark goes quite beyond that immediate target, and challenges the assumptions of all progressive thought since the Enlightenment. The humanism of the Renaissance sought to reclaim the value of man in this life and on this earth. The treasures of Greek and Latin civilization—humane letters and classical art—would be recaptured to enlarge the mind and refine the spirit. With the development of science in the seventeenth century, this humanism acquired a new ally. Science, reason, progress—these became the sacred watchwords of the *philosophes* of the Enlightenment in the eighteenth century. Humanism thus subtly changes its coloration: with his instruments of technology and science, man prepared to build a place for himself further and further from the rest of nature, and in his capacity for limitless progress he would in time cut himself off altogether from the man of prehistory. The thinkers of the Enlightenment thrilled with the faith that they were just at the beginning of history, true history, in comparison with which the achievements of the past would all seem like the night of prehistory: a darkness of myth, superstition, and ignorance.

Nietzsche was one of the first to question this overvaluation of modern history. In man's long existence upon this planet, he remarks, by far his greatest labors and achievements lay in the long centuries of prehistory. Anthropolgy has confirmed this insight. Our civilization today still rests on the great discoveries made by early man: how to plant seeds and till the earth, how to weave cloth, fire pottery, and smelt metals. (Also to ferment plants for alcoholic drinks, an accomplishment which for some puritanical reason anthropologists seem sometimes to pass by.) This is a banal item of schoolboy knowledge, and therefore we do not reflect upon it. I am enormously impressed, however, because I am unable to do any of these things. If civilization were to founder, I would not even know how to set about rediscovering these arts. I have planted, but the seeds were bought in a store; imagine beginning with the grasses of the field, sifting out the proper strains until eventually one got the seeds of wheat. Walking out of doors I occasionally pick up curious stones, but I don't know which are metallic and haven't the least idea how I would go about extracting the metal if it were there. And the leap from flax to cloth is beyond my powers of imagination. Dear reader, do not be blasé and underrate prehistoric man before you ask yourself whether you too could start from scratch as he had to and accomplish what he did. On this point the intellectuals of the Enlightenment were very rude guests: they lived in the house that archaic man made possible for them, ate his bread, used his metal in their forks and knives, wore his clothes, drank his wine—and all the while scorned him as a creature of darkness.

And if we begin at last to admire properly his prodigious feats of invention, we might then go on to believe that archaic man may have also been wise about things other than material crafts. The more the anthropologists tell us about primitives the more we are impressed by the subtlety of their ways of thought, by the elaborate structures they built—unlike ourselves—to live within their limits and to maintain a balance in their trans-actions with nature. Archaic man would have understood, transposed into his own terms, the intent of Camus' saying that we "can reject all history and yet accept the world of the sea and the stars." That indeed was the strategy of his culture, which in the interests of stability sought to absorb the extraordi-nary event—and by absorbing it cancel its shock—into some ordinary and permanent structure of behavior. History, after all, deals with exceptional and extraordinary events. And since the French Revolution, particularly, the sense of world history that has prevailed among Western intellectuals is that the only really significant events must be so exceptional that they trans-form the whole fabric of human life from top to bottom.

Perhaps by now we have had more of that kind of history than we can take, and we could use a little of the cushioning strategy of archaic man. This archaic creature would also have under-stood the reason behind Faulkner's fondness for the word "im-memorial," for what needs most to be remembered has to be absorbed into some ordinary social structure or rite to become engraved deeply upon the subconscious below the shaky conscious memory that goes with dating. However, he would *not* have understood the modern ideologies that exalt man above nature and divide him from it. Archaic man finds no meaning in himself apart from the cosmos he inhabits.

Why this brief excursus into anthropology? Well, we began this book with a double quotation from Hegel via Sartre to the effect that history takes place behind our backs. The sense there was that history is never completely calculable but always takes surprising turns contrary to our intentions. Now, however, we give the aphorism another twist: we may have to go behind the back of history (with all its twists and turns) to find man. Back of history there lies prehistory. And "back" here does not mean past in the sense of finished and done with, but a background persistently present; or, to change the spatial metaphor slightly, underneath us as a foundation on which we rest. Perhaps some day history will be reabsorbed into the matrix of anthropology, from which it emerged in the first historian, Herodotus (who was really half and half). Then all the extraordinary events of the historical chronicles—wars, dynastic intrigues, and revolutions—will be seen for what they are: variations, and for the most part erratic and violent ones, upon the few themes of those basic relations man has to establish between himself and the environment.

There is an interesting comparison that can be made here between anthropology and literature on the one side and history and journalism on the other. James Joyce once remarked wisely to a friend: "Literature deals with the ordinary; the unusual and extraordinary belong to journalism." Man bites dog is news, but dog bites man is a pretty tame story for the papers. What the newspapers headline as news are unusual and extraordinary events. If these events get reported often enough and lengthily enough and in big enough type, they may pass on into magazines and get into books, and then they become history. History is only news on a grand scale, the continuation of journalism on a higher and more selective level. But art addresses itself to the ordinary, and therefore more archaic, part of man. Joyce's observation holds true even for the strange material of a writer like Kafka, who derives his power precisely from laying hold of the fantastic in the ordinary. Where it loses its grip on the ordinary reaches of experience, fantastic art degenerates into mere whimsy.

We have seen three writers engaged, each in his own way, in salvaging that archaic part of us. Let us now try to put as briefly and tidily as we can what they lead us to conclude:

Man cannot find meaning in himself, not in himself alone anyway; he must feel part of something greater than himself. And to belong simply to a social group will not do, for then we may all be together but we are just the lonely crowd in a void. No, he must feel that he belongs to something cosmic that is not of man and not of men, and least of all man-made, but toward which in the deepest part of himself he can never feel alien. This is not the Nature of the Romantics. We are pushing back here toward something more primal than that. The intimations of deity behind the sublime veil of nature lay too easily at hand for the Romantics. Theism has become too remote for us, one more man-made construction, an abstraction placed over the mystery of things, and above all we must get beyond abstractions even if in the end we shall have to come back to them. God maybe later, but right now we must get closer to the things themselves, particularly the things that are not of man, so that we can discover our lost kinship with them and a cosmos can be born for man again. For man as an alien to the cosmos has always been, and must continue to be, a Nihilist. We have to learn to live again in the presence of mystery that forever baffles the understanding but renews us even as it goes on baffling us. And, let us make no bones about it, this is a nature that cannot be prettily sentimentalized in the manner of some of the Romantics, for lavish as it may be it is also implacable and harsh in the limits it imposes upon us so that at times we must cry out with Faulkner's dirt farmer speaking to his land in a fit of exasperation and love: "You got me, you'll wear me out because you are stronger than me since I'm jest bone and flesh." Yet that was the source out of which came the life-giving energy that created our species in the first place; and ultimately it is the source out of which must come the energy that will carry us beyond Nihilism.

A rather old-fashioned conclusion to have arrived at through the tortuous bypaths of modern literature. And a very slender and tentative conclusion perhaps; but we may be able to give it more body if we push on now to examine some further testimony that the age (through the voice of its artists) has rendered about itself. Perhaps matters will be a little more visible if we turn now to the more primordial plastic arts, sculpture and painting, to find out what images of himself man in this century felt compelled to paint on canvas or carve on stone. Here we enter a more archaic domain of reality than the written word evokes. Man painted pictures and fashioned images before he had any written language and the capacities for abstraction that literacy brings with it. It may be this older habit of image making that still haunts us when we are driven to blackboards and charts and feel dissatisfied with an exposition in words until we have a picture before us to which we can point and then can declare to an audience: "Look here, now you must see, really see, what I mean!" It is as if we do not know what we mean until we have a picture of it. (And is this not the force behind Wittgenstein's statement that "every proof is a picture"?) So I turn now to the painters and sculptors for the picture—or pictures —of what I have thus far been laboring to say.

The reader should thus be forewarned that he will be meeting the same story again. The same but not identical, for in art as in nature no two things exactly repeat each other.

Part II

Interlude for Pictures

Don't think, look!

—WITTGENSTEIN

5. Heads and Bodies

"What has modern literature to set beside this?" André Gide asked—but really exclaimed!—at a retrospective exhibition of Picasso in Paris in 1932. He was referring to the bold dislocation of forms, the arbitrary distortions of the so-called real world, and generally the freedom of the painter to go beyond the cramping and rigid molds of a too literal realism. It was the first large retrospective of Picasso. There have been so many since that we have become dulled to such spectacles, but to go through such a show for the first time is like stalking a jungle proliferating with exotic shapes, primitive figures lurking through the thickets, cacophonous voices blaring from the trees, and here and there clearings of lovely and blessed calm, which also turn out to be troubling when we get there and look. Gide himself had just recently attempted his own boldest experiment against realism in *The Counterfeiters*; but the book was too hesitant and self-conscious about its own technique to achieve any monumental effect, and the characters seem not so much to live as to be perpetually gazing at their own reflections in the mirror of the novel. Poor Gide! His own genius lay in a taut and graceful classicism. He could not escape it, and so he was overwhelmed by this brute flood of life that was poured out before his eyes. He was the right person to ask it, and his question does hit the mark. Painting and sculpture, of all the arts, have most freed the imagination of this century from the forms of the preceding; and so show us most vividly, at a glance as it were, that we live in a very different time of the human spirit.

The reasons for this greater boldness and freedom lie in the nature of the media themselves. On the face of it, the plastic arts seem to be the most limited in their materials: the painter has just so many square feet of canvas at his disposal, the sculptor so many cubic feet of stone or metal. But within these limits he is free to shape whatever autonomous image may be visited him by chance, talent, or the unconscious—or all three together. This image can be taken in with a glance. It does not need to tell a story to hold our interest. If it bores us, we can turn away in a moment. The writer, on the other hand, committed to words, is also held by the laws that govern language. For one thing, the words must be heard or read, and this takes time. We do not know how the story turns out until we have read to the end of the novel, and the author must keep our interest alive from page to page until we get there. The novelist who would empty his fiction of plot altogether, like Samuel Beckett in *The Unnamable*, has to draw desperately on all the resources of invention to keep the words moving from line to line. The poet like T. S. Eliot who would abolish the usual connectives of traditional verse must make sure that his fragmentary images are sufficiently charged so that they hold the interest of the reader and fuse together into one imaginative whole. Language is bound to the world of meanings that always involves some sequence in time. By contrast, the visual image is self-contained; we can look at it with the absorption we give to a simple natural object—a shell or piece of wood polished by the sea that we pick up along the shore.

This autonomy of the visual image, however, can be misunderstood. If we grasp it in too one-sided a way, we end up in a sterile formalism. Then line, shape, and color by themselves are claimed to be sufficient for the visual arts. These claims and counterclaims became vociferous and heated in connection with the rise of the American school of Abstract Expressionism several decades ago. The artists—or more exactly, their partisans—wished to defend their abstract images against a public which, it seemed to the artists, wanted the pictures they looked at to bear some definite resemblance to things they knew. We were at that time a provincial country where modern art was concerned. Since then, we have perhaps swung to the opposite extreme and have become complacent about anything that wears the look of experimentation. The artists, of course, were right to defend their freedom to put upon the canvas whatever shapes they pleased. But their partisans rather overplayed their hand by implying that painting had always been abstract at heart but only recently discovered this truth about itself. Those were the days when art teachers would hang a print of El Greco upside down in front of the class to show that what the painting was really *about* was shadow, mass, spatial arrangement, and the rest. A very good pedagogical device perhaps for making beginners sensitive to formal values. But what would El Greco himself have thought of this reversal? He had intended the painting to depict the burial of Count Orgaz.

Curiously enough, the painters themselves in their private conversations were not given to this violent either/or dichotomy between abstraction and representation. Privately Jackson Pollock could ruminate for hours about what each loop and squiggle in one of his abstract paintings represented to him. De Kooning was compelled to do his women pictures—much overpraised, in my view, because they are in ceaseless quarrel with their subject; but no matter, the compulsion to tie the image to the world beyond was there and had to be yielded to. Unfortunately, Abstract Expressionism, lionized too quickly, faded too quickly. Pollock and Franz Kline died prematurely; De Kooning sputtered out in impotent rage. The movement might have settled down to establish itself as a style, become conscious of its own aesthetic, and prepared itself for some major statements in paint. But the rapid turnover, which seems to be the law of American capitalism and its cultural market, demanded that it be replaced by the newer models of Op and Pop and Minimal art. The artists, no longer traditionally starving in a garret, had instead become victims of a booming market. Abstract Expressionism had been the first American school that became a leader of the international avant-garde, and buyers were willing to snap up anything new in the hope that the miracle would strike again. The owner of one of the best-known galleries in New York has remarked that he never asks himself whether a picture is good or not but only whether it will have "historical value"; that is, whether it will sell at a good price because people think it may be part of a major trend. Naturally enough, this inflation in the market has led to a corresponding deflation of aesthetic values in the art that is being produced right now.

The result is that there has been a weakening in the power of the visual image. The autonomy of the image has to be understood always in connection with this other aspect of its power. True, the image stands there alone; we can look at it for itself; but it has power over us to the degree that it is resonant—even when not directly representational—of a world of forms beyond itself. In any case, the devotees of abstract art might have remembered that some of the most revolutionary artists of our time have been concerned beyond the obsession with formal questions, with giving us images of man and woman. These images, which haunt our imagination and have long since become a part of our modern sensibility, are more than abstract shapes. Picasso has been the dominating figure in the art of this century; and he is also the supreme counterexample to the dogmatisms of abstract art. For what is the work of Picasso but a torrential volcano of forms in which the human image is perpetually being smelted down and recast anew? The fashionable dictum that the medium itself has become the message— that the technique of painting has become its subject matter; or, in another formulation, that this subject matter is the action of painting itself—simply does not square with the large body of significant art (and I do not mean academic art) in this century.

Picasso, to repeat, is the dominating figure in the plastic art of the twentieth century. This does not mean necessarily that he is the greatest; we are still too close to him to judge him on that, and his genius bristles with many questionable aspects. Indeed, he has yet to be done up in print: no monograph—so far as I know—has gathered together all of his facets into some thematic unity and so plucked out the heart of his mystery. But dominating he is, and with a kind of ruthless and swaggering boldness. (The story is reliably reported that a palmist whose genuineness was being tested was shown a photographed impression of his palm without being told whose hand it was: "A gangster with genius," she observed—not a bad summation really of the painter who has hijacked all the museums of the world.) No interpretation of modern art could be offered without mentioning him, and so we shall have to give him a brief sidelong glance here if only to place certain other works of other artists in their proper context. After all, what is troubling the psyche of the twentieth century in its deepest layers must somewhere come to the surface in that immense panorama of images that Picasso unrolls before us.

Even in his very early, relatively realistic period, there is still the aura of the mythical about Picasso's figures. At first glance they might seem to continue in the genre of Degas' ballet girls or Lautrec's café performers. But these latter are the products of a sharply observed, if also a very expressive, realism; they belong to a definite milieu, in the opera house or the Moulin Rouge. Picasso's circus folk, on the other hand, are situated in an indefinite landscape, nowhere, and a strange wind seems to blow over them. His acrobats and harlequins make one think of the first figure of the tarot deck, the Juggler, who is the initiate to be led through all the experiences of life symbolized in the other cards. These circus folk are figures that begin Picasso's long descent into the nether world of the unconscious. If one could imagine all his paintings spread out before us like the cards of the tarot we would have a panorama of the progress of Picasso's soul through the archetypes of the unconscious.

The invention of Cubism, which preoccupied him with the

Picasso, *Three Musicians*. 1921 (summer). Oil on canvas, 6′ 7″ ×
7′ 3¾″. Collection, The Museum of Modern Art, New York. Mrs.
Simon Guggenheim Fund.

formal properties of painting, does not halt him in that descent into the nether world, for he was always ready to place the formal dislocations of this style in the service of his own expression. In fact, Cubism itself has two opposing, but closely linked, aspects. It decomposes bodies into surfaces as seen from any side, and flattens them out in a space that is also flattened. The objects are familiar ones—bottles, vases, guitars, tables, and so forth—but now they look strange and mysterious. This space is untraversable; these objects cannot be grasped simply the way I might put my hand directly across an ordinary table and lay hold of a bottle. There is an opacity, a strangeness, at once mysterious and close about the world of the ordinary—not unlike the effect conveyed in literature by some of the works we discussed in the first part of this book.

This sense of mystery pervades the early Cubist pictures, around 1911 to 1912, by Picasso, Braque, Juan Gris. But there is another, less deeply metaphysical, side of Cubism that has to do with its purely decorative capacities. After all, this style was a technical triumph that permitted the painter the freedom to reshape objects as he chose but at the same time under strict control of a design that used the total area of the picture space. This freedom evoked a certain gaiety in the painter; he could be witty, ironical, and playful as he cut up familiar objects around him and manipulated them into some surprising pattern for the eye. Moreover, the flat painting permits the use of flat color for a gay poster-like effect. Picasso himself has made full use of these decorative and light-hearted possibilities of the style. There is, after all, a considerable bit of the rogue about this man, and more often than not a touch of mocking humor in some of his most somber efforts. At the same time he was always driven by the restless urge (not really shared by other Cubists) for those peculiar visual images that emerge from the nether world of myth and the unconscious. Sometimes the two impulses converge in one painting, as in the famous *Three Musicians*. These three creatures are dressed in carnival costume,

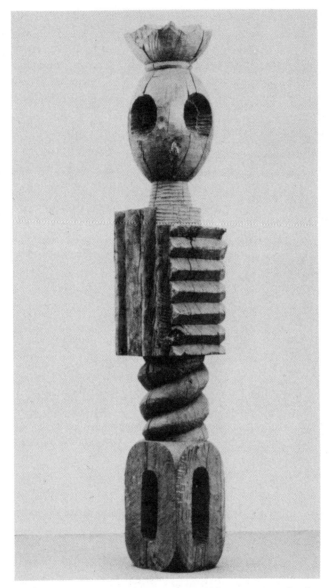

Brancusi, *King of Kings.* No date. Wood, 118⅛″ high.
The Solomon R. Guggenheim Museum.

itself very decorative, and the freedom of Cubist style permits the colorful elements to be further manipulated into a decorative pattern. Yet there is also something uncanny and mysterious about these three musicians, who are both human and inhuman, like many of the figures out of myth. They happen also to be comic, and we do not know whether to laugh or be frightened by them.

This self-consciousness and irony in handling myth, which we shall meet later in James Joyce's *Finnegans Wake*, keeps cropping up in modern artists. After all, the rational mind of our culture had apparently long since discarded myth, and we should therefore expect the artist, however his heart yearns for it, to be a little gingerly and awkward in trying to recapture it.

Brancusi's is a temperament altogether opposed to Picasso's —all elegance and refinement where Picasso is stormy and turbulent. Yet like Picasso, Brancusi is in search of primordial forms that pull our imagination beyond the strict confines of realistic art—figures of the bird, the fish, or some other unknown prehistoric creatures. But there is always the note of elegant irony, almost as if Brancusi, being a self-conscious modern, must caricature a little these primeval shapes that he rediscovers. His *King of Kings* evokes the ruined splendor of some monarch out of prehistory. There is an imposing and awesome mystery about this strange and solitary figure. But as you walk about it, it seems to shift into another range of feeling, like those optical puzzles that can be seen now one way and now another; it ceases to be solemn and becomes funny. This pompous king could be the prototype of innumerable cartoons in the *New Yorker*.

In Picasso, as he goes on during the 1920s and particularly in some of the great lithographs of the 1930s, the self-consciousness and irony lessen as these images from the unconscious seem to become more urgent. One notes, among others, these archetypes: (1) The woman. Picasso has done her in so many moods and aspects that it would take a book in itself to follow

Picasso, *Minotauromachy*. 1935. Etching, 19½″ × 27″. Collection, The Museum of Modern Art, New York. Purchase of the Museum.

this theme through his works. (2) The bull. Since Picasso was a Spaniard, one might see here merely the influence of the bull-ring. But unlike in Hemingway, the bull is the center of attention and the matador has disappeared. The bull, for Picasso, embodies primitive energy, cruel and destructive. But he too goes through metamorphoses and becomes the minotaur, half beast and half human. The minotaur is somber and ferocious at first, but then becomes more humanized and poignant, with a kind of suffering wisdom to his bestial face. In some of the late drawings he is the old man painfully held in thrall by a younger woman. (3) The child with a lamp enters into this macabre world as if an innocent vision were still possible amid its horrors. These motifs all appear in *Guernica*, which is only incidentally a work of political art. The bombing of this city during the Spanish Civil War merely served as the occasion for the eruption of figures that Picasso already harbored in his unconscious.

But enough of such motifs. We have cited them in passing only in order to indicate that the visual image, far from being a mere matter of abstract decoration, has the strange power of attaching itself to and speaking for the deep life of the unconscious. But there is another kind of power, connected less with myth and the unconscious and more with human history and culture, and that is the power, again quite strange and over-whelming, by which a single image can sometimes sum up a whole civilization or epoch. For proof, we turn now to the pictures that make up the chief business of this chapter.

I

They are six pictures in all, in two pairs of three: three faces and three bodies. The bust and the reclining figure are standard subjects throughout the history of art; and this choice seemed advisable, for it would avoid any eccentric or angled-camera snapshots upon the history of art. We are, after all, trying to generalize about our time from what is plainly there before our eyes if we only take the trouble to look.

Two of the reproductions are from older periods, and only the last in each group of three is contemporary. The older pictures are needed as a framework in order to highlight the extraordinary change that has occurred with the moderns. The reader ought to look at these pictures one at a time, if necessary hiding the later ones with his hand so that he imitates imaginatively the movement of history passing from one image to the other.

The first is the face of Agrippa, a great general and three-time consul under Emperor Augustus. There is a short poem addressed to him by Horace, but it is a very slight one and more in the manner of begging off. Horace was on terms of intimacy with some of the great, but he seemed to shy away from this young general, and this bust perhaps tells us why. It is a handsome face, certainly, but also an arrogant one. The unknown sculptor, most probably a Greek residing at Rome, intending to flatter, seems to be remembering the figures of Alexander the Conqueror. Pride, power, arrogance—here is the face of the *Imperium Romanum* gazing out at you across all those centuries. But if you look closely, you will also find a petulant quality in these good looks; petulance and sullenness—as if the wielding of power were perhaps not altogether satisfying, though the man himself cannot grasp what it is that he lacks.

With the second face—John the Baptist from the Cathedral of Reims—we are in a different epoch and a different world: the high Middle Ages of Christendom. Man is being-in-the-world, says Heidegger, and this world is always historical through and through. History does not fall upon us like a force from without, but shapes our being from within outward. Man is within history, and history is within him. The artist's image is like a lens that gathers into focus all those scattered rays of the period that converge upon it, and hence the remarkable power of a simple visual image as here, to portray two wholly different epochs of the human spirit. The Greco-Roman sculptor of the first work could not have fashioned the second face, not that he lacked the technical skill but simply because he could not have imagined anything like the second face since his world had not arrived at that historical phase of the spirit that looks out at us from the medieval face. We, on the other hand, can no longer create a face like the second because we have already lived beyond the power of Christianity that passed through the medieval sculptor into his work. Before the philosophers had pronounced their intellectual v∍rdict on His demise, the death of the Christian God had become evident from the time that painters could no longer portray convincingly the face of Christ. Manet, as Edgar Wind points out, painted a *Christ Mourned by Angels* that follows the same pattern as a work of Mantegna. Yet we admire Manet's work simply as a piece of technical virtuosity; it is not convincing, whereas Mantegna's painting was intended to make its viewers bend their knees, and probably still would if our knees could bend. Looking then both forward and back in time from the work of art, we have to say there is a curious inevitability about it that it belongs to its time, and could not be created either earlier or later than it actually was.

This inevitability is not to be confused with historical determinism. Whatever else he may hold, the determinist must believe that the future is predictable if we know all the hidden historical forces now at work. But determinism always founders when it comes to the question of art, for the work of art is a genuine creation, and creation implies, in its concrete detail, some measure of unpredictability—even for the artist himself, who cannot be sure just how the work will turn out. To predict a future work of art in detail would mean that we ourselves would have had already to have created it. The Greco-Roman sculptor could not have predicted art like the face of the Baptist unless he could already have created it. And we today cannot predict what the art of the future will be because that would require that we ourselves already stand in that future state of

Head of Agrippa. 1st century A.D. Courtesy des Musées Nationaux.

Head of John the Baptist. 13th century. Cathedral of Reims.

Giacometti, *Head.* 1928. Marble, 15″ high. Courtesy Stedelijk Museum, Amsterdam.

being, from which alone its genuine and convincing works will flow. Let us bear in mind the full force of this point—that art belongs uniquely to its epoch in the simple sense that it could not have been created at any other time—when we come to the third of our three images: the face of modern man.

The face of St. John, we commonly say, represents spiritual man, while Agrippa is worldly. But both belong completely to their worlds, only the world in each case is different. Each sculptor has represented not merely a human face but the metaphysical reality of his epoch. What man is, Heidegger has said, is a question of the horizons of possibility open to him. There are horizons of the spirit open to St. John that are closed to Agrippa, handsome and sullen with power, but locked within the bounds of his own finitude. This medieval face has been touched by some transcendent power that has descended vertically into history to become incarnate in human flesh. This is the secret of what has been called medieval humanism: God by taking upon himself human flesh ennobled it, left it still humble but touched with immortal longings. Here again, the question of reality is linked with the meaning we assign to time. For Christian faith, the universe was created, and time with it. Time, which thus has a beginning, consequently has a direction and moves toward an end—which will be the consummation of time itself. St. John the Baptist looks beyond this earthly present toward that eternal future his coming was intended to announce. For Agrippa—whether he was Stoic or Epicurean in his philosophy, and he was probably both at different moments, as most noble Romans were—the universe was eternal, and his being could never transcend those eternal cycles of time ever changing yet ever changeless.

What, then, are the horizons of possibility open to our third face—modern man? The figure is by Giacometti, a fairly early one from 1927. The face is blank, but it says a good deal to us. The philosopher Max Scheler, in one of his more Existential moments, declared that ours is the age when man has become, for the first time in history, fully and thoroughly problematical to himself. The frameworks—of religion and tradition—that once contained us no longer hold, and we face the world without presuppositions. The two earlier faces have so definite a character; in each case the individual knows who he is and what man is. This blank face, on the other hand, makes us think of Sartre's dictum that man has no essence: he exists first and then has to create what he is. Yet, empty as it is, this is not the face of a mindless zombie. Giacometti has put energy, boldness, and power into it. It is the face of a conquistador—and not the conqueror of this or that particular historical kingdom, but of nature itself. Indeed, we know that this creature in our time has mastered the secrets of atomic energy, soared into space, and girdled the earth in his networks of communications. Yet if one continues to look at this face, one begins to feel a haunting and poignant quality about it. Despite all that power that he has amassed, this strange creature still finds his existence questionable: he does not know who he is or what his meaning is. We could appropriately inscribe this bust with a sentence from Samuel Beckett: "There somewhere man is too, vast conglomerate of all of nature's kingdoms, as lonely and as bound."

But, it may be argued, this is only one among the countless pieces of sculpture that have been fabricated in our period. True, and it is not altogether typical of Giacometti either, for many people are surprised, on seeing the reproduction, that it is by him. But let us also remember the previous point about the uniqueness of the visual image: it belongs to its time and can be created only in that time; and even if only one such figure had been created, it would be a symptom of that time and no other. No artist before the twentieth century could have imagined this face as a finished piece of sculpture, unless as a hoax in which he himself immediately disbelieved. But we today find it an image that haunts us. We look at the ancient and the medieval figures, and we say, "There is the face of Rome. There is the face toward which the Middle Ages aspired." Someday in the future men will look backwards and say, "There is the confused and questioning face of the twentieth century."

Moreover, this work is not at all atypical of Giacometti. He is better known, of course, for his thin men, which for many have become his creative signature; but elsewhere in dealing with the human face, as in his later paintings, the end result, though it operates through different means, brings us before the void face again, though by a different path. We know what agonies Giacometti went through, and how he exhausted his models, in order to paint these faces. "Impossible," he claimed to one sitter. "There is an infinity between the chin and the jaw." Here, instead of being blank, the face seems to contain too much in order to be represented. But the effect is the same: space is untraversable, as always with Giacometti; the shortest distances, as between chin and jaw, are too long to be crossed. In these later faces by Giacometti we watch the face decomposing into the void out of which it is ultimately composed. His people pulsate between Being and Nonbeing. If they thrust aggressively into the void like the beaked conquistador, or decompose inwardly into it like the painted faces, it is all one. They all, in the words of Sophocles, "come to nothing."

Let us turn now from the head to the body. The head, of course, is part of the body, though traditionally we tend to set one off against the other. Mind and body—these are the two opposites into which our culture has divided our being. The mind—which is more or less assumed to inhabit the head and express itself through the face—is concerned with the meaning of things, with questions, puzzles, predicaments and paradoxes, and hopefully their solutions; the body meanwhile binds and preserves us in the earthbound life of the instincts. But this body also—the intricate structure created by nature through millions of years of evolution—may have a wisdom of its own that we come to forget or quarrel with or question. So the body itself can become as problematical as the mind and haunted with as many meanings, which you can see if you look carefully at the next triad of reproductions.

These—two sculptures and one fresco—all represent the human figure in reclining form, a subject that has attracted artists since the Greeks. The first is from the Parthenon, from the high period of Phidias, and perhaps even done by Phidias himself; the second is Michelangelo's painting (in the Sistine Chapel) of Adam just after he has been created by God; the third is by the contemporary English sculptor Henry Moore. The three are but variations upon the same theme, yet these variations tell us a great deal about the historical vicissitudes of Western humanism.

The Greeks are often spoken of as the first humanists. At any rate, their civilization, compared with those of their Asiatic and Egyptian neighbors and predecessors, seemed to bring the world into human focus. The Homeric poems present us with a radiant and sunlit world in comparison with the swarming and febrile darkness of the Babylonian epic *Gilgamesh*. The images of animal gods, or figures half human, half animal, that haunted the imaginations of earlier peoples have disappeared with the Greeks, leaving only a vestigial trace in an epithet—like owl-eyed Athena—addressed here and there to one of the gods. In striking contrast to their Oriental neighbors, the Greeks took pride in the naked human body, and their statues glorified it as it had never been before—or perhaps since.

Yet we must not forget that the most beautiful of their statues are those of the gods. (The reclining figure here, for example, represents Dionysus.) The greatest Greek sculpture is from the sixth and fifth centuries before Christ. That was also the heroic age in which tragic drama emerged and reached its peak. From the one as from the other—from the heroic images of sculpture as from the stark characters of tragedy—we know that the gods were still real and present, and that though man might wrestle with this presence, as in the Greek tragedies, he did not do so to abolish, but to preserve it. Socrates had not yet appeared to make the world safe for Rationalism, and the Greek myths had not yet degenerated into the charming aesthetic fables they became for a later age. This point must always be held in mind if we are to see Greek humanism in any proper balance. Though the Greeks could glorify the gods in no better way than by giving them the beautiful figures of men, the human form on the other hand could attain a beautiful ideal of balance and harmony because man was understood to be in the presence of the gods. It is only in the later Hellenistic period, when the gods have retreated, that "humanism" as a conscious ideal becomes transmitted to the Romans as a mark distinguishing the cultivated man from the barbarian. Art is then regarded as a product for consumption by a refined sensibility; no longer, as in Greek tragedy, an open ritual celebrating the god and shared in by the whole people.

Yet there is a sense in which it is true to say that Greek civilization does mark the emergence of man from the night of the unconscious, and therefore the establishing of his humanity in a way that is new in history. For the primitive, man is not the first of the animals. Some African tribes, it has been noted, rank the elephant first, the lion second, and man somewhere further down the list. In these other beasts, after all, power is so evident and overwhelming that man seems feeble by comparison. Even the fact that man has language does not weigh heavily in the balance, since the very silence of the animals is taken as a sign of some secret and superior wisdom. At this stage of his development man is so much a part of nature that the distinctive implications of his being human are not grasped. The Greeks, on the other hand, were obsessed with this question: What is distinctive, what really marks off man from all the other creatures of nature? And the question did not have to wait for the philosophers. The earlier poets and tragic dramatists return again and again to the question of this most questionable creature, this unique, puzzling, enigmatic animal that is man—most awesome of all awesome things, Sophocles calls him. To the degree that

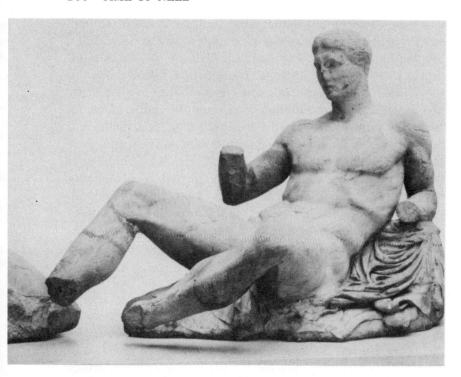

Phidias, *Dionysus.* 438–432 B.C. Marble, over life size. Courtesy Trustees of the British Museum.

Michelangelo, *The Creation of Adam*. 1508–1512. Courtesy Fratelli
Alinari.

Henry Moore, *Recumbent Figure*. 1938. Stone, 54″ long. Courtesy The Tate Gallery, London, and Henry Moore.

we look for what is absolutely distinctive about the human species to that degree must we set it apart from the rest of nature.
The historical achievement of the Greeks was to separate man
enough from nature that the full dimension of his humanity
might emerge in all its radiance. This reclining figure by
Phidias, beautifully relaxed and self-sufficient in its own balance, has been cut out from the swarming nightmare of forms
that infests the imaginations of earlier peoples.

Something much more sharp and drastic divides Michelangelo's *Adam* from the rest of nature: he is the individual creature of God. True, the whole universe has also been the product
of the divine creation; but in Christian belief each individual
soul itself issues directly from the hand of God, and all the rest
of creation, according to Genesis, has been placed under the
dominion of this human creature. There is an individuality in
this Adam that is absent from the timelessly ideal figure by
Phidias. We see Adam at the unique and dramatic moment just
after creation. Lassitude and weakness cling to him as to a
newborn infant; in his face a loving passivity and gratitude
acknowledge his creaturely dependence upon the Creator. But
this supine form also ripples with power. This moment is the
beginning of human history, and this figure has within it the
latent energy that will never be quiescent. Time which has just
begun with the creation itself will hereafter move ever forward
toward its providential goal. The Dionysus of Phidias, on the
contrary, remains locked in a timeless and eternal balance, part
of a cosmos that has no beginning and end, and where time
itself is without direction. We see Adam at one chosen moment,
which is pregnant with drama and history; there is no chosen
historical moment, amid the eternal cycles of his life, at which
this Dionysus is now reclining. Despite his schooling in the
Greeks, Michelangelo was perpetually violating the strict classical canons because he had to pour into his figures a dynamism
not found in ancient art. His Adam gives us a different version
of Christian humanism from the medieval John the Baptist. The

two are obverse sides of the same Christendom, which raised church steeples pointing toward heaven but also was the only civilization that colonized the globe and forced its missionaries upon primitive peoples.

With the reclining figure by Henry Moore we have come full, or rather half, circle to a point directly opposite to the statue by Phidias. The dynamism has gone, and tranquillity and repose reign again. But the effect is altogether different: for where the Greek sculptor sought to cut out a figure sharply defined from nature, Moore seeks to make the outlines less definitely human in order to reintegrate this body with the earth. The features have disappeared as if eroded by weather (the real weather of time did that to Phidias' sculpture, or we would see it as even more clear-cut), as if the stone itself were sinking back into the earth again. The sculptor seems trying to persuade us that we are not looking merely at a human artifact, but at a geological product of earth and air and wind that has been deposited here by natural forces. This statue would not look nearly so good indoors in the room of a museum. It belongs here in the open air and on the earth to which it quietly clings. The hole through the center of the figure, Moore has told us, serves to unify formally the whole mass by bringing front and back together. Beyond this formal use, however, its more expressive purpose is to bring the body that much closer to earth because, looking through it, we see the ground. In its repose there is also an immense yearning. The head is greatly reduced in its proportions, and the features of the face have almost vanished, and properly so, for the being of this creature is absorbed into the body which yearns to belong again to its earth.

What has happened to bring about this historical circle from man beautifully isolated from the subhuman world to man (or woman) struggling to sink back to earth like a rock worn by the tides of the sea? The needs that clamor for aesthetic expression at one time may not do so at another. An attitude pertinent at one stage of history may be irrelevant and empty at another.

Those who talk nowadays with enthusiastic facility about humanism would do well to take a long look at this statue by Moore. The artist, of course, does not produce at the dictate of some intellectual thesis. Moore created this figure long before people knew what ecology meant and before public crusades were beginning to be launched in behalf of our earthly environment. Looking back now, we see that in the last century and a half the human world has expanded in every direction. Our roads cut across the earth, flatten its contours, and obliterate its green surfaces. The animals disappear except for the few who are preserved in man-made zoos. We have covered the earth with our human wastes. In the Western nations, for the first time in history, the bulk of mankind—70 percent or more—now lives in cities or in sprawling conglomerations attached to urban centers. Of all these developments art had been prophetic: the poet Baudelaire spoke of nineteenth-century Paris, which was hardly populous by present standards, as the "city swarming like an anthill" *("fourmillante cité")*, where "the tyranny of the human face" overwhelms one in the crowds from which one can never escape. Baudelaire also went on to speak of a future city from which all life (except man of course) would be excluded, and glittering metallic replicas would replace real trees in the streets. Perhaps one can have too much of the man-made world, and to find oneself one must lose it. Moore's statue speaks to us out of that need.

The painter Dubuffet offers a rather surprising if somewhat oblique illumination of this Moore figure. Dubuffet is not a great painter perhaps, but he is a very witty and sensitive man, and extraordinarily responsive to the currents of the time. Moreover, he writes well, and his own words do help us know what is going on within him and behind his canvases. He was, to begin with, a thoroughly urban and sophisticated character, having started in the worldly trade of a wine salesman, which he subsequently abandoned in order to become a painter. Among his early works, we find childlike paintings that look like

Dubuffet, *The Geologist.* 1950. Oil, 51½″ × 38½″. Private Collection, Pierre Matisse Gallery, New York.

graffiti scratched on some public place. The people he portrays on a city street look like very flat figures scratched on the wall of the houses along which they walk, as if they had no other life than the narrow street that encloses them. The decisive experience for Dubuffet was a journey into the desert of North Africa. Here was a landscape not yet subdued by man, where one could lose the "tyranny of the human face" and find oneself by entering the company of things as simple as stones.

Perhaps it was the time I spent in the deserts of White Africa that sharpened my taste (so fundamental to the mood of Islam) for the little, the almost nothing, and, especially, in my art for the landscapes where one finds only the formless—flats without end, scattered stones—every element definitely outlined such as trees, roads, houses, etc. eliminated. . . .

One will find also, among these pictures, certain ones called Stones of Philosophy, which represent only a large stone. . . .

It appeared to me that the facts—the pure and simple facts—presented by the formal texture of these big stones, could make these big pictures, at least with time, companions to which one could be strongly attached. . . .

The kingdom of formal ideas always appears to me of very little virtue beside the seignorial kingdom of stones.

In a world swarming with humanists, why should not the sudden glimpse of the nonhuman—the contour or metallic gleam of a stone—come like a ray of salvation? He went on to do a series of paintings depicting the "Life of the Soil," full of strange and squiggling shapes that represent the busy, immensely fertile, and indefatigable life of nature that goes on apart from man. In most of these paintings the human figure does not appear; but in one, *The Geologist*, a tiny and grotesque man, a humanist no doubt, is perched near the top of his canvas. The figure is dwarfed by the immense and complex life of the soil on which he ridiculously stands. We forget that our whole man-made world, in which we have lost ourselves, is only a tiny fragment within the total life of nature that goes on not at our bidding.

But, oddly enough, we shall find in the thin men of Giacometti the best commentary on Moore's reclining figure. At first glance, the two sculptors look antithetical: the figure by Moore is monumental, its body voluminous and overflowing; Giacometti's figures are small and so thin as to be almost vaporous. They are also antithetical temperaments: Moore the hearty and robust countryman from Hertfordshire, and Giacometti, the introverted Swiss-Italian who spent his creative life on the Left Bank of Paris. But when we look longer, we see that these seemingly antithetical visions open doors on opposite sides of the house but nevertheless lead to the same center.

Giacometti's invention of the thin men is one of the most striking cases of unconscious visitation in the history of art. At the time he had not the least intention, or even the faintest idea, of creating such figures. Whenever he set about to make a figure in the more usual size and proportions, something strange and unaccountable happened: under his hands it became smaller and smaller until it was finally reduced to almost nothing. He tried to fight what was happening to him. In vain, the figures still got smaller and smaller. This obscure compulsion, which was pushing its way forward to a vision he did not yet grasp, was stronger than consciousness and will. During that period, Giacometti tells us, he could carry around in a matchbox the work of a whole year.

Whence this obscure need to let the human figure crumble away into nothing—or almost nothing? Whence this urge to bring man down, to reduce his pretensions, to turn the traditionally grandiose form of *homo humanus,* which had become a sterile shape in the hands of academic humanism, to a strange *homunculus?* It is time perhaps that we stopped speaking of negative and positive in this simple-minded black-and-white dichotomous fashion. The so-called negative, pushed far enough, may secrete its own positive that we could not have guessed without going through the process of negation. Out of this remorseless reduction of man to matchbox size there were to emerge the lean and solitary figures of undeniable grandeur. For that is one of the most remarkable things about his small sculptures: they are more grand than most of the gigantic figures on monuments. One simple reason is that because they are small and we cannot escape seeing them in scope we are always seeing them as if at a distance. Nietzsche spoke of "the pathos of distance" as a characteristic of the lonely individual isolated by his own greatness. Giacometti's figures have this pathos; but, something more, they also exude distance. Man is *"ein Wesen der Ferne,"* a creature of distance, Heidegger has said, referring to the fact that man has distant horizons that outstrip the animal's. Giacometti's figures are not only seen at a distance; they create a distance between themselves and us because they seem always haunted by distant vistas of their own.[1]

The Humanism revived at the time of the Renaissance— really, re-created, for it had necessarily a different spiritual identity from its Greco-Roman model—insisted among other things on the classical canon in sculpture. Thus distortions, which had been very expressive in the earlier forms of Gothic, were severely condemned and banned. This classical canon persisted in sculpture more strictly than in all the other arts. In the nineteenth century when painting was already finding a new freedom in the Impressionists, the sculptors remained bound within the Humanist convention. Sculpture, after all, was more bound to Humanism because its predominant subject remained the human body, male or female. Rodin is one of the last great sculptors who, despite other liberties, still basically

1. It is important here to call the reader's attention to the fact that Giacometti's thin men suffer in reproduction to the flat page. Someone who has seen them only in reproduction is not likely to get this impression of the distance they invoke. One has to see them in a hall or large room, move around them, in order to become aware that as one moves toward them, and however close, they still remain distant. No stronger indication than this could be given that the sculptor has remained strictly faithful to the medium of his art—three-dimensional space.

adhere to this tradition. After him, modern sculptors destroy, distort, or deliberately bypass this classical convention. The mold of classical humanism can no longer contain their vision of man.

Giacometti is one of these innovators, but in a curious way his figures are haunted by a remembrance of the classical tradition that they would at the same time subvert: his *Man Pointing* can be regarded as a contemporary incarnation of the *Apollo Belvedere!* The stance, the gesture, and the general orientation of the figure are similar. But the classical form has undergone a strange metamorphosis. Anxiety has entered the Greek pantheon, and the gods lie sleepless at three o'clock in the morning, while the fat drips away from their bones. But this anxiety, so modishly contemporary as it may seem, also invokes a past more archaic and haunting than the images of a late Greco-Roman humanism.

The fact is that any statue that violates the classical canon and yet succeeds as a work of art is bound to bring us back in imagination to a period of art when the accurate realistic depiction of the human body was an irrelevant issue for the artist. Giacometti perpetually reminds us of this past. It has become almost fashionable to take his *Figures in a Public Square* as the emblem of modern alienation. These men walk in a public place, but they will never meet and will never talk to one another. Could one have a more compelling image of the lonely crowd today? True. But the loneliness of man is also recalled to us in various places of the world where he has mysteriously vanished and left images but no written records of himself. Imagine the figures of Easter Island diminished to miniature size and set at appropriate angles on a two-foot-square base, and you would get much the same effect. Nothing reminds us of the loneliness of man in the cosmos more than the images left by a vanished race. *Chariot* takes us back to a prehistorical period of men and their battle wagons long before the robust and legendary Homeric heroes. Giacometti, of course, was simply following the dictates of his sculptural vision. "I thought of the chariot," he has remarked, "because I wanted something that would raise the figure higher for the viewer." But a strange thing happens when the figure is elevated: it becomes more isolated and more lonely. This woman, impaled upon her chariot, will never drive it into battle. Between herself and the objects of her use the void has intervened. Man's essential loneliness is to be a presence that haunts a world that must ultimately be strange to him. The fragility of Giacometti's figures suggest a species that may have already vanished from the earth.

Now turn back to the body by Moore. Between it and the thin figures of Giacometti we can now observe not contradiction but a complementary dialogue. Moore's figure yearns to belong to the earth, to be reintegrated with nature and instinct, to become almost a simple natural object "rolled round . . . with rocks, and stones, and trees." But this yearning comes out of a lack, a need with which this needy time desperately threatens it. The threat is expressed in the Giacometti figures, where the body has become so meager that it seems on the point of vanishing altogether.

If you keep in mind Giacometti's later portraits of faces, and then put your eyes a few inches from the head of one of his statues to observe it closely, you will see that there is a strict continuity between his work in these two different media. The faces of these tiny statues are modeled with infinite care, delicacy, and expressiveness. The whole being of the figure has been sucked up into the head and face. In the Moore figure the head is smaller and the features of the face eroded, as if these were drained back into the body in its thrust to rejoin the earth. While Giacometti's have lost nature in the anguish of the void, Moore's forms must lose their human features in order to find themselves once again in the nonhuman world. Here is a tension of opposites that divides our contemporary being.

In the foregoing we have made the experiment, admittedly

Giacometti, *Chariot*. 1950. Bronze, 57″ × 26″ × 26⅛″. Collection, The Museum of Modern Art, New York. Purchase of the Museum.

speculative, of offering two images, a face and a body, as representative of our time. These then would be two separate portraits of ourselves done from two different points of view. But now let us compound the felony and push the experiment one step further: let us superimpose that particular head on that particular body, and we should then have the composite portrait of ourselves—not of course how we look outwardly but what we are inwardly. The result is aesthetically monstrous, to be sure, but if we can bear with its dissonance, it may be worth a moment or two of reflection. Indeed, the effect of this composite is also humanly monstrous. That sharp beaked head of the conquistador seems ready to tear apart the inchoate and passive body beneath it. The conflict of opposites: male principle at war with the female principle! The imperious thrust of rational consciousness against the more diffuse life of the unconscious, instinct, emotion. Or, as Robert Graves might put it, the baleful god Apollo, prophet of false enlightenment, supplanting the old matriarchal goddess of nature.[2] But pause a moment; think of that other aspect of this blank face that we have previously noted: the poignancy of its emptiness. This is the face that becomes lost in empty space and finds at last no answer to its questions. It has need then of that earthlike body to carry on its life. What have we here but a picture of the situation we encountered in the three writers we examined in the first part of this book. The head ends by finding a world without meaning, and can survive only by surrendering to the vital and natural thrust of energy that can carry it past its paralyzing questions.

2. Graves must have chuckled at the fact that the first moon flights were named after Apollo. We have indeed to admire his accuracy as a mythmaker, for those were the first flights in which men, by rational calculation, broke free from the gravitational field of mother earth. And with the arrogance typical of this god who ruthlessly supplanted the older maternal deities, they left the old mother in very dire straits—choked with garbage and sullen with the conflicts of her human children, which are ultimately instinctual and unconscious in nature. NASA could not have been so far-seeing as to plan the name this way; one can only assume that some very obscure promptings out of *anima mundi* bestirred their scientific consciousness.

But, you may say, the two in tandem are at least a workable solution for the time being. Unfortunately, two such uneasy yokefellows make us anxious, for at best they can only be in a state of unstable equilibrium. This "for the time being" is, alas, this time in which we live; we have no other—and it may be a very short time. Can we really make do for long with such a patched-up and superficial alliance between the opposites that divide us?

POSTSCRIPT AND TRANSITION

The thin men of Giacometti are in danger of losing their bodies. Amid all the words spilled, all the embroideries of ideas lavished in interpretation of these works, let us hold fast to this immediate and obvious fact about them.

But are these images pertinent today to us who have become sensually liberated and make a great parade of the body? We have long since overcome Victorian prejudices and take the naked body for granted. Our athletes, on better diets and vitamins, outstrip the competitors of the past and make mockeries of their records. And do we not have Esalen, the institute in California where people go to throw off inhibitions and are able to establish direct bodily rapport with others? Still, one can't help being a little skeptical. Would such an institute be necessary if something very drastic had not gone wrong elsewhere? And is it not a highly artificial and synthetic way of making people natural as beauty parlors are supposed to make them beautiful? The bravura acceptance of nudity does not mean necessarily that we have become capable of real physical intimacy. It would seem more likely that such intimacy happens, not by callously bypassing shame and modesty, but only when these latter are freely surrendered to the other person.

In all this parade of flesh the real meaning of the body—at least as we have intended it in the preceding—is lost. The body is not a physical container that we inhabit. And we have not given it its due when we are able to exhibit this container in public without flinching. Existentialist philosophers have spoken of "the lived body" in order to suggest the degree to which one's own body is internal to oneself. But even such a phrase cannot do justice to the intimate sense in which the body is an inseparable phase of our total being. The body is an immensely complex structure created by nature through millions of years of trial and error through whose operation, of which we are mostly unconscious, we carry on our daily lives. We live by the tides of the blood, the rhythm of breathing, the vast and intricate processes of unconscious mind without which we could not carry out the most elementary sequences of rational thought. The body is not a physical container but a region of Being—a network of living processes that sustains us but also binds us to the whole chain of life upon this earth. The body connotes life, vitality, directness, spontaneity, the natural. The opposites that have come to be set up against these are reason, intellect, tradition, social respectability, culture. It is the war of these opposites broken loose in modern culture that we proceed to examine in the next section.

Western civilization, as we now know it, begins with Plato dividing mind and body. Out of that split came philosophy. Out of philosophy science, and out of science technology. There was no necessity that this development take place. The world could have been left to Homer and the Greek poets or patterns of social stability developed, in the manner of classical Chinese civilization, without our ever building up these elaborate conceptual structures that make up science. It happened nevertheless; and we are today working out the consequences of that historical eruption. When the cause goes back so far, and reaches into all parts of the civilization, we cannot expect that its effect will be cured so easily because the masses now wear bikini suits on public beaches, nude bodies are exhibited on the screen, and the nudity of a whole cast is accepted on the stage. After all, those bikinis were mass-produced and thus required the complex organization of technology and mass marketing. Man does not step outside of nature and choose to return to it whenever and however he pleases without struggle and anguish.

It is this struggle and anguish that we shall now take a look at. In Symmetry with Part I we choose three writers, each of whom represents a progression in the drasticness (which does not mean necessarily a ranking of their artistic stature) with which they treat this theme. In Hermann Hesse the war of the opposites rages openly and is explicitly named and discoursed upon; on the one side intellect, tradition, bourgeois respectability, and the awesome and heavy weight of culture; on the other, emotion, instinct, the unconscious, and the rebellious struggle of the individual against the social establishment in order to achieve his wholeness. But however tormented and anguished the battle, the prognosis is optimistic. Hesse is a teacher, a didactic writer, who feels he can instruct us on the way toward reconciliation with ourselves. In Franz Kafka the battle is not joined, the protagonist is too meek for that, but it is there in the wings. The hero seeks to find his place within the community, to share in the simple and natural emotions of the commonplace; but despite his yearning, he is prevented from doing so by the heavy apparatus of the mysterious powers who rule this world from behind the scene. With Samuel Beckett we are past yearning; the battle has been fought and lost; nature is dead or moribund, or man has long since left it. "Kill it," Hamm roars as Clov is scratching at a flea in his trousers, "or it will start life all over again." Here we have reached the end of the line . . . or perhaps not. We shall have to see.

In the meantime we should observe that our subtitle is neither strained nor flippant. However we may conceive the chief protagonists of these writers, we can hardly think of Steppenwolf, Joseph K., or any of Beckett's waifs as fat men, or even of a moderately robust physique. The juices of life here are not that rich. Decidedly, they are lean, very lean.

Part III

The Thin Men

6. Journey to the East

Some children repeat the lives of their parents, even down to omitting all those things the parents themselves avoided. So the continuity and stability of the race are assured. Other children, and they are fewer, seem driven to search out and experience the unlived life of their parents. These are the voyages of discovery that broaden the mind and enrich the spirit of the race. But even when successful—and most of them are not—they are always paid for in suffering, as if the children must make atonement for the sins of the parents, and perhaps most of all for their sins of omission.

Both parents of Hermann Hesse were connected with missionary work in India (his mother had actually been born there). They continued, back in Europe, to maintain a lively interest in Indian languages and culture. But they were able to return to European Christianity without any break in their lives, and were completely contained within that framework. Accordingly, these good and pietistic parents had slated young Hermann for the theological seminary. He rebelled, had a religious crisis, and on two separate occasions ran away from home. From some of his earlier stories one might get the impression that his parents were stern, heavy-handed, and unsympathetic. On the contrary: years later in writing to his sister, Hesse spoke of how much both children owed to the kindness, sensitivity, and culture within the atmosphere of their home. Parents, alas, can never be sure what will make their children rebel. In any case, Hesse's revolt was against a parental figure far larger and more awesome than his individual father and mother. The parents, however, with their remembrances of India and its culture,

187

were to supply him with the instrument of his rebellion—and ultimately of his salvation. They reminisced about India, but it was he who would be compelled to make the real journey to the East—the journey inward—that they had never taken.

This frustration with the Christianity of his time was only part of Hesse's rebellion against European civilization as a whole. He was at the midpoint of his life when the dismal catastrophe of the First World War broke out; but years earlier he had felt a malaise and desperation chafing within the European spirit, and shortly before 1914 he left Germany, with its oppressive atmosphere of nationalism and militarism, to take up residence in Switzerland. He remained always a "good European," in Nietzsche's sense: a man who thought national boundaries were silly and served only to provoke the insanity of wars. In the 1920s he went back to Germany, but it was no use. Years before Hitler came to power, Hesse sensed in the German soul that festering resentment and arrogant patriotism that would lead to the Second World War. He therefore removed himself to Switzerland and became a Swiss citizen—a proper home for a true internationalist.

But political realities are always secondary for Hesse to the things of the spirit. Our historical textbooks usually present us with the picture of social upheavals and their consequent and accompanying psychological dislocations, and so unconsciously we tend to think of the causality going only in this way. But in fact it may happen in just the opposite direction: the psychological atmosphere may become so sick that it finally erupts in panics, wars, and revolution. Very early, at the beginning of his career, Hesse had felt there was a drying up, a death of the spirit within European civilization itself. Europe has become a graveyard, he wrote; the great culture it had once created could continue now only in an inert and mechanical way that stifled the individual's spontaneity. What was needed was some renewal of Being. When the mold of a culture is shattered, or its rituals become stultifying, one may have to step outside it to find renewal. Hence the journey to the East.

A culture, as the anthropologist sees it, is an extension of nature by human means. It is the marvelous device by which man gives expression and form to his own natural needs and which allows him at the same time to cope with nature of which he is a part. Man's so-called high culture, which satisfies needs —for order, beauty, meaning—as natural as his needs for food and sex, is also originally part of this structure. But what happens when this higher structure becomes top-heavy, inert, and cumbersome, and instead of promoting the needs of life stifles them? The individual must then seek renewal within himself, for there are no available social means to help him. The forms of an alien culture may be suggestive, but they too present themselves as dead letters unless the individual travels the path inward that will give them life for him. Renewal, real renewal, must mean a descent into the unconscious. When a culture is working, the unconscious takes care of itself and becomes invisible because it is contained and expressed within the overt rituals of life. When the culture ceases to work, the unconscious becomes troublesome and obtrusive.

This is what Hesse felt had happened to European civilization. Europe, he wrote, had conquered the whole world and lost her own soul. For a century she had built factories and ceased to think of the spirit. Hesse belonged to that generation when the case histories of Freud, just appearing, were making clear that Western civilization, whatever its enlightenment and progress, was harboring within itself some grievous sicknesses of the human soul. It was also the generation which felt the first full impact of Nietzsche; and here the message was an uncompromising and, if necessary, ruthless individualism if that were the only means to secure health and wholeness.

Hesse has now become extraordinarily popular with the younger generation in this country, and it is easy to see why. His early novel *Beneath the Wheel* could be taken—with a few changes of names and locale—as the story of a college dropout

as it is happening all around us now in America. Hans Gieben-
rath is a gifted and diligent student until under the influence of
Hermann Heilner (the intitals H. H. keep cropping up in Hesse)
he begins to feel that the System is stifling the spontaneous and
emotional side of his nature. He quits the seminary, works at a
number of jobs that seem demeaning to his bourgeois parents,
takes to the taverns (nowadays it would be marijuana and
drugs), and finally drowns in an absurd accident. No matter;
Hans has failed, but others will take up his fight to recapture
natural man beneath the heavy apparatus of social man.

Two decades ago one could scarcely have foreseen this current popularity of Hesse among the young. Yet here is a clear
case of art's being prophetical of life. Forty or fifty years before
the hippie culture was to erupt among us, Hesse was its prophet
—even down to the Oriental trappings with which it fits itself
out. And rereading him now should help us to see what the
revolt of today's youth is really about. It is only secondarily
political. Sometimes political causes are grasped only in order
to externalize or objectify the more nameless malaise within. At
bottom, however obscurely grasped, the revolt is for some psychological and spiritual wholeness which our civilization seems
to these young to frustrate.

But there is one part of Hesse's message that his youthful
admirers tend to forget. His theme is the polarity that divides
human nature. The opposites are not so much isolated traits as
whole constellations of qualities that tend to make up two eternal manifestations of the human psyche. On the one side, the
constellation revolves around: reason, reflection, tradition, discipline, social order, bourgeois steadiness and reliability and, in
its inferior manifestations, respectability. In the other constellation are: spontaneity, emotion, intuition, instinct—and the
product that issues from them, art. Nietzsche had spoken of
these as the Apollonian and Dionysian sides of human nature,
borrowing the names, respectively, of the gods of enlightenment and of enthusiasm. In an older philosophical tradition

they had been referred to as the opposing claims of culture and nature which man is forced to live by. Hesse's theme, repeated from story to story and novel to novel, is the conflict between the two. But—and this is precisely where his youthful admirers are apt to miss his point—victory cannot belong to either side. One force cannot conquer the other without also eventually inflicting defeat upon itself. The triumph of reason and order can bring about emotional paralysis, neurosis, and the blank wasteland of Nihilism where all values lose their meaning. But pure spontaneity of emotion could turn life into a blob without form or order. True, Hesse grew up under the heavy pressure of bourgeois society in Germany, and his emphasis tends to be placed on the side of vitality, emotion, and instinct. In another historical atmosphere, however, the emphasis could just as well go the other way. Man is condemned to live forever in the tension of the opposites; but his salvation lies in maintaining, not civil war, but a fruitful dialogue between them. In the ancient Chinese symbol of psychic wholeness the dark and the light lie down beside each other and each must give to and receive from the other.

Two other European writers—Gide and D. H. Lawrence—in this same period spoke up for the individual and his instincts against the oppressiveness of society. In fact, Gide was even earlier in the lists with *The Immoralist* (1902), one of his most remarkable novels. In a striking parallel to Hesse, the influence here too is Nietzschean, and the hero's career is in fact modeled somewhat after Nietzsche's own. Michel is a young professor who comes to find all his learning and culture turn into dust and ashes while the forces of life become atrophied. In North Africa, a climate different from Europe's, he breaks through the barrier of conscience, discovers his body and freedom, and becomes whole and healthy for the first time. But Gide is aware of the dialectical tension within his subject matter: Michel has destroyed the order which once held his life together, and his existence has now become so elementally sensory that he sits all day in the shade pressing the coolness out of pebbles, aware that he has to begin again and begin from the beginning. No such dialectical subtlety infects the more blunt, straightforward British mentality of Lawrence. However amazing a poet he could be at times, there was about Lawrence the persistent and cantankerous spirit of a nonconformist preacher always delivering the same sermon: the necessity of rediscovering mystical consciousness and organic wholeness with the body against the dark satanic mills of modern industrial society. Both of these writers bear confirming witness that Hesse's theme does not come out of personal idiosyncrasy but out of the needs of his time.

Yet there are two good reasons for choosing Hesse as the representative figure for this particular theme. First, he suffered the conflict of the opposites within himself in the most agonizing way. Gide made the breakthrough that permitted him to square his Protestant conscience with his homosexuality; and while his life thereafter was not placid, it had nevertheless the steadiness of the French bourgeois about it. Lawrence found his Queen Bee, eloped with Frieda; and while his life continued to be restless and rather foot-loose, he had early found the relationship that contained him. Hesse, however, suffered and went on suffering the worst torments of the modern neurosis: mental breakdown, a tragic marriage, psychoanalysis, sanatoriums; and only toward the very end did he arrive at any safe harbor of serenity. The second, and more significant, reason is that this conflict between sensuality and spirit is the chief theme of German culture, both in its poetry and in its philosophy; and Hesse, working within this tradition, is able to give the whole question deeper philosophical reverberations.

Why this conflict between flesh and spirit—or spirit and nature, as the philosophers put it—should be so much a German obsession may be left to speculation. No doubt, people will speak of "the German soul," though a national soul is usually a pattern of national history that has taken a grip upon a people.

In any case, with Goethe's *Faust*, German literature virtually begins as the exploration of this struggle between the rival claims of nature and spirit, vitality and intellect. The aging scholar Faust is suffering a death of the spirit; all learning, all the highest values of man's culture, have lost their value for him. Here again, Nihilism is the product of declining vitality, of the gray waste of emotion undischarged, of instinct stultified. He seeks renewal through a pact with the devil, and his youth is restored. Out of this old medieval tale, which originally intended simply to portray the destruction of a Christian soul by trafficking with the black arts, Goethe made a psychological parable for modern man. In the second part of the drama Mephistopheles has ceased to be the capering and melodramatic devil of tradition; he has now become Faust's lieutenant in the prodigious labor of reclaiming the wastelands of the earth. The idealistic ego has to come to terms with its opposite, the devil in ourselves, if it is to release the life-giving energies.

Nietzsche is simply Faust lived over again, but with more agony, and thought through to the most drastic conclusions. Thomas Mann (the contemporary often linked with Hesse) plays his own variations upon the strife of the opposites: the division between those healthy spontaneous natures capable of "the blisses of the commonplace" and the more introverted, reflective temperament of the artist who is alienated from the immediacy of the common life. And finally, Freudian psychoanalysis itself is a reprise, this time an ultimately pessimistic one, on the old motif. For what in its simplest terms, Freud tells us, is the unhappiness of modern man but the fact that he finds it more and more difficult to bear the heavy burden of culture at the price of the instinctual renunciations it entails?

Behind this modern wrestling with its modern devil there stand of course Luther and the Protestant conscience. He had launched his Reformation with a psychological split that had been smoothed over in the images and rituals of medieval Catholicism. On the one hand, he would demand a loftiness of faith and a severity of conscience that the practice of Catholicism, out of its compassion for human weakness, did not exact. At the same time he was an extremely sensual man himself and hard put to suppress the demands of his body. Honesty of conscience, however, could not allow these demands to be satisfied by the back-alley lecheries of monks in the Middle Ages. Therefore the clergy must marry! It is interesting to observe that one extreme evokes the other: the further one pushes toward a more lofty spiritualism the more troublesome and compelling become the desires of the body.

It was the fate of German literature to arrive late, a century and a half after France and England had produced the master-pieces that would be the framework of their own national litera-tures. At one time Goethe was able to remark, and he was being only half jocular, "German literature is me." As newcomers, they would have to work feverishly to make up lost ground. The Germans went through a prodigious labor of assimilation in their effort to appropriate all that was known. The German spirit became, as it were, top-heavy with culture. In the latter half of the eighteenth century, when modern German litera-ture began, the two contending European movements in the world of letters were the Enlightenment and Romanticism. The Germans had to do justice to both, appropriating what was positive in each. On the one hand, all the intellectualism of the Enlightenment; on the other, the passion and freshness of feel-ing of Romanticism, which to the more nationalistic critics seemed to breathe the youthful spirit of the Germanic races that were only now arriving on the stage of world history. Ger-man literature was thus born with two souls dwelling in its breast. And the language itself was the fitting vehicle for this duality. The fascination of the German language, its unique beauty, to the foreigner is its materiality and concreteness on the one hand, and on the other its capacity for an almost prodi-gal abstractness. It would almost seem as if the conflict of opposites had been embodied in the language itself from the very start.

I

To come back now to Hesse from this brief divagation upon German destiny. His chosen strategy in dealing with the conflict of the opposites is to embody them in two contrasting characters. In story after story there will be on one side the sober, rational, reflective, studious, and disciplined conformist; on the other, the spontaneous, instinctual, and Dionysian individualist. The rational character is usually altered by contact with his opposite, sometimes to his downfall; the latter seems never to be transformed into an Apollonian.

In *Demian* (1919) there is the added note of the occult: Max Demian, who draws his sustenance from the darker part of his being, seems endowed with almost superhuman powers. The achievement of individuality sets a man so far apart from the herd that they see on his face the mark of Cain, which is really a sign of their fear of following their own inner destiny. But here too the conflict of the opposites has a more favorable result: Emil Sinclair, who begins as the more commonplace of the two, comes so under Demian's tutelage that he too begins to wear that secret mark of the individuated one on his face. In *Narziss und Goldmund* (1930) the opposition acquires the further dimension of the artist versus the thinker. Goldmund must leave the medieval monastery to give himself to the sensual life for which he is destined; but this sensuality becomes spiritualized in the art he is able to create out of it. Narziss, the reflective scholar, also moves toward reconciliation with his opposite; very late he comes to realize that these statues of Goldmund, which formerly he would have judged to be mere sensory objects, are perhaps more spiritual than any philosophy or theology. But he is able to reach this development not by himself alone but only in reflection upon the life of his friend Goldmund. In the end, the thinker learns the truth of the spirit from the artist. However, Hesse departs from his regular strategy in one work, *Steppenwolf*, and chooses instead to lodge the conflicting opposites within one character alone. And here their conflict becomes worth watching in some detail.

The Steppenwolf, Harry Haller by name, is a middle-aged bachelor, immensely cultivated, but whose culture—like Faust's—has turned to world-weariness and despair. He thinks of himself as a wolf of the steppes, that shy, lone, forever restless beast of prey. Underneath the crust of civilization there is a wild beast lurking in him. Like Faust he can say, "Two souls, alas, dwell within my breast." But matters of the psyche are no longer so simple in this century as they were for Goethe. The divided parts of the Steppenwolf's soul can in turn be divided indefinitely:

The breast and the body are indeed one, but the souls that dwell in it are not two, nor five, but countless in number. Man is an onion made up of a hundred integuments, a texture made up of many threads. The ancient Asiatics knew this well enough, and in the Buddhist Yoga an exact technique was devised for unmasking the illusion of the personality. The human merry-go-round sees many changes: the illusion that cost India the efforts of thousands of years to unmask is the same illusion that the West has labored just as hard to maintain and strengthen.

And Hesse turns this philosophical doctrine into a criticism of the old-fashioned realistic novel that sought above all to establish the solid identity of its characters:

In literature too . . . we find this customary concern with apparently whole or single personalities. . . . each character makes his appearance unmistakably as a separate and single entity. . . . These conceptions are not native to us, but are merely picked up at second hand, and it is in them, with their common source in the visible body, that the origin of the fiction of an ego, an individual, is really to be found. There is no trace of such a notion in the poems of ancient India.

"Je est un autre"—the I, the ego, is a stranger—Rimbaud declared toward the end of the nineteenth century. Quite
fittingly, as he was one of the last to claim the traditional powers
of the poet as seer, his words were to become prophetic of that
vast tide within the modern novel that has sought to disintegrate the once solid ego into the shifting and uncertain layers
of personality beneath it. Perhaps the logical last step in this
movement is that taken by Samuel Beckett in reducing the Ego
to a No-thing, a void, whose only identity comes to it through
the words it has been taught by others and the babble of language from which it can never break free. Has this movement
within literature been produced out of mere psychological curiosity and the will to technical experiment? Hesse's words suggest that this literary quest comes out of a deeper convulsion
within a culture that has lost its identity and must go in search
of its own soul. Hesse has merely been more fortunate than
other writers in finding in the Orient an explicit philosophy for
the search.

And yet nothing could seem more saturated with the West
than this novel so thick with the atmosphere of postwar Germany. Though the story is set in some unnamed provincial
capital, one cannot read it without thinking of Berlin in the
twenties, with its *demi-monde* of cabarets, jazz bands, the music of the *Threepenny Opera* throbbing offstage, and figures out
of Grosz cartoons wandering in the background. If Haller's
excessive cultivation has estranged him from his own emotions,
it also painfully sets him apart from the popular culture around
him. It is the period when cultivated sensibilities had to endure
the first full bruising encounter with the mechanical instruments of mass culture: movies, the phonograph, and the squall-
ing infant of radio. Here is the unhappy Steppenwolf being
assaulted by a gramophone: "The devilish tin trumpet spat out,
without more ado, a mixture of bronchial slime and chewed
rubber; that noise that owners of gramophones and radios have
agreed to call music." The violence of this reaction might amuse

us today. We who have been battered by television and singing commercials, and by all the more subtly mechanized marvels of our civilization, are likely to think that Hesse's generation had it rather easy. But the years after World War I were precisely the point of transition at which the first impact of mass culture would be felt more sensitively by those who had matured in a less democratic period.

Out of this same background (he too had been a student in Berlin) Ortega y Gasset wrote *The Revolt of the Masses*, in which he recognized that the whole face of Europe had been irreparably altered. The masses had arrived on the stage of world history, they poured out all over the public places, and with them they brought their shattering weapons of noise. Today, of course, we can smile indulgently at Hesse's raucous gramophone; we have hi-fi sets that provide better listening than all but a few seats at a concert hall. But it is questionable whether as the instruments of mass culture become slicker, smoother, and more functional, the level of culture generally is really helped. The hi-fi set and a copious library of records could be an invitation to passivity; one thinks of music as an object of comfortable consumption, and less and less does one have to go about producing it for oneself, as in the more old-fashioned private chamber and singing groups. Movies are altogether more instantaneous in their impact, but also far less subtle in their implications, than the novel. The words of a television commentator are consumed on the spot. Language becomes more brisk, more immediately public, and more banal, as if everything must be grasped on the instant. For one reason or another people read less. Though the instruments that may have provoked Hesse's anxiety were very archaic, his premonitory tremors were not pointless: the problems of mass culture are still very much with us.

In any case, the Steppenwolf has to come to terms with these newer gods. His old gods—his cultural idols—are Mozart and Goethe, but these no longer release the healing waters for him.

The highbrow is doubly immured in his own prison: on the one hand, his sensitive veneration of the highest products of human culture cuts him off from the common life, while on the other hand all this cultivation leaves him only in a wasteland of spiritual drought. The movement out of this impasse comes through a young woman Hermine, a pretty *demi-mondaine* whom Steppenwolf has picked up in a cabaret.

The name Hermine has some interesting reverberations. In ancient mythology one of the functions assigned to Hermes— the god, among other things, of hermeneutics or interpretation —was to guide the souls of the dead into the underworld. Analogously, Hermine will guide Harry Haller on his descent into the underworld of his own unconscious. There is a suggestion of something vaguely hermaphroditic about her: she reminds Haller of a boyhood friend named Hermann, and in a costume ball at the end she is dressed as a young man, and Steppenwolf mistakes her as such. In the old traditions of symbolism the figure of the hermaphrodite, as the reconciler of the duality of sex, was one embodiment of wisdom. It may seem making things a bit thick, the reader might think, to have a pretty and quite superficial *demi-mondaine*, whose mind is mostly on pleasure and dancing the foxtrot, to be the vehicle of such subtle meanings; but Hesse succeeds remarkably in making us feel Hermine's quite ordinary and charmingly feminine personality as inseparable from the trembling overtones she awakens in the Steppenwolf's unconscious. Besides, from the Oriental point of view, the distinction between grand and insignificant, high and low, belongs only to the relative world of practical realities. From a deeper point of view, any object may mirror the world, and the deepest revelations may come through the apparently most trivial things or people.

Hermine introduces Haller to the jazz musician Pablo, who becomes his initiator into that part of experience that has hitherto escaped him: physical immediacy and the life of the senses, and who, above all, teaches him to laugh. The paradox here is that at first this handsome Latin musician of unreflective animal rhythms had seemed so absolutely mindless that he and Steppenwolf could hardly talk at all or only at cross purposes, but he has now become a vehicle of instruction. Above all, he introduces Haller to the supreme experience of the "magic theater."

Here the novel departs altogether from the restricting claims of realism. Hesse had begun by setting his character in a realistic enough framework. Haller is observed from the outside within that neat and scrubbed world of the bourgeois rooming house where he is a perpetually wandering and homeless tenant. Then it had passed into the more lyrical, subjective, and didactic vein which is typical of Hesse. But now the narrative launches itself into the fantastic directly and without any explanatory scaffolding—a wild, surrealistic vaudeville before Surrealism had become a program among the French.

It would make an interesting study to examine the role of dreams throughout the history of the novel. Dreams had been presented in fiction before, and sometimes with considerable elaboration of detail. A supreme example is the dream of Ivan in *The Brothers Karamazov*, which occupies a whole chapter to itself and is not only a stunning example of Dostoevsky's insight but a crucial dramatic link in the story. That dream, however, is still anchored firmly in a realistic framework. We are told that Ivan is dreaming, and we are aware throughout that all these details, however vividly they are brought before us, are fantasies passing through the mind of the dreamer. But the freer an art form becomes, the more readily it dispenses with transitional scaffolding, the more abruptly it can juxtapose conflicting and diverse images, allowing the observer to supply the connectives. (This same development, and over the same period, has taken place in poetry, painting, and music.) So with Hesse the novel has arrived at the point where the author can present fantastic material with a point-blank matter-of-factness as if he were narrating simple and external happenings.

Indeed, the division between real and imaginary, objective and subjective—on which not only the whole realistic novel but our conscious understanding of the external world is absolutely based—ceases to hold. This technique is entirely consistent with Hesse's Oriental point of view: since the psyche is at least as real as any outer event, what occurs within it must be accorded at least as much reality as anything that takes place in the so-called real—viz., external—world. After all, the division between inner and outer can only be provisional when the outer fact is always to some degree a projection or fragment of the mind itself. There are days in our lives when a dream can fall on us like the heavy blow of a stone hurled against our body.

A lurid sign flashes over this symbolic showplace:

TONIGHT AT THE MAGIC THEATER

FOR MADMEN ONLY

PRICE OF ADMITTANCE YOUR MIND

In this magic theater everything that lurks hidden within the psyche is allowed to flash forth in its own super-real reality. It is "for madmen only" because the adventure into the unconscious will seem bizarre and even lunatic to the unimaginative who remain within the security of rational consciousness. And "the price of admittance" is "your mind" because, as Pablo explains, you must lay aside the point of view of rational consciousness in order to understand the revelations that the magic theater brings forth. The point of view of the unconscious is not necessarily that of the conscious, and it may in fact simultaneously embrace two opposed attitudes. For Westerners this fact is all but incomprehensible; but for Orientals it is a deep part of the wisdom of life that they assimilated over thousands of years. The Buddhist initiate declares, "I spit on the name of Buddha." For the Western mind, with its Aristotelian logic, this statement can only mean a denial of the object the believer is supposed to venerate. For the Oriental, it means that the love of the Buddha is not held rigidly within the framework of doctrine, that the attachment to the Buddha is also able to embrace the detachment from what it venerates.

So Mozart appears in the magic theater, but not as a solemn Olympian out of the mausoleum-museum of high culture. Instead he is a mocking figure, playing the buffoon, turning somersaults and playing trills with his heels. This visitation is not meant to persuade Steppenwolf to give up his love for Mozart; he is only to take that love more in the spirit of life than of the museum. In their solemnity museums become mausoleums, and the art caged therein ceases to live. Steppenwolf, the earnest highbrow, has become too one-sided and rigid in his worship of high culture. And where consciousness has become too one-sided, the unconscious must compensate, in order to restore balance, and assert the opposite point of view as valid. The logic of the magic theater—which is the logic of the unconscious—proceeds by opposition and antithesis.

But the revelations of this theater can also be quite frightening to the conscious mind. In a wild sequence—which resembles a crazy and frantic chase in the movies—Haller is involved in a mad scramble of pursuing automobiles, shooting, and killing. Modern culture has become everywhere violent through its possession of guns and automobiles; but here Haller, the declared pacifist, learns that he harbors the same seeds of violence within himself, for he is able to shoot and kill in his own war upon the automobile. More disturbing still is to see the projection of the duality between man and the animal in himself. A trainer leads out an emaciated wolf and puts the famished animal through its paces. The wolf is so cowed and obedient that when a rabbit is placed in front of him he does not touch it. Then the roles are reversed; the wolf commands and the man crawls on all fours. The rabbit is placed before him and now, horror to behold, the man tears into the shrieking creature with his teeth and devours it. Starve the animal in man, and the so-called human side of us will become infinitely more ferocious. What cruelty on his fellowmen cannot man inflict in the name of his sacred ideals! No other animal could have carried out the prolonged and organized carnage of the world war. And Steppenwolf (who is Hermann Hesse the pacifist above the battle) goes away from this exhibit of the theater thinking: "Today I knew that no tamer of beasts, no general, no insane person could hatch a thought or a picture in his brain that I could not match myself with one every bit as frightful, every bit as savage and wicked, as crude and stupid." The fear not of the Lord but of the evil in man's own heart may be the beginning of wisdom.

Steppenwolf must also enact the ritual murder of Hermine. He must pass beyond the love of the woman who originally opened the doors of wisdom for him. To clutch too tightly to any value is to absolutize it, distort it, and tear it out of the stream of life to which it belongs. "What is enlightenment?" asked Hui Neng, an early patriarch of Chinese Buddhism, and answered his own question: "It is to awaken the mind without fixing it upon anything." Pablo takes Hermine's body, which shrinks to figurine size, and puts it in his pocket. The unconscious must deflate any value that consciousness might tend to overinflate. It must even deflate itself if necessary. Even the magic theater must not be taken too seriously, and there is a brief mock trial of Steppenwolf in which he is condemned not to be shot but laughed at by a firing squad. Steppenwolf-Hesse is always in such a dreadful danger of being taken in by his own earnestness.

But this wild and whirling vaudeville must be brought to some crashing finale. Mozart snaps on the radio, fiddles with the dials, until the tin horn spits out its own particular mixture of bronchial slime and chewed rubber. The music is Handel, and Haller is bidden not to turn away in disgust at the imperfections of the instrument but to listen closely until through all the mechanical distortions and ugliness of tone he can hear the beauty of the original. In life itself the sublime and the beautiful are always inextricably mixed with the tawdry and ugly, and the ideal is never glimpsed except through imperfect actuality. The stream of becoming is the eternal interplay of these opposites. And Mozart gives his final instructions: "You are to live and to learn to laugh. You are to learn to listen to the cursed radio music of life and to reverence the spirit behind it and to laugh at its distortions." Laughter is the instrument of detachment; it breaks down the spiritual rigidity that seeks to clutch at its values as if they were so many coins hoarded by a miser.

And now, at last, Mozart suddenly turns into Pablo. The ultimate opposites have passed into one another, and this witches' Sabbath has been concluded. (In actual life, of course, Mozart and Pablo would have had an immediate understanding, but the opposite here is Steppenwolf's falsified idealization of Mozart.) But though Hesse is willing to adopt a wholehearted Oriental embrace of the opposites, he is not left with an Oriental tranquillity. What he has experienced of himself must become the beginning of a new stage of strenuous effort:

> I understood it all. I understood Pablo. I understood Mozart. . . . I was determined to begin the game afresh. I would sample its tortures once more and shudder again at its senselessness. I would traverse not once more, but often, the hell of my inner being.
>
> One day I would be a better hand at the game. One day I would learn how to laugh. Pablo was waiting for me, and Mozart too.

The Westerner who journeys to the East in search of his own soul comes back to find himself on his own doorstep: inescapably a member of Western civilization, and therefore a Faustian man of perpetual striving. But it is salvation none the less, and do not think that nothing has been accomplished. As the old Zen master has said, we are saved such as we are.

Such ambiguity is perfectly understandable to the Oriental, for what else does that compassionate but also ironical smile of the Buddha mean? In an earlier novella, *Siddhartha* (1922), Hesse had already dealt with this more occult meaning of salvation. Siddhartha is one of the variant names for the Buddha himself, and the life of this character is lived out somehow in parallel with the hidden side of the Master. Siddhartha does in fact encounter the Buddha, listens to his teachings, and is won over not by the man's words but his being—his gestures, movement, glances—and he suspects that this man, whom he cannot help revering, must conceal another message behind the precisely tabulated morality he preaches to the public. In any case, Siddhartha—like the typical Hesse character—has to follow the law of his own being, and throw himself into the world of commerce and the life of the senses. Years later, having known wealth, status, and love, but having given them up, he settles down by a river with an old ferryman and there at last he finds *his* salvation. But it is a salvation that will seem curious to some. When an old friend from his youth, Govinda, who has never ceased to struggle tensely for Nirvana, turns up and asks for instruction, Siddhartha tells him: You are always seeking and therefore you do not find because you get lost in abstract words; what is real is things like this stone and this river before me:

"I can love a stone, Govinda, and a tree or a piece of bark. These are things and one can love things. But one cannot love words. Therefore teachings are of no use to me; they have no hardness, no softness, no colors, no corners, no smell, no taste—they have nothing but words. Perhaps that is what prevents you from finding peace, perhaps there are too many words, for even salvation and virtue. Samsara and Nirvana are only words, Govinda."

Where have we heard these words before? It is Ernest Hemingway speaking, but now he has found a justification of his faith in the senses on a trancendental level.

Hesse is not inventing here, but simply following the teaching that Mahayana Buddhism elaborated through centuries of meditation upon the life and the message of Buddha. The dialectic of the Oriental mind works in a way that is true to its own principles but seems bizarre to the Westerner. The young Bud-

dhist becomes apprenticed to a Master through whose guidance
he hopes to find Nirvana (enlightenment).[3] He lives in Samsara,
the realm of becoming and blindness; on the other side of the
river lies Nirvana, release; and Buddhism is the raft to ferry him
over to that blessed farther shore. There follow years of self-
discipline, of sweat and tears, and—rebuffs. Today I almost
reached Nirvana; but no, I was striving too hard, I must try to
relax; then, trying to let be, he may find himself becoming all
the more self-conscious, and of course self-consciousness divides
us from reality. After ten or fifteen or twenty years of this, there
comes the day when the Master takes him aside and tells him:
"One secret I have held back from you: there is no Nirvana, no
special state of mind that can be called Enlightenment."

For the Westerner this might seem a cruel hoax, and the ten
or fifteen or twenty years of the disciple's life thrown away. But
the Oriental is far more logical in following his own lights. If
reality is one, and we seek not to be cut off from it, then how
could there be a special state of consciousness without separating us from it? On this side enlightenment, on that side nonen-
lightenment; and so the world has once again been cut up by
another dualism. No, Samsara is Nirvana, and Nirvana is Samsara. There is no hither and farther shore, and no raft to carry
you across; you are already there, though most of mankind does
not know this. As one Chinese sage puts it, "The Tao is your
ordinary mind." The Buddhist stories reiterate this message
time and again, in parable after parable: The young disciples ask
the Master, "What was the world like before the Buddha appeared?" And the Master, saying nothing, only raises his arm.

3. Usually, when this word is used throughout this book it refers to the
meaning it has had for the West: intellectual clarification and scientific understanding. The enlightenment the East spoke of, however, has to do with the
integral person, and usually involves his will and emotions more than his reason.
The difference between the two civilizations might be summed up in these two
different understandings of what it means to be enlightened. Of course, we may
be talking of the East of the past, since it now looks as if it were being dragged
into the orbit of Western civilization.

Baffled, the disciple asks, "What was the world like after the appearance of Buddha?" Same gesture. Here for the Buddhist the most important event in human history leaves the world just as it is. For the Westerner that would be a paradox too frightening to be swallowed; but life, as Steppenwolf-Faust had to learn, is one paradox after another. Salvation, to the man who has been saved, only brings him back to the world as it is. But it is something to be given back the world, as Siddhartha touching his stone or trailing his hand in the river has come to know.

II

Almost twenty years after the neurotic turbulence of *Steppenwolf*, the atmosphere has cleared and tranquillity reigns in Hesse's last major work, *Magister Ludi* (*Das Glasperlenspiel* in German; literally "The Glass Bead Game"). The novel appeared in 1943, when Europe with its old ferocity was plunged in another war. The First World War had been a convulsion in Hesse's life, involving him in public polemic and scandal. The second, which was far more global and destructive, seems to have left him relatively untouched. True, he had sensed the coming of this war as early as the twenties, and if you have been predicting a disaster that long you are perhaps inured to its coming. But he was also nearing seventy, and there had already been enough earthquake and upheaval in his life. From the serenity of tone of this last book one can believe that he had—in the words of the Buddhists—"crossed to the other side." Now the present age and its turmoils have receded far into the distance as he writes about a world of the future that looks back upon our civilization with contempt and pity.

The collapse of our world has come about not through Armageddon, but through boredom and emptiness. Ours was the "Age of the Digest"—writes Hesse's imaginary historian, looking back at us from the security of that future vantage point—when the curiosity for information became so enormous and the sense of real significance so absent that mountains of memoranda and documentation accumulated on the most trivial subjects. A hundred years before Hesse, the Existentialist philosopher Kierkegaard had predicted that ours would become the Age of Journalism: men would be driven toward information rather than wisdom, preferring the slick digest, the compendium, the instant formula, and generally the secondhand to the original until the whole existential core of life becomes gutted and covered over with empty stereotypes. Hesse follows the Existentialists' critique of modern society: behind the frantic externalization of life there lurks a void. Even with all the intricately organized escape into triviality man cannot escape himself and his mortal condition:

> They [i.e., we of the present] learned with persistence to drive motor cars, to play complicated card games, and devoted themselves dreamily to the solution of their crossword puzzles, for they stood almost defenceless in the face of death, fear, pain and hunger, spiritually unadvised and no longer able to find consolation in the Church. They, who read so many theses and listened to so many lectures, allowed themselves neither the time nor energy to fortify themselves against their stark fear, to struggle against their inherent dread of death, and lived in trembling, believing in no to-morrow.

This (from *Magister Ludi*) is what the Existentialists have called *Angst vor den Angst*—the panic flight from the anxiety that is inherent in life itself. This is only one, but perhaps our ultimate, form of Nihilism. The epoch collapses because it is no longer able to bear the burden of its own anxiety.

What will replace us? Not, as Hesse sees it, the mechanical horrors of Orwell or Huxley. Presumably, the world will by this time have had enough of all that machinery. No; in accordance with the eternal law of opposites, we shall pass over into our antithesis: after the mindless extroversion of the present, mankind will relapse into the monastic contemplativeness of the Middle Ages. Among the various monastic orders there is Castalia, which is devoted to the Bead Game. What the game is like we never clearly know. Hesse writes at great length about it, and very poetically, but with a calculated vagueness that reminds one of Henry James draping veil after veil around the situation in *The Golden Bowl*. Originally, we are told, the game developed out of music as a way of seeking out new arrangements of musical motifs. Gradually it began to assimilate new materials; formulas of mathematics could be combined with musical themes or with basic patterns of architecture. It could thus develop a kind of intricate counterpoint between different areas of culture. So the Bead Game emerged as the fulfillment of the idea of a *mathesis universalis*—a universal system of symbols embracing all knowledge—that had been dreamed of by a few ancient thinkers. Above all, however, it is also a method of meditation analogous to the ancient techniques of the East by means of which the self converges upon its own center.

Hesse's Oriental influence here is more Chinese than Indian, and he draws particularly on the *I Ching*, or Book of Changes. It is easy to see why this ancient Chinese classic should have become a repository of wisdom for him. The *I Ching* is composed of sixty-four hexagrams—arrangements of six lines, broken or unbroken—that are supposed to represent the archetypes for all human or cosmic situations. The book is built on the principle of contraries: the yin and yang forces are in perpetual interaction with each other within the universe. Nothing is stable in this world, but the sage always looks for the archetypal pattern which any passing human situation illustrates. Presumably the Bead Game, whatever it is, would involve the same kind of insight: the Master gazing at the pattern of beads sees there the archetype of which any particular historical situation is only a variation.

Joseph Knecht, the hero, grows up within the order and eventually becomes Magister Ludi (master of the game). Little is told of the biographical details of his life. In Castalia—as in the

Middle Ages, which did not bother to write biographies of the great masters who created the cathedrals—the trivial details of "personalities" that preoccupy us are no longer considered significant. What counts is the inner content of a life, and for Joseph Knecht this resides in the spiritual realities that have been woven into the Bead Game. Of course, this takes the novel far beyond any form of realism. The realistic novel, as we have seen with Erich Auerbach, develops from the modern consciousness of history: because the actual situations of history seem to be the crucial arena in which man works out his destiny the novelist feels compelled to depict them in all their objective detail. If this sense of history is given up—if the historical situation is understood simply as a variation upon some archetypal theme—then the preoccupations of the realistic novel also become irrelevant.

The reality of time also becomes changed. The Castalians live in a continuous and unchanging present. Hesse virtually brings all action to a standstill—which will seem like an irritating doldrums to some American readers. Yet the book stays alive through its language. This is the one book of Hesse's that has really to be read in the original. Most American readers have a curious idea of the German language formed from the snarls and squeals of the Nazis in war films. In fact, when German is well written, it has an almost hypnotic and incantatory effect quite unlike English or French; and sometimes of course this quality can seduce the writer to go on and on and on. So Hesse, without plot and without the bric-a-brac of realistic fiction, sustains his long narrative within this everlasting present of Castalia almost solely by the extraordinary power of his prose, musical in its grace, evocative and ironical in its resonance. Perhaps no German book has been so mellifluously long-winded since Goethe's *Wilhelm Meister.*

However, nothing stands still forever in Hesse's world. Having risen to a position of eminence in the order, Joseph Knecht begins to feel signs in it of the rigidity and sterility that always fasten upon elaborately organized institutions. The Game itself, this exquisite mandarin's pastime, may be swept away in some violent eruption of history. It is as if, Knecht writes to a friend, a man is sitting in an attic room intent upon a subtle work of scholarship, and suddenly becomes aware that a fire has broken out in the house below. (Is Hesse recalling here those lofty German souls who chose to ignore the first smolderings of Hitlerism?) Here a surprising and ironic reversal seems to take place in Hesse's thinking. Hitherto, Castalia has been extolled for its pursuit of the timeless as compared with the greedy thirst for trivial historical novelties that marks our own Age of the Digest. Now, however, Joseph Knecht feels that he must warn his superiors that the Order has been too little concerned with the reality of history. The eternal pendulum of the opposites has begun to swing again—this time from the timeless to the historical. Immerse man totally in his historical situation and he becomes lost in journalism, in the welter of facts and the changes of fashion. The pure withdrawal into the timeless, on the other hand, leads to stagnation. The Castalian Order has to learn that it does not stand outside history, but will in fact perish historically unless it can renew itself.

Here the impatience with which we have been chafing must break out. Why has Joseph Knecht taken so long to get to this point? Why did he not see that danger of sterility at the start? Has Hesse merely been putting us on throughout this long parable? The fact is that the Bead Game is never quite convincing as a spiritual exercise. To combine a theme of baroque music with a formula from the calculus is a fanciful piece of historical scholarship—something out of Spengler, and Spengler was the first to insist that his own thought belonged to a culture whose vitality was in decline. The Castalians are really librarians of a sort, rearranging and cross-indexing the relics of culture that they have retained. Real creation always plunges deeply into the specific matter and medium with which it works; dallying between the disciplines is the work of sciolists. The fact is that the Castalians are Alexandrians through and through.

Alexandria became the center of learning in the ancient world at a time when Greek culture had lost its pristine vitality. No longer able to be poets, they became scholars. They could not create tragedies like those of Aeschylus and Sophocles, but they could edit the works of these masters; the divine simplicity and straightforwardness of Homer belonged to a heroic age that mocked theirs, and so they must trick him out in endless footnotes and invented symbolisms. Alexandrianism has since become the name for this phase of a civilization when culture becomes top-heavy and Talmudic and stifles the springs of life beneath it. It is the fear of Alexandrianism that has prompted the suspicion of, and sometimes outright revolt against, culture through the whole of modern art, from the mustache drawn on the *Mona Lisa* by the Dadaists to the mocking puns in James Joyce's *Finnegans Wake*. It is the same fear that runs throughout all Hesse's earlier works that the routines of tradition and culture can crush individual spontaneity. How, after we have seen the agonizing disassociation in Steppenwolf, could Hesse have expected us for a minute to accept Castalia as a possible resolution for Haller's torments?

Perhaps Hesse, out of a spirit of irony, wished to warn those who might dream of some new and tranquil Middle Ages that we cannot be delivered thus from the turmoil of the present. During the present disturbances in the American colleges some professors have whispered secretly that the university may have to form some inner core like the Monastery of Cluny that kept civilization alive during the Dark Ages. Such a core would be a secret brotherhood that outwardly granted the students everything they wanted while devoting itself secretly to "irrelevant studies" and so might carry us through the dark ages into which we are passing. An understandable dream in this period of frustration. But it would be well for its advocates to remember Castalia.

But, however late, always better late than never, and at least

Joseph Knecht has made his discovery. Having made his stand known, he has no recourse but to resign from the Order, and he sets out from the monastery to become tutor for the child of his old friend Designori, who had long ago argued with him for the claims of the world. Joseph meets the boy, Tito, in the mountains. The next morning, as he wakes, he sees the youngster, who does not know he is being watched, dancing before the rising sun, executing a ritual he has never been taught but which, in the ecstasy of the moment, comes out of ancestral memory as man's primal salute to the dawn of light within the clearing of nature. Tito dives into the mountain lake, crying to Joseph to follow him. Caught up in this enthusiasm, Knecht runs and plunges, but the shock of the water is too much for him, and he is too old. After floundering for a few strokes, he is overcome and drowns.

In the eternal dialogue between spirit and nature Hesse again seems to give the latter the last word. In throwing himself to the elements, Joseph Knecht has perished. He could have been more prudently self-protective by staying with the Order, but in that cast he might have died the slow death of stagnation. There is no resolution; life is a perpetual movement toward a resolution that never ceases. The last hexagram of *The Book of Changes* is entitled "Not Yet Completed." After the universe (and man with it) has gone through sixty-three stages, pulsating between opposing forces, with each fresh situation the reversal of the other, one arrives at—what? Not at an end, for that would be death; but at another beginning, always a beginning, where there are things yet to be done and a man must walk warily. There is no escape from the wheel of birth and death. Man's only salvation is to learn to live in balance with the eternal and ceaselessly shifting play of opposites.

7. The Atonal World

Writing as a form of prayer.

Yesterday with the Jews . . .

The spike was still there, crookedly protruding from his shattered forehead . . .

The word "Kafkaesque" has become part of the common language. But what does it mean?

A man wants to ring up somebody whose number he does not know; the telephone book is unaccountably missing, and he searches in vain for it in all the cubicles of the enormous office; he will have to try Switchboard; she gives him the Central Operator, who tells him to ask Information; he does not have Information's number, but Operator has already rung off and he has lost the connection with Switchboard; he will have to try again; but Switchboard is busy and he will have to wait; when he gets her and tries to explain she immediately gives him Operator again, and a fresh voice, unaware of what he has already gone through, tells him he will find the number in his telephone book. Repeat several times with variations. He hangs up. Downstairs there is a drugstore with a telephone booth and its book that he has in fact sometimes used to make calls which he did not want Switchboard to overhear; this is not such an occasion, which makes the present confusion more absurd. Waiting for the elevator, slow descent of seventeen floors, frequent stops for people getting on and off. Down at last; but something has happened to the drugstore in the last week: the telephone booth has been removed, and the book with it, to make space for a display of greeting cards. He could send one of the cards instead of telephoning, but decides not to. He gives up—but, like Joseph K., only for the time being.

Later, when his exasperation has subsided, he may tell this true story as a humorous anecdote about himself and the telephone company, and the word "Kafkaesque" may pop out of his mouth, even if he has read very little of Kafka, or perhaps nothing at all, but only heard that these are the kinds of things that happen in that writer's world.

But is this what Kafka is all about—these tedious and banal comedies of frustration, these baffled failures to make connections in the midst of a society too intricately organized? Surely there is some significant and uncanny discrepancy between this lonely writer in his death and what the world later comes to make of him. This most isolated of men dies alone and unknown, and with that continuing sense of failure that had been with him all his life he asks his friend Max Brod to burn his manuscript novels as being "completely bungled from the start"; and yet his name passes into a common adjective. The mockery of this triumph, if it be such, which would not have been lost on his ironic intelligence, is significant on at least two counts. He must strike some deep and uneasy chord in our being for his name to be pressed into this common coinage; and surely it is just as significant of something in our civilization that in spreading his name it must also dilute his meaning.

I

To find out what Kafka is about it helps to turn to the *Diaries*. They are not his least considerable production, and humanly speaking they are the richest in content. Max Brod's adoring biography is indispensable for facts, but it can really mislead us about its subject. Brod was the good-hearted idealist, an energetic and enthusiastic Zionist, the extrovert who could not altogether comprehend his introverted friend. Besides, he feels that he must defend the dead, and therefore must make palatable the more gruesome and noxious aspects of the writings. There is always the hint that Kafka's heart, after all, was in the right place and that the conflicts within his breast—especially in the matter of religion—had been reconciled. The *Diaries* show us the Kafka that remained hidden to Brod.

We meet at first an eager alert mind, intent on what is going on around him. Such diligent awareness is, after all, demanded of a young and aspiring writer—who else in our time would struggle to keep a long diary after a tiring day at the office? But then we begin to notice that the observations of the life around him are very decidedly restricted by the temperament of the diarist. A great deal is going on in Prague, but if we had to reconstruct the life of that city from these diaries we would be at a loss. The life of the Austro-Hungarian capital before the First World War was at once a glittering and a seamy affair. The aristocracy, still visible and unworried, made a parade of light-hearted dalliance. Among the bourgeoisie the respectability of the family reigned publicly while privately the amount of illicit sex was staggering. In Vienna alone—the city of Freud's early casebooks—one out of three births at this time was illegitimate. Country girls who came to town for work usually went into domestic service, where they were fair game for the males of the household, for otherwise they might find themselves unemployed again and have to turn to the streets in prostitution.

There was also the floating *demi-monde* of traveling players, who were much more numerous in a period which lacked the mechanical entertainment of the cinema. When a Yiddish troupe came to town Kafka was much in attendance. He was attracted by one of the actresses, a Mrs. Tschissik, and we catch a fleeting but very sharp impression of a coarsely attractive and vigorous woman who might have wanted to go further with him. Kafka flitted around her, but nothing happened. She emerges for a moment, like one of those ardent Jewesses out of a story by Isaac Babel, and then is gone. What would Babel have made of this occasion? What, indeed, would a diary of Babel have made of the life of Prague, both within and without the Jewish enclave? But Kafka does not have this robustness of temperament; his talents lie elsewhere. This diarist, we quickly perceive, is a virginal young man. The note of abnegation sounds early and persists throughout these pages. Kafka trod his own duty-bound and narrow path averting his eyes. One brief passage records that he liked to walk down a certain street that was frequented by prostitutes; but the thrill was of fear, for if he happened to meet the glance of one of the girls, he quickly turned and fled in panic.

And where, one asks, are the Czechs in all this? A few brief references, that is all; they might almost not have been there. Yet they were there, we know; Prague was their city, even if not yet politically. Kafka spoke their language, and as a functionary in the State Workers Insurance Agency he had often to deal with them. Yet friendship or even a single personal contact is missing. He did have a brief affair with a Czech woman, who seems to have served as the original of Frieda in *The Castle*, but that was toward the end of his life, and even the indefatigable Brod did not find out about it until after Kafka's death. So far as these earlier years of the diaries are concerned, Prague seems like a ghost city peopled by the silent shades of the Czechs. Kafka complained against the city as another curse that had befallen him, and at various times he tried unsuccessfully to move to Berlin. He was disposed to see many things in his life as a curse, and perhaps even life itself, but Prague did set a triple seal of the outsider upon his lonely destiny. It was within, but outside, a conglomerate empire, with which one could in any case hardly identify as a nation. The Czechs, who might have provided an alternate sense of a fatherland, were strangers to him. And—third, but really first—he was a questionable member of the local Jewish community that was painfully aware of its own precarious and isolated position outside the

Austrian crown and the Czech population.

Historically, of course, the Jew is the archetypical outsider. Made homeless by others and among others, he has nevertheless managed usually to be intensely at home among his own. Kafka was not at home there. When Brod took him to a Sabbath ritual, he came away cold and stern, remarking that what he had observed there was "the sheerest superstition." Yet secretly he began the study of Hebrew, and later surprised Brod by the progress he had made in it. He could not join with others, but had to pursue in secret and alone the things that mattered most to him. To Brod's repeated preaching he flared up one day, "What have I in common with the Jews?"—but then added, acknowledging his own division on the subject, "I have nothing in common with myself." At the same time he began to read with intense interest books on Yiddish literature and on Zionism, and carefully noted down passages from the Talmud and stories from the Hasidim. But it was all done with the meticulous detachment we find in his fiction. "Yesterday with the Jews," begins one entry recording his attendance at a performance by the Yiddish troupe and an evening with them afterward. Cool and ironic, the phrase falls upon our ears as if he were speaking of an alien group. To be an outsider within a people who had been historically forced into the role of the outsider is about as far as one can go in estrangement.

Nevertheless, he must turn back to the Jew in himself to find the words adequate to express his ultimate loneliness. One of his remarks has been frequently quoted as the devastating expression of the utterly alienated man: "Without forebears, without marriage, without heirs, with a fierce longing for forebears, marriage and heirs. They all of them stretch out their hands to me: forebears, marriage and heirs, but too far away for me." Modern writers and intellectuals express their alienation in a variety of ways; industrial society has become too materialistic and routine, the culture has become superficial and middle-brow, and politics presents us with no meaningful alternatives for action. And so on. Kafka, however, must experience his alienation in the most ancient and essentially Jewish way: unmarried and childless, he is cut off from the line of Abraham. In the covenant, after all, God had pledged his word to the seed of Abraham. The survival of this people, throughout all the disasters of history, is not only a matter of life and death for themselves but a continued vindication of God. Frederick the Great liked to engage his court physician, Mendelsohn, in philosophic discussion; one day he asked the latter what evidence there was for the existence of God, and Mendelsohn answered, "Sire, the Jews." The hypothesis of God's existence would be refuted if there were no more Jews. Kafka was plagued all his life by a sense of inadequacy, but nowhere more than by the fact that for complex personal reasons he could not bring himself to get married. To die childless is to die alienated from the race. Beside that all his other alienations—from the ghost city of Prague, the glittering emptiness of the Austro-Hungarian empire, the gray monotony of the office in which he was a prisoner most of his life—must seem merely external and accidental.

Jews divided about their own Jewishness are a common enough thing. In this country we know all about this self-hatred of minority groups: Jews, Negroes, Irish, Poles, and others who harbor resentment and shame at the degraded roles that history forced upon their people. Kafka's division within himself is of another order altogether. There is something almost saintly in this retiring and gentle character, so extremely scrupulous about personal and social obligations. We think of him as a kind of Zaddik, one of those unorthodox saints of the Hasidim. A religious yearning breathes through all his writings. The other side of his nature was a profoundly skeptical and ironic intelligence.

Moreover, his life falls within a peculiar and fateful period for European Jewry which was bound to intensify these conflicting tendencies within him. In the nineteenth century the Jews in

the German-speaking world had become successfully assimilated and now felt compelled to ask after their own Jewish
identity and inheritance. The Zionist movement had been
launched, and talk of it was very much in the air during Kafka's
youth. That was one possible answer, but there was another,
and almost diametrically opposed, attitude toward the question
of Jewish identity. Where Jews had risen to eminence, they had
done so in professional and intellectual circles, and consequently they were—certainly in proportion to their numbers—
the people of the head. As products of the nineteenth-century
Enlightenment, they were also among its chief standard-bear-
ers. But the Enlightenment of that century was hardly favorable to any religious yearning. Kafka is the suffering witness to
this war between the head and the heart within his generation.
"The spike was still there, crookedly protruding from his shattered forehead as if it bore witness to some truth."

He returns in the *Diaries* to draw a line through the last part
of this sentence as if he were unsure that this spike bore witness
to any truth at all. Did it perhaps prevent him from the truth
that might have been his? Years later in aphorisms written
toward the end of his life, when he began to surrender himself
more to his religious impulses, he was in no doubt about what
that spike meant: "The bony structure of his own forehead
blocks his way; he batters himself bloody against his own forehead." The forehead had been a barrier between himself and
his profoundest religious yearnings. For another person that
frustration might not have mattered; for a genuine religious
temperament like Kafka's it produced a crippling neurosis. The
result is that subtle paralysis of will and the grayness of feeling
that pervade his life.

A narrower Freudian view seeks to explain Kafka by his relationship to his father. He is the case of the son who cannot stand
up against the dominating father and so succumbs to the feelings of guilt and inadequacy. In this connection a good deal is
made of the story "The Judgment." Here the authoritative fa-

ther opposes the son's engagement, and in an amazing outburst condemns the latter to death by drowning; the son obeys, and as he slips from the bridge into the water he exclaims, with that fatalistic but mocking compliance to authority found throughout Kafka, "Dear parents, I have always loved you." As much as its matter, the manner of writing of this story is significant. Kafka completed it at one sitting, between ten at night and six the following morning—a remarkable performance in one who always worked at a halting and hesitant pace. Some mental blocks must have been lifted so that the unconscious poured through in a breakneck flood. Afterward, Kafka tells us, he experienced a feeling of lightness and exaltation as if a heavy weight had been lifted from him. The neurotic mass had been momentarily lightened and the patient breathed in freedom for a while. The son had stood up to the father through the weapon of his art.

All very tidy and clinical, and true as far as it goes; but it is not the whole picture, and the facts are not altogether in accord with events in the story. It was Kafka himself, not his father, who broke off his own engagement. He was too solitary by nature, he felt, and the pursuit of literature, which was the only thing in life that interested him, made marriage impossible. At the time he had begun to read Kierkegaard, and he was struck by the parallel between his own case and that of the great Existentialist. Kierkegaard had broken off his engagement to Regina Olsen because his isolated disposition and a religious vocation condemned him to the single life. Kafka had also his religious calling: "Writing as a form of prayer," he jotted down in his diaries. He would dedicate himself to the priesthood of letters. But one other parallel between the two cases is not usually noted: years after the event, Kierkegaard took another view of his broken engagement and wrote in his *Journals:* "If I had had faith, I could have married Regina." The wholeness of genuine faith would have healed his divided and unhappy spirit and made it possible for him to enter the ordinary life of mankind. And Kafka? Might not he too, if he had made peace with his own deepest religious yearnings, have been able to enter the life of the commonplace and establish his link with forebears and heirs?

Nor was his actual father anything like the capricious and overpowering tyrant in "The Judgment." On a number of occasions Max Brod tried to argue with him that he was building fantasies on his relationship with his father. It is to Brod too that we owe publication of Kafka's "Letter to His Father," which surely is among the most amazing personal documents ever written. Here Kafka embroiders charge upon countercharge between son and father with all the implacable and meticulous dialectic of his fiction. One is immediately suspicious of all that close-knit reasoning. Why go to such intricate lengths to prove one is right unless one is hiding something from oneself? The diaries do not give us a picture of a family circle riddled with hostilities. On the contrary, if anything seems to be wrong, it is that the atmosphere is a little too close and stifling. There is something disquieting in this young man who sits around hour after hour with his parents, bored and listless, waiting until it is time to go to bed. "You are reserved for a great Monday," he writes—but this interminable bourgeois Sunday through which he sits will never, it seems, come to an end.

No, it is not Kafka's individual flesh-and-blood father that explains his fearful sense of authority, but the other way round: his attitude toward the mystery of authority leads him to make much more of the actual father than he ever really was in life and to project upon him the image of an overwhelming power. The forces of authority in his writings are cosmic rather than human, and consequently invested with a numinous rather than factual reality. Probably nowhere in the world's literature will you find images of greater cruelty than in his story "The Penal Colony." In a penal camp of cold and implacable justice the inmates have their crimes engraved on their bodies. There is no relief, no break, anywhere within this relentless world where to be is to be punished. One thinks of the wrathful and punishing God in some of the more archaic passages of the Old Testament. The inheritance of Judaism was alive in Kafka, but to the degree that he could not appropriate it, it had to take on this alien and threatening form. He ended by projecting it upon the father.

But here, unwittingly, we seem to have been drawn into questionable matters of "interpretation." Something in Kafka provokes the army of interpreters, and their interpretations have piled up to a point where they obscure the text of his fiction itself. They all fall, with some variations, into two groups: (1) Kafka is the neurotic artist *par excellence;* in fact, in the words of one critic, he is "the artist of neurosis." By giving artistic expression to neurotic states, he touches chords that are latent in us all and so wields a kind of magical power over the reader. But of course a clinical picture, done with the most consummate artistry, would remain only that, and would not pass over into literature. Something else is resonant in Kafka, something in our human condition that is transcendent of the materials of the clinic and the case history. And hence the need of another kind of interpretation: (2) Kafka is fundamentally a religious writer and, specifically, a religious humorist, in whom the Higher Powers are hidden and inscrutable, but comic in their transactions with men. Thomas Mann has given the most notable expression to this point of view.

But Mann's elegant essay is also typical of what can so easily go wrong when the commentator has substituted his own ideas for what one actually finds in the author. Kafka, for Mann, emerges as a mystical and tender soul, a latter-day Romantic in the style of Novalis, smiling through tears. If one had not read Kafka, one would get no idea from Mann's graceful eulogy of what one is to encounter in those pages: a world that is gruesome, repelling, stifling, wearying in its grayness—multiply the adjectives as you will. This is the palpable surface of Kafka's fiction which commentary cannot brush past. Otherwise we lose the author himself for the ideas we can spin out from him. We had best, then, let the interpretations take care of themselves while we turn to examine the surface of Kafka's fiction as it presents itself to the reader—that artistic surface that is, after all, the end-all and be-all of the artist himself. And there, as it turns out, we shall encounter once again the author of the *Diaries*.

II

Indeed, no writer has labored harder in trying to bring everything forward onto the pure surface of his narrative. Among all the modern efforts to get beyond the restrictions of realistic fiction Kafka's stands alone—and is in some ways the boldest. We find in him none of those intricate devices for rendering the multiple layers of time and personality. There is no attempt to interiorize reality by dissolving the continuous flow of external action into the multiple and subjective reflections within the minds of various characters. Kafka is not concerned with anything like a stream of consciousness or *monologue interieur*. Everything is to be objectified in the continuous and sequential course of the narrative itself, in the actions and talk of the characters. Their thoughts are not reported except as they are expressed in dialogue, which is often of a most intricate and dialectical nature, or in their overt response to the objective situation. Thus Kafka would take us in one bold step beyond the intricacies of modern subjectivism back to the pristine sense of the narrative as simple myth—as the unfolding of the actions of the protagonist one after another in chronological time.

Yet this scrupulous externalization of the novel is totally different from what we find in "the American novel," to use that tidy category that the French have invented for us. In the first part of this book we analyzed at some length this tendency toward externalizing the narrative in physical events or actions. This technique was also connected with a deliberate effort toward the fragmentation of experience: the sensory fact is rendered vividly but in disconnection from the facts that follow it. It is as if, to use our earlier metaphor, we have the bright beads of sensation adjacent to each other but without the connecting thread of meaning that would bind them together. The effect is to disconnect the narrator-observer from the events he relates, which in their disconnection confront him as a reality alien, opaque, and absurd. The narrative structure is event A, then event B, then C, etc.—not A therefore B therefore C. In Kafka, on the other hand, the connecting and inferential links are not abolished but insisted upon. We do not get merely A, then B, then C; but A therefore B therefore C. Every attempt is made, even by a mimicry of logic, to make the following event appear to issue, almost dialectically, from what preceded it.

Nevertheless—and this is the amazing thing—the opacity and prima facie unintelligibility of the Kafkaesque world are much denser than what we find in Camus or Hemingway or Faulkner. No detail in this world is ever presented as possibly not having its reasons, and the protagonist may in fact get involved in endless debate about them. But these reasons themselves may be absurd; they do not fit in or connect the facts together; and if they do connect and fit the facts into some larger context, it is this whole context itself that looms up as opaque and unfathomable. Nor is there any chance that Kafka will let this world seduce us by its sheer sensuous charm. Hemingway's Michigan woods may not be a world with the traditional structures of meaning, but the details in it, taken one by one, are so vivid and engaging that most of us will make do with them without the connecting thread. What matter if facts A, B, and C are disconnected so long as each is enchanting enough to stand by itself! Kafka does not seek even that fragmentary identification with the world. It is a mistake to speak, as one critic has, of his "lovingly exact portrayal of the actual world." Exact, yes; but loving? And even the exactness is not the physical vividness of sensation of a painter so much as the gray sobriety of a lawyer duly taking note of all the facts in the case. In an admirably flat and precise style—which makes us feel that he never forgets his training for the law—Kafka renders the details of his story as scrupulously as if he were writing a legal brief for the most banal case. Yet everything in this world is just a little bit askew, a little bit off focus or focused too sharply. A remark from his journals conveys better than the words of any critic the effect he aimed at and achieves: *"The perpetually shifting frontier that lies between ordinary life and the terror that would seem to be more real."*

Earlier we spoke of a certain effect of flattening at which certain modern writers (and painters) have aimed. Kafka's dry and meticulous style is perfectly adapted for achieving a peculiar kind of flatness. The classical view, enunciated by Aristotle, held that the plot should have a beginning, middle, and end. A situation is given; further actions and events complicate it, and the general tension is heightened until a climax is reached, after which there is a denouement and subsiding of this tension. If daily life moves more or less along a horizontal line, with irregular bumps of excitement up and down, then a dramatic plot would be represented by two sides of a triangle, one tracing the rising and the other the falling action. The realistic novel, in its aim to present "a slice of life," tended to flatten the sides of this triangle so as to bring them closer to the horizontal. Nevertheless, the triangle remained, the traditional schema of the plot persisted. If the slice of life were not going to spill over into some shapeless blob, the writer had to exercise some principle of selection and he had further to organize this material with something of a "story" in mind in order to hold his audience. In some of the classical realists, indeed, the underlying plot is as neat and orderly as a well-made play, even to the extent of having definite curtain ringers at the end of appropriate sections.

Against this realist convention, Kafka sets out to achieve a flattening of the action more radical perhaps than in any other writer. The beginning, usually abrupt and startling, seems to contain within itself everything that follows. Instead of a developing plot with beginning, middle, and end we have a beginning, continuation, and termination. The story "Metamorphosis" is a good example. The hero, Gregor Samsa, awakens one morning to find himself transformed into a gigantic bug. The rest of the story proceeds calmly and implacably from this initial situation; there is no dramatic heightening toward a climax, but only a prolongation of distress. When the reader has had enough, indeed can hardly take any more, the author quietly snips off the horizontal line of action by having Gregor die. The heroes of Kafka remain stuck—like the mole in its burrow in another of his stories—in a situation that is already their whole destiny. And here again, as we have seen throughout, technique is integral with the writer's vision: these devices of Kafka—the flat style and the flattening of the action—are the means through which he conveys a thoroughly anticlimactic vision of everything on this earth. "The end of the world," he writes in one of his notebooks, "will not come on the last day, but the day after that."

With all this flatness, however, Kafka's surface always reaches toward some unknown meaning beyond itself. Take the opening pages of *The Castle:* though you may be reading them for the tenth or twentieth time, they are still astir with the air of something strange and uncanny. The snow, the village, the castle under distant cloud—some unexpected mystery is about to unfold from all this. You know, of course, that the rest of the novel is going to grind down these expectations to the gray and monotonous banality of K.'s repeated frustrations at making contact with the distant castle. Still, the air of mysterious expectancy, of something untold and unknown, is there in the first chapters. The whole of Kafka's art might be described as one of baffled transcendence. The narrative seems to open toward depths upon depths, but we are always brought back to the banal surface of things. The transcendent is perpetually evoked and at the same time perpetually deflated—Kafka's art is made up of this dual tension. Everything must suggest something much more than itself, and yet be nothing more than itself. Here again Kafka offers the best commentary on his own technique in his notebooks:

> . . . as if one were to hammer together a table with painful and methodical technical efficiency, and simultaneously do nothing at all, and not in such a way that people could say: "Hammering a table together is nothing to him," but rather, "Hammering a table together is really hammering a table together to him, but at the same time it is nothing," whereby the hammering would have become still bolder, still surer, still more real and, if you will, still more senseless.

In pursuing this aim, the voice goes on in the same flat and even tone, never raised or lowered. Kafka permits himself no outbursts of lyricism or poetry. The extreme form of flattening —and here Kafka goes beyond any other writer—is to achieve a flatness of feeling. His world must be drained of emotions; he must offer his own heart as a victim that is no longer allowed even to feel. And yet between the implacably even-toned lines one senses always the immense tenderness of the heart denied —and denied over and over again, and denied even the lyricism of crying out its own heartbreak. This gray monotony is not a matter of mere length, as one might think from the novels, but of tone. Long before the sixty pages of the "Metamorphosis" have ended, we are drained and exhausted and can hardly crawl forward to the finish. At first we are shocked, appalled, repelled by the freak of the young man transformed into a bug; there follows some grotesque humor from the responses of his family and the lodgers; then gradually we become numb, drained of feeling, enveloped in a kind of stifling void. The feeling of monotony is itself an emptiness of feeling. Kafka uses it to drain us of all our habitual and natural feelings so that the world becomes distant and uncanny to us, as if we were to step out exhausted into a gray and empty street in the blank dawn after a sleepless night.

These happenings that always seem somewhat off key, where the usual or expected developments do not occur, are also found in the atonal world of modern music. The comparison is neither far-fetched nor arbitrary. Tonal music is one of the unique inventions of our civilization, and if what we have been observing of the transformations of another major form, the novel, are to the point, then we should expect to find comparable disruptions and metamorphoses within music too. And indeed we do. The whole of tonal music was a magnificent and elaborate artifice built upon a very simple foundation: the key with its tonic and dominant tones. However intricate his variations, however surprising and complex his harmonies, the composer must return to the tonic. After many wanderings, through which we were never homeless, we do in fact come home.

Inevitably, with all great forms of art once securely established, the complications set in: dissonances, exotic chromatism or tone coloring, and polytonality—a system of multiple perspectives, as it were, which makes use of several keys at once without any dominance necessarily accorded to any single one. Yet, within these conflicting keys, there is still the hierarchical order of the first (tonic) and fifth (dominant) tone. The next step, taken by Schoenberg, was to go beyond the system of tonality altogether, abolish both the home key and any hierarchical order within the sequence of tones. The composer chooses a series of twelve tones out of which to construct his piece; and, note this well, all of these tones are of equal value. Atonal music thus begins with the premise of Nihilism: that all the elements in its world are indifferently equal. Here again we have our principle of flattening, but now applied within music. By varying these twelve tones—which are taken to exist equally alongside each other on the same horizontal continuum of sound—rhythmically and contrapuntally the composer seeks to create a work that will have unity within variety, and will also hold the attention of audiences that have been used to traditional structures and developments within music.

What led to this demolition of the marvelous edifice of tonal music, one of the greatest achievements of the Western spirit, and its replacement by a style that leaves us much more insecure and homeless? One might try to answer this question solely from the viewpoint of technique: the possibilities were there in the medium, and human restlessness, being what it is, had to move on to exploit them. Unfortunately this explanation, true enough as far as it goes, does not tell us why the restlessness took the form it did or how it seems to fit in so aptly to the pattern of events outside music. After all, the world was not getting noticeably calmer or men more at peace with themselves while music was becoming more complexly dissonant toward the end of the nineteenth century. Nor had our world become more secure when atonality entered. These mutations in musical form, let us not forget, occur within the same historical framework within which modern literature has also undergone its upheavals.

Atonal music, though it has been with us for some years now, still strikes our ears as eery and uncanny. Even where we have grown accustomed enough to find beauty—and even great beauty—in some of its creations, the quality itself of this beauty is of a strange and disquieting kind. Is this the effect of nature or habit? We come to this music after long exposure to the great tradition, and psychologically, an even more potent influence, all the musical habits and expectations engrained in us by songs, hymns, and ballads from childhood on. Perhaps then we listen for the wrong things. Our ears, feeling homeless, search inevitably for a key that is not there. Something like this happens in our encounter with Kafka. On first reading we feel that something is off key, and inevitably we listen for a key that is not there but that we expect always to be on the verge of hearing; and then we take refuge in "interpretations" that would seem to supply the key but ultimately fail because they do not accord with the actual texture and surface of the narratives themselves; until finally it dawns on us that this is an atonal world and without any key at all.

But what works in one art may not do so well in another. The twelve notes of the atonal musician are a pattern that he can weave and reweave. They are there as a binding form behind the ordinary keys that disappoint us by not taking shape. In fact, it could be argued that the twelve-tone series becomes a kind of surrogate key in place of the traditional diatonic structures. But a narrative in words is not so abstract a form and has other more material exigencies to satisfy. Stretched beyond the length of the stories, where it works, the flattening of the narrative begins to pall in Kafka's novels. They begin to drag and become monotonous, and not merely through the reader's inattention, but because through the repetitiousness there is a continuous thinning out of substance to the point where it becomes a gray mist.

Some years ago Edmund Wilson wrote the now famous "Dissenting Opinion," in which he argued that Kafka's stories were masterpieces that could be ranked alongside those of Poe or Hoffmann but the novels were failures. The essay was a shock, but a momentary one only, to the intelligentsia, who promptly took it as a sign of Wilson's blind side as a critic. It is too easy in reading Kafka to get lost in the play of one's own ideas and cease to follow what the writer has actually managed to put down in words. Wilson at least stuck to the novels as novels and not as charades of ideology, and his judgment has moreover the concurrence of Kafka himself. In the farewell letter to Brod he delivered his last judgment on his own literary efforts;

> I am not enclosing the novels. Why rake up old efforts? Only because I have not burned them yet? . . . Next time I come I hope to do so. Where is the sense of keeping such work which is even bungled from the aesthetic point of view? Surely not in the hope of piecing together

from all these fragments, some kind of justification for my existence,
something to cling to in an hour of need? But that, I know, is impossible; there is no help for me there.

These words will never cease to amaze us. Literature had been
his single passion and his religion; he had staked his life upon
it and lost, and yet he can judge his efforts as a failure with
calmness and dispassion, and without a trace of whining. Despite misery and frustration, he remains morally intact. His true
vocation was a merciless honesty.

The novels are certainly failures. But we need not follow the
implication of both Kafka and Wilson that they are therefore
insignificant. We have long since become accustomed to the
aesthetic power of ruins and fragments. The ideal images of
antiquity come down to us eyeless and limbless, eroded and
scarred and pocked by weather, and in that form they repose
in the pantheon of our imagination, not diminished but possibly
gaining a haunting power in their ruined state. In this time of
need when we have to begin at the beginning again (and indeed
back of that to find a beginning, in order to return to "the things
themselves" at the roots of experience), when our thinking, as
Heidegger says, must learn to descend once again into the poverty of its materials, in such a time we should not expect or
demand the vast and finished syntheses of an earlier period.
The painter Miro, when he took up ceramics, produced not
polished urns or vases but potsherds that might have been dug
from some ancient midden. Kafka's novels are fragmentary because he had not found, could not find, the form toward which
he was groping. Even among the stories only a few are complete and realized; the rest remain fragments and sketches,
overpowering in the nuclear image—as in "The Great Wall of
China"—that generates them. The power of the myth is still
vibrant through the crumbling ruins.

Myth has been defined as what holds "everywhere, for everybody, and at all times." Kafka's bare narratives have been emp-

tied of all the bric-a-brac of the realistic novel; all the heavy furniture of documentation by which Balzac's heirs among the novelists might tie their characters down to a particular historical period and milieu has been eliminated. Fairy stories begin "once upon a time," but the time of the true myth, however it may seem to be recounting the events in the past, is really anytime—a perpetual present. Grammatically, the events of *The Trial* are related in the past tense, but a remark in Kafka's notebooks makes clear the real sense of time that pervades this novel: "Only our concept of time makes it possible for us to speak of the Day of Judgment by that name; in reality it is a summary court in perpetual session."

In particular, Kafka's two principal novels reach back to a distinct medieval type of epic: the story of the quest and the search. The hero goes in search of the Grail or the chapel perilous, and after many adventures his quest is attained in some miraculous fashion. The greatest example of this kind of epic, of course, is Dante's *Divine Comedy.* Here the hero, Dante himself, is on a pilgrimage toward the greatest goal that mankind could ever possibly conceive: the experience of the Beatific Vision itself, in which by being united to the Divine Nature he will also grasp the mystery of existence itself. And the quest turns out to be successful, as the title implies, since a comedy is a story with a happy ending. But we might guess this success immediately from the opening lines:

> In the middle of the journey of our life
> I came to in a dark wood
> Where the straight way was lost.

The straight way! There is not only a way, but one and only one; however far we may have wandered, we have only to get ourselves back on the road and it will lead us to the goal.

But what a difference if we turn now to Kafka, taking Dante —as we did earlier—as the peak from which to measure our progress from the Age of Faith! *The Trial* is the story of the hero's search to find out why he stands condemned; *The Castle* tells about his quest for a home within the community of the castle and for work of his own to do. In both cases he is doomed to failure. The way becomes more entangled by red tape, more confused by the senseless and conflicting voices of authorities, as the search continues. "There is a goal," Kafka remarks in one of his aphorisms, "but there is no way." At the end of *The Trial*, two men appear and lead Joseph K. to the outskirts of the town, where one of them thrusts a knife into his heart, turning it twice. "Like a dog," the dying K. murmurs in final abjectness. We do not have a last chapter of *The Castle*, but Kafka—according to Max Brod—had told his friends what the ending would be. K. dies out of sheer exhaustion from his efforts to contact the castle authorities and to have his job and his place confirmed by them. At last, word comes from the castle that owing to "certain auxiliary circumstances" he will be permitted to be buried in the village.

Thomas Mann, so intent on turning Kafka into sweetness and light, sees in this ending a clear sign that "at last, grace is vouchsafed." On the contrary, it seems very much like the last twist of the knife that the higher powers, after playing cat and mouse with him all along, should assign K. a place after his death— precisely when such an assignment is no longer of any use to him. That is Kafka's final touch of mocking humor. Camus too, like Mann, seems much too hopeful when he associates Kafka with existentialists like Kierkegaard and Shestov, who despite the cruelty and absurdity of existence make the paradoxical leap into faith, *Credo quia absurdum*. Kafka—at least if we stick to his fiction—makes no such leap into transcendence. His world is sealed off in its finitude more drastically than Camus' in *The Stranger*. True, this world is also pervaded by humor, but too grim to provide reconciliation or comfort. Steppenwolf, in his dream-vision, had been told by Mozart that "You must learn to laugh; and as you learn this, you will understand that all humor is gallows humor." Kafka's is gallows humor, not robust and coarse in the manner of Brecht's jailbirds, but always dialectical—the ironic jesting of a Talmud without God.

Epics, of course, tend to be episodic. Even Homer has his longueurs. And, who knows, had not the Homeric poems been subjected to a strict recension sometime in the seventh century B.C., they might have come down to us as diffuse and sprawling as the Norse *Eddas* or *The Nibelungenlied*. Editors have been at work on a recension of Kafka too to rearrange the structure of *The Trial*. He had not numbered his chapters. When Brod undertook their arrangement, he was guided by his own judgment as well as his remembrance of the order in which Kafka had read some of them to him. Subsequent examination of the text for internal signs of chronology—the passage of the seasons, references to events that have already happened, or K.'s steady deterioration under the burden of his arrest—seem to yield a different order. E. M. Butler, Kafka's translator, gives a qualified endorsement of this new arrangement because "it makes the novel appear less episodic and more of an organic whole." Perhaps, but not enough to matter. What difference do minor matters of chronology make when the story as a whole is about a man stuck in one spot? At a certain level of the self—and this is the deeper truth behind the Kafkaesque narratives—every human life remains stuck at its center. The separate chapters thus become variations upon one central situation. Max Brod is entirely right when he says the story could be prolonged to infinity—except of course that the human finitude, both of author and reader, must break off somewhere. Where a human life is stuck at one point, and its story merely a prolonged duration at that point, the accuracies of historical chronology cease to matter.

Yet if editorial rearrangement makes little difference, we can nevertheless imagine quite clearly what the form of these novels, if realized, would have been like. They would not have given us anything like "organic" development in the usual sense. They would have preserved their flatness to express his anticlimatic vision of the world, and yet they would have to be renewed by invention and surprise in each section if they were not to thin out into a monotonous insubstantiality. They would have remained episodic in line with their own peculiar epic, quality, yet each episode would have to stand forth in its own vividness and actuality but return us always to the hero exactly where he was, or perhaps only a half step forward, thus reminding us always of Giacometti's remark, "Inches are eternities." The project would have been ambitious and exhausting for any talent; and Kafka, in poor health and chained to his desk at the office, died young—at forty-one.

It is the mark of a neurosis that it sometimes sets its sufferers an impossible task to accomplish. Perhaps Kafka understood that his reach had exceeded his grasp when he wrote to Brod that the novels were "aesthetically bungled" in the first place. But this failure is more than an incident in Kafka's case history. Sometimes an art develops to the point where it presents us with a richness of possibilities that becomes almost self-defeating for the artist to pursue. The comparison with the atonal composer is again pertinent. While atonality has opened immensely new resources to the musician, it has also brought new and horrendous difficulties in finding a unifying form to replace the old diatonic structure. André Hodeir, one of the most brilliant interpreters of this new music, writes:

Serial [that is, atonal] music cannot fail to be even more artificial and abstract than the most artificial and abstract works from which it originally derives. . . . There is, of course, reason to fear that future composers may simply collapse beneath such a tremendous weight. Even now, the raw materials of music seem to resist the composer's manipulation as they did not in the eighteenth century. . . . In the future more real genius will be required to write a piece of great music. . . . There is a real danger that music may actually breed its own death, not through its inability to break away from its traditions, as would have been the case if the neo-classical reaction had its way, but from having set its sights infinitely high.

It makes one uneasy to think that in the future more genius will be required than in the past to write great music. An art is in trouble when it sets its sights so "infinitely high"; perhaps it is breeding the conditions for its own paralysis of will. Here again, whatever the unique roots of failure in his personal life, Kafka is a key to some wider crisis in the arts today.

In any case, a failure in form may become a form expressive of failure. Kafka's vision is one vast image of impotence. Both gods and men are ultimately powerless. However cruel the higher powers are, however arbitrary and capricious their exercise of authority, the institutions they wield are themselves passing into disarray and ruin. The penal colony, which had perfected one of the most horrifying instruments of punishment, is now falling into decay, and its legends and traditions are defunct and almost forgotten. The Chinese empire, the embodiment of Oriental despotism, can no longer maintain contact between the center and its extremities. The functionaries of *The Trial* are as incompetent as the crumbling Austro-Hungarian empire. The authorities in *The Castle* never know their mind from one moment to the next. "That's how people work their own confusion," Olga explains to K. "Is there any reason why it should be different in the Castle?" If one were to construct a theology out of Kafka, the gods would be decidedly anthropomorphic in nature. Mysterious and transcendent as they may be, and baffling for man to communicate with, they are nevertheless projections of the most bumbling and self-frustrating sides of human nature. Perhaps in the end we can be reconciled to their capricious cruelty by knowing that they stumble into as many ridiculous pratfalls as the characters on earth.

An ancient Jewish story tells about a student who once came to his rabbi and asked, "In the old days there were men who saw the face of God. Why don't they anymore?" The rabbi replied, "Because nowadays no one can stoop so low."

Is Kafka able to stoop that low? Everything in his imagination bends toward the banal and the ordinary, toward the simple act of a man hammering a table together. Everything in his heart inclines him to the gentle and suffering victim, the hare that is already fleeing from the hunting dogs that will catch it, the bird that is destined for the cage that has gone in search of it. Yes, he would stoop that low, but . . . the spike that protrudes from his forehead gets in the way. He cannot bend far enough; or if he does, he has to bend his neck so that he must see everything at a weird angle. K. wanders from the street into a peasants' kitchen; as the steam clears, he discerns two men in the corners bathing, children playing on the floor, and a young woman suckling a child. For a moment we have the outline of a scene out of Breughel, strange and earthy; but click, the focus goes awry, and these peasant characters fade into the general phantasmagoria. In the aphorisms written during his last days—published under the title "He"—Kafka ceased to let his head come between his heart and himself, and he surrendered to his feelings in a series of religious reflections that are among the deepest and most moving ever written. But it was too late to find this healing reconciliation with his own natural longings. Tuberculosis had done its work, and he had only a short while to live. "My head conspired with my lung behind my back"—here he names, with an uncanny precision, the two agents of his mortal sickness. The one had stifled his bodily, the other his spiritual breath.

"I represent the negative elements of my age," Kafka wrote in his *Diaries;* and here again he is the accurate diagnostician of his own case. For a final image of him we may turn to the story "The Hunger Artist." It was one of the few works he told Max Brod that he wanted preserved, and it may be a useful reminder of some of the meanings we forget when we toss the adjective "Kafkaesque" about so casually. The hunger artist is the practitioner of a once venerated profession. Seated on straw in his small barred cage, pallid in his black tights, and with his ribs sticking out, he is marveled at by the gaping throngs. After forty days his fasts are terminated in triumph; his impresario makes a speech, the band plays, and one of the ladies leads him in his weakened state down from his cage. But the days of glory pass, and fasting ceases to be understood and appreciated by the people. The hunger artist has to join a large circus, where his cage is placed next to the menagerie. Here he is depressed by the stench, the restlessness of the animals by night, the raw lumps of flesh carried past for the beasts of prey, and the roaring at feeding times. The people hardly glance at him as they hurry in order to get to the menagerie. The attendants fail to count the days of his fasting, and he wastes away. His emaciated body is discovered underneath the straw, and expiring, he tells his secret: ". . . I have to fast, I can't help it. . . . Because I couldn't find the food I liked. If I had found it, believe me, I should have made no fuss and stuffed myself like you or anyone else." Into the now vacant cage they put a young panther. This wild creature, the incarnation of animal vitality, seems to carry despite the bars his freedom with him in his noble body. And the joy of life streams with such ardent passion from his throat that the onlookers crowd around the cage and never want to go away.

Had Kafka found his food, he might have appeased the hunger for the natural life that with him was inseparable from the hunger for the spirit. As it turned out, he became the hunger artist himself—the artist of spiritual starvation. He is perhaps the most negative artist of the time; but in pushing his sheer negativity to the extreme, he becomes also one of the most compelling and positive of modern figures. In this time of need he is the saint of spiritual anemia called to witness what lies most hidden in this need. No doubt, we shall find ways of hiding it still, and we shall continue to spout the word "Kafkaesque" for any number of adventitious occasions. When the scapegoat is loaded with our sins and turned out into the desert, mankind can forget about him. We can even go on concocting interpretations in which Kafka will appear much less frightening so that, evading his meaning, we also evade ourselves.

8.The Body in the Bottle

There is no having, only being, only a being panting for
its last breath, panting to be choked out.

—KAFKA

We may as well begin with Samuel Beckett at the moment of
his career that made him famous: the play *Waiting for Godot,*
first staged in Paris in 1952.

Two tramps, Vladimir and Estragon, are on stage. They are
there to wait. What they are waiting for is the coming of a man,
Godot, who is expected to provide them with shelter and sustenance. Meanwhile, they try to make time pass with small talk,
jokes, games, and minor quarrels. Tedium and emptiness.
"Nothing to be done" is the refrain that rings again and again.

In the midst of the first act, two strangers—Pozzo and Lucky
—storm onto the stage. Pozzo seems to be a man of affluence;
Lucky, the servant, is being driven to a nearby market to be
sold. Pozzo tells the tramps about Lucky's virtues—the most
remarkable of which is that he can *think.* To show them, Pozzo
snaps his whip and commands "Think!" and there follows a long
hysterically incoherent monologue in which fragments of theology, science, sports, and assorted learning jostle in confusion
until the three others hurl themselves on him and silence him.
Pozzo and Lucky go off. The tramps are left in their old void.
A boy arrives, announcing that Mr. Godot will not come today
but promises surely to come tomorrow.

The second-act curtain finds the tramps in exactly the same
situation. The only change is that a bare tree in the rear of the
stage has put forth some leaves—which may be some sign of

241

hope, or merely the course of nature. Pozzo and Lucky return from the opposite direction. Pozzo has gone blind, and Lucky dumb. Pozzo, so powerful and brutal the day before, is now a ruined and feeble man. The two go off, the dumb leading the blind. Vladimir and Estragon are left alone once again with their void. A boy enters—a different one from the day before —and announces Mr. Godot will not come today, but surely will come tomorrow. After he goes off, the tramps make an obviously futile gesture at suicide. The final curtain finds them exactly where they were at the beginning of the play.

This exiguous plot—if it can be called plot at all—brings to the stage that tendency toward a narrative of purely horizontal line that we have already noticed in Kafka. There are moments of heightened intensity, some times of great excitement, in *Godot*, and then of relative détente; and Beckett manages to keep the ball going by one bit of business or comedy after another. The tedium of waiting is not at all tedious in this play. But there is no logical concatenation of actions leading to a probable or inevitable climax, to be rounded off finally by a satisfactory denouement—the structure of the usual "well-made play," whose neat final curtain allows the audience to file and forget the whole matter in some neat pigeonhole of the mind. The tramps end where they began. The formal question of the proper length of the play is only to be judged by the limits to the intensity with which the single situation can be maintained. "The play has two acts," Beckett observed with his usual simplicity, "because one would have been too short, and three would have been too long." (Precisely this same problem of length—not too short and not too long—has become a delicate one for atonal composers, since they too have thrown away their kind of plot: the sonata form within the tonal system.)

Now, it is to be expected that a good part of the audience, in the grip of a *habit* that can be satisfied only with the well-made play, would have found *Godot* hard to take. But the most amazing part of the public's response was the universal clamor for "the meaning" of the play. On the face of it, this was a singular request to make of a work written in the simplest and most understandable language. True, there is one incoherent speech, Lucky's long tirade in Act I; but that is not to be understood as anything else but incoherence, since human thinking is meant to be portrayed at best as merely a hodgepodge of fragments. Why, then, should this play have been considered baffling and obscure?

The reason may be that art itself has ceased to be an ultimate and irreducible mode of experience for the modern audience. The work of art is an irritant to be covered over as quickly as possible with the plaster of a conceptual "meaning." It is understandable that the practical mind, immersed in action, has to proceed by prompt classifications and will suffer language to go no further than easily assimilable labels. But the remarkable thing about our time is that there has arisen a whole host of erudite minds who are only the reverse side of the coin of this philistine tendency, and who cannot rest until they have wrenched "symbols" and hidden "meanings" out of the text— as if the work itself did not exist until those symbols were found or imposed.

But doesn't Beckett use the name "Godot" in his title and even have the messenger boy refer to Mr. Godot as an old man with a beard? Why Godot instead of Smith, Jones, or Dupont if the author had not meant that this was a play about waiting for God?

On this solemn business of symbols I think it may lighten— and possibly enlighten—the atmosphere a little if we remember the joke about the man who goes to the psychoanalyst for the first time. He tells the doctor he is suffering from a recurrent and frightening dream:

"Night after night I dream I am in a rowboat, at first close to shore. Then I row out—farther, farther. Suddenly the oars break, and I am alone and helpless on the wide ocean. At that moment I wake up, sweating and frightened. What does that dream mean?"

"Very simple," says the analyst. "It is a symbol of castration anxiety. Your dream means that you are afraid of being castrated."

At which, the session for the day being over, the man departs. He does not come back; and the doctor, puzzled at first, finally forgets him until a few months later they chance to meet at a party.

"Why didn't you come back to see me?" asks the analyst. "We could have discussed your dream."

"Oh, doctor, that was unnecessary. You explained to me its meaning." Then, after a pause: "But you know, I've taken to dreaming again. I'm wakened almost-every night by a dream that I'm being castrated."

The doctor now becomes all solicitude. "Why not come in so that we can discuss it?"

"Really, doctor, it's not necessary. I know what this dream *means.*"

"? ?"

"Yes, doctor. It means that I am in a rowboat, I row far from shore, the oars break, and . . ."

This story (the spirit of which might amuse Beckett himself) has its own special lesson for psychoanalysis, but it also says much about symbols in general. Why should not the ax of symbolism cut both ways? If A is *the* meaning—and notice the definite article signifying one and only one meaning—of B, then might not B be *a* meaning of A? If the waiting in Godot is a waiting for God, then what does it mean to wait for God? It means that you get up each day to roll the Sisyphean rock, scrounge for food, endure the boredom and squabble of intimates, fill time, and even wait for other people to come and go, persisting, and, among other things, make up stories about a man with a gray beard. If you propose to wait for God, there is really no other way to go about it. What else were men doing during those long Ages of Faith when they were in fact waiting for God?

"No symbols where none intended," Beckett has explicitly warned the critics in *Watt*. And he might well have added: no philosophical system where none is indicated. The interpreters have overloaded his writings with elaborate philosophical constructions as well as contrived symbols. True, Beckett is an intensely intellectual writer. He is a man of apparently enormous erudition, who has read widely in philosophy as well as literature. It is only natural that scraps of learning and tags of ideas should bob up again and again in his work. Suppose an author had spent much of his early life as a lumberjack; would we not expect references to trees and logging to recur again and again in his writing? But Beckett is not a thematic writer in the likeness of Camus or Sartre, who construct their fictions in parallel with certain orderly sets of ideas that they also take the trouble to work out and publish in separate books. Where ideas appear in Beckett, they are more often than not spat out in disgust or played with ironically. If we follow Beckett's earlier anguished gropings for his own form, it is quite clear that he is not one of those writers whose inspiration is launched from some more or less tidy system of ideas. Speaking of Proust, Beckett remarks on "the labors of poetical excavation" that are the writer's real task. This excavation runs far below the stratum of ideas. Not that the work does not give rise to philosophical reflection; it does. But there is a great difference between reflecting upon a work of art and reconstructing it as a mere motif of ideas. The gnarled tree seen through my window gives rise to endless meditation; but I do not propose thereby any demiurge who has woven it out of bloodless categories. The philosophical significance of Beckett, such as it is, is that he brings us to a realm of experience beyond ideas altogether, where they do not apply, cannot be formed.

Having cast off these clouts of symbol and idea mongering, we may now proceed to a more positive effort at understanding.

I

Beckett's actual beginning, though it won a prize, was far less sensational than *Godot:* the long poem *Whoroscope* (1930). The young poet imitates T.S. Eliot's *The Waste Land* to the point of including notes; but in the more choppy and intramural character of its erudition it more nearly resembles Ezra Pound's *Cantos.* The speaker is Descartes, which means nothing for or against the author's supposed Cartesianism. As a student of French literature, Beckett has simply found the seventeenth-century philosopher a fascinating figure. This—as well as most of his other early poems—is the kind of avant-garde antipoetic poetry that young men wrote in the twenties and early thirties. In retrospect now, we can see the signs of genuine talent in those early poems; but in general Beckett is carrying on an unresolved quarrel with the poetic medium itself. Some of his later poems, though slight, are haunting and memorable, and are likely to endure. It is clear that Beckett, had he stuck to that medium, would probably have become a first-rate poet. But his most genuine poetry, as it turned out, was to be achieved in prose.

His real beginnings as an author—in the sense that we find him there intact with almost all his themes—is the remarkable little book *Proust* (1931). He was only twenty-four when he wrote it, and it bears all the traces of youthfulness: passages of overwriting, some intellectual posturing and arrogance, pugnaciousness, and . . . genius. In the light of Beckett's later work, this early confrontation with Proust might seem an unlikely encounter. Beckett's material is so elemental, plain, gross, and scabrous; while Proust, even where he is depicting a monstrous and demoniacal world, must enwrap it with all the refined complexities of high society. The differences of temperament

between the Swiftian Irishman and the neurasthenic Frenchman are so striking that one would wonder beforehand what
the former might extract from the writings of the latter. Beckett sees himself, as we all must do, but what he sees is also Proust
—or a part of him—and seen perhaps more profoundly than any
other Proustian interpreter.

Proust himself occupies a most remarkable place in that dissolution of the realistic novel within this century. Like Joyce in
Ulysses—though altogether unlike him in literary means and
goals—he stands at the confluence of the two separate streams
of Realism and Symbolism that flow from the nineteenth century. He speaks with a great deal of contempt for realistic fiction
for its preoccupation with external facts and documentation—
for superficial rather than interior reality. Yet Proust was also
a careful student of Balzac, and his great work *À la Recherche
du Temps Perdu* is quite Balzacian in conception, for it is,
among other things, the detailed story of the breakdown of one
social order and its replacement by another. And Proust, despite his antirealistic outbursts, is a diligent and waspish reporter on all the rituals in the game of social status.

But with Proust, the novelist of manners, Beckett is scarcely
concerned. Underneath that Proust lies the poet, whose vision
of life as essentially suffering is as stark as that of Buddhism or
Schopenhauer, and it is upon this Proust that Beckett seizes. To
what extent is the suffering in the Proustian world due to the
author's own bodily sickness, his asthma and neurasthenia? Certainly the quivering nerves of the narrator are carried on inter-
minably at times, and D. H. Lawrence had his justification for
his impatience at Proust as a hothouse and perfumed neurotic.
But with Proust, as with some artists, the sickness seems to be
the condition of a vision that is not available to healthy organisms. Certainly too, there is an impossibly refined narcissism
in the torments of love experienced by his characters. The
desired object is not attained, and therefore there is the suffering of craving; if attained, there is the boredom of satiation. So

far Schopenhauer. But the Proustian pessimism extends to a more fundamental fact of the human condition: that man is plunged irremediably in Time. The Proustian architecture of time is an elaborately irregular baroque edifice, full of cunning corridors and passageways, where turning a sudden corner one comes upon a vista of time longer than the longest straight line and a character who has been changed by the years beyond recognition. No other novelist has made time as real as Proust as the agent of deformation and transformation of his characters in a manner incalculable to the reader from his first encounter with them. Proust's chief themes thus are Time and the Self in their hidden and manifest, subtle and overpowering, interplay. They will also be the themes on which Beckett strikes his own very personal variations.

The mutable self is many selves. Can it always be sure which one it is, or that there is a real self at all? The nonself (the Anatman of the Buddhists) seems to be as real as that provisional self that we present for public purposes. Burrowing from layer to layer of the self, Proust wonders whether or where there is any bottom. And what about speech then? If one seeks to speak to oneself, to whom, to which of the many selves, is one talking? And when one seeks to speak sincerely as oneself, out of the depths of oneself, from where does that voice come? If we cannot be sure that we can speak to our own Self, how can we ever be confident that we can ever communicate with another Self? So Proust is driven to conclude that communication is impossible and each individual is unredeemably alone: "We are alone. We cannot know and we cannot be known. 'Man is the creature that cannot come forth from himself, who knows others only in himself, and who, if he asserts the contrary, lies.'" Beckett, borrowing here from Proust only what he wants to know because in fact he already knows it, will go on to put this lonely individual, noncommunicating and noncommunicable, at the center of most of his plays and novels.

Proust believed in art as the sole redemption from time. The artist catching the Idea, the essence, adumbrated by the flux, retrieves it from Cronus' devouring maw. Later writers have been denied the solace of this fate. Camus, meditating in *Sisyphus*, remarks that in ten thousand years the works of Shakespeare or Goethe may be without value, and may in fact not even be understood. For man, as a radically temporal being, no recourse to the eternal is permitted. Proust's faith remains still with the aestheticism of the nineteenth century and the Flaubertian cult of the priesthood of letters.

For Beckett the position of the writer is far more human and humiliating. As we have said, his sensibility is more grossly and plainly physical than Proust's, but such coarseness may also get him more directly to the heart of his matter. In any case, even where following Proust's thought on art as a reality that escapes our ordinary life in time, Beckett gives it his own bodily twist in the very last words of his essay: ". . . the 'invisible reality' that damns the life of the body on earth as a pensum and reveals the meaning of the word: 'defunctus.' " "Pensum" is a favorite word of Beckett's. The dictionary tells us that a pensum is a task imposed on a scholar (schoolboy) as a punishment. Life in the body, then, is a punishment imposed on the scholar, schoolboy, intellectual—the man who lives by the head, "the seat of all the shit and misery," as Beckett exclaims in *Molloy*. Bad enough; but the further etymology of this word has even more somber revelations. It comes from the Latin verb meaning "to weigh," and originally designated the amount of flax weighed out to each slave in the morning which he was responsible for spinning that day. And "defunctus" comes from the verb "defungor," to pay a claim and be quit of it. The defunct—the dead —are those who have spun out their bit of flax, paid the debt of life, and are free. For the enlightened modern middlebrow, these will seem morbid reflections, but it is worth noting that the morbidity here is not the invention of a contemporary writer, but the judgment of the race embodied in an ancient language.

But if Beckett was already in possession of his own point of view at the age of twenty-four, he had hardly found his own form for fiction. Three years after the Proust essay there appeared a collection of stories, *More Pricks Than Kicks* (1934), which, though often brilliant, very funny, and mordant, is also something of a hodgepodge of styles and influences. Indeed, the number of influences that the young Beckett, indefatigably literate, had to absorb at this historical juncture of international literary experimentation was multitudinous. For the young Dubliner, who had already lived in Paris, the example of his former townsman who had made a sensational entry into international letters, James Joyce, must have been overwhelming. There are, among these stories, plays with language in imitation of the later Joyce of *Finnegans Wake*. Beckett had also been exposed to the rising winds of the surrealist movement, and these stories at times cut very loose from ordinary realism. At other times they apply the sharp surgical scalpel of realistic deflation. As a first volume of stories, this work of Beckett does not have the achieved unity of form and style of Joyce's first book, *Dubliners;* but then from 1904 to 1934 the twentieth century had gone through artistic changes with breakneck speed, and the young Beckett emerged within a much more dense and confused literary milieu than had Joyce.

These stories do introduce us to an image that will persist throughout Beckett's later writings: the hero is named Belacqua after the character who appears in Canto IV of Dante's *Purgatory*. Belacqua is among the slothful on the first ledge of the Mount of Purgatory. Seated in almost fetal position, his head down between his knees, he is not recognized by Dante until he speaks. Then Dante shows irony and good humor in the meeting—evidently the real Belacqua, despite his lethargy, had been an amusing fellow on earth. There is here, no doubt, a certain amount of personal identification: Beckett had been nicknamed Oblomov (after that celebrated sloth of Russian fiction) for his own apparent indolence. Nearly all Beckett's later heroes will be, like Belacqua, decidedly not men of action, to say the least.

But there is another wonderfully ironic attraction about this figure: the indolent Belacqua has just made it out of hell by the least possible exertions. He has escaped the devils of eternal perdition but without having surrendered most of his life to the YMCA devils of strenuous duty. His is a strategy that Beckett might easily cherish as his own: to do just enough to escape torment, to be able to sit on one's ledge enjoying one's reverie —"the Belacqua bliss," as Beckett will later call it—watching the dawn break crooked over the sea. Our images, however, usually choose us rather than the other way around: and it will be interesting to see how the later part of Belacqua's revelation to Dante may or may not apply to Beckett. He is in the lowest rung of purgatory, Belacqua tells Dante, because he put off his repentance until the last moment. Clever fellow, to have leaped aboard just in time. Thus far Beckett has continued along his own unrepentant ways.

The real breakthrough in fiction came with *Murphy* (1938), a first-rate comic novel, totally differing from the early Evelyn Waugh but in its own way just as good. Yet it sold only forty-five copies—which makes one wonder about the insular obtuseness of the British literary market. True, the book has its faults; it is self-conscious and almost precious in spots. But in the precision of its writing, fertility of invention, its macabre humor, it already establishes Beckett in a class by himself.

Murphy is a young Irishman (one may think of Beckett himself, though the identification is unnecessary) roughing it in the Bohemian drab lands of London. He is having a love affair with Celia, a prostitute, and to get her off the streets he forces himself to look for a job. Meanwhile, some of Murphy's friends in Ireland, a group of amusing puppets, come to look for him. The job Murphy finds is, appropriately for him, as attendant in an asylum outside London. When he moves to his room in this hospital, he does not tell Celia, and now she too joins the Irish friends in the quest for Murphy. Meanwhile, he turns out to have a great way with the inmates, who recognize him as one of their own; both they and he have turned away from the howling fiasco of the outer to the inscrutable peace of the inner world.

When the friends find Murphy, it is too late. He has been destroyed by a fire accidentally started from the gas heater in his room. The menial who is to carry Murphy's remains back to Ireland gets involved in a bar brawl, hurls the packet of ashes at another man: "By closing time the body, mind and soul of Murphy were freely distributed over the floor of the saloon; and before another dayspring greyened the earth, had been swept away with the sand, the beer, the butts, the glass, the matches, the spits, the vomit."

The point of this macabre puppet show, Beckett tells us, is the mind of Murphy, about which he gives us a remarkable digression (Chapter 6). The section cannot be used to establish anything like Beckett's "philosophy," though he refers to philosophical ideas in the course of it; it is not a system of ideas but a description of his *experience*—the experience of withdrawal from an outer world into another and more satisfactory reality. But the passage does establish a map of the mental world or worlds within which much of his later writings can be placed.

As Murphy, bound to his rocking chair, sluffs off the body, he finds three zones within his mental world: light, semidark, dark. In the first, or upper, zone the world without is present, but he has the power to invert or change it where he will. He can return kick for kick for its indecent savageries. This is the zone in which a good deal of the ferocious satire of Murphy is cast. The second, or semidark, is the zone of "the Belacqua bliss"— the dream of the contemplative watching the dawn break crooked over the sea. To this zone belong the marvelous chiaroscuro reveries of landscape, dawn, and twilight we later find in *Molloy* (1950).

The third zone introduces us to a more difficult reality, where we must follow Beckett's own words:

Here there was nothing but commotion and the pure forms of commotion. Here he was not free, but a mote in the dark of absolute freedom. . . .

It was pleasant to lie dreaming on the shelf beside Belacqua. . . . But how much more pleasant was the sensation of being a missile without provenance or target, caught up in a tumult of non-Newtonian motion. So pleasant that pleasant is not the word.

Thus as his body set him free more and more in his mind, he took to spending less and less time in the light, spitting at the breakers of the world; and less in the half light, where the choice of bliss introduced an element of effort; and more and more and more in the dark, in the will-lessness, a mote in its absolute freedom.

The difficulty is how a literary work can descend into these depths, which of their very essence fend off all language. Beckett's attempt to enter this third zone is *The Unnamable* of the early 1950's. But fifteen years or so later, Beckett is older and wiser, and this zone, as we shall see, is not so easily reached, and its bliss has given way to panting and anguish.

II

But if *Murphy* charts Beckett's work to come, the progress is hardly logical. If for a moment, in this first novel, he has found his form, it is at best only a provisional one. The work is too brittle, too self-conscious, too circumscribed in its scope. (Beckett himself remarks disdainfully that all the characters except Murphy are puppets.) The next step, the novel *Watt* (written in 1942–44, but not published until 1953), shows him once again floundering toward his form. It has many wonderfully funny things, but it is also tedious, as Beckett usually is not; and on the whole it records his personal quarrel with the novel form as such. The novel—and Beckett's progress at this point—seems to lurch along much like Watt's walk:

Watt's way of advancing due east, for example, was to turn his bust as far as possible towards the north and at the same time to fling out his right leg as far as possible towards the south, and then to turn his bust as far as possible towards the south and at the same time to fling out his left leg as far as possible towards the north, etc. etc.

Tedious going indeed! Beckett is all too plainly mired alongside his subject, too involved with it to permit himself any proper aesthetic distance. What he required for that distance was the transparent screen of the French language between himself and his material. Turning to French after 1944, Beckett found the release through which he finally became Beckett, and so the first persistently bilingual author in modern letters. This bilingual virtuosity is quite different from the case of Vladimir Nabokov, who dropped his native Russian as a literary vehicle and turned permanently to English after 1937. Beckett, on the other hand, has continued to vibrate between these two poles of French and English, each of them feeding its own juice into the current.

He has said that he turned to French because it was easier to write without style in that language. This remark is straightforward, but not completely self-explanatory. English, being richer, catches up the writer more in its poetic possibilities, and form gets lost. French is more formal, more precise as prose, more pointed. It carries with it its own imperatives of form. Moreover, anyone who undertakes to write in French must carry with him the associations of this literature, which from the seventeenth century onward has cultivated polished form more than any other national literature. At any rate, the marriage turned out a happy one, blessed with fine offspring, beginning with the novel *Molloy*,[1] an extraordinary mingling of incantation and earthbound humor, in which all of Beckett's gropings hitherto find an exquisite balance.

---

1. In point of fact, three stories—"L'Expulsé," "Le Calmant," and "La Fin" —were written before this, though not published until 1954. Beckett also had some groping in French: a play *Eletheria* and a story, "Mercier et Camier," neither of which he allowed to be published.

Molloy is writing in his mother's room, which he has finally reached by some means he does not remember. His long soliloquy tells us of this search for the mother. The story, then, like Kafka's writings, belongs to the literature of the quest. But such a thread of plot and unity is only nominal. Molloy's amazing soliloquy breaks down into disconnected episodes and humor, which Beckett keeps feeding with a tireless invention so that the tale keeps driving forward at a breathless pace. In fact, Beckett gives us here a briskness of movement absent from his earlier fiction. In *Murphy* the writing had moved forward slowly and self-consciously; in *Watt* all movement has become mired. But Molloy's soliloquy hurries us forward, even though it leaves us at the end exactly where we were at the beginning. After all his fragmentary encounters with women, policemen, social workers, Molloy the tramp tells us at the end that he "could stay where he happened to be."

The second, and complementary, part of the novel is the tale of Moran, a cop sent to hunt out Molloy and dispatch him. Moran is notified of his assignment by a secret agent, and we get the sense of a mysterious Kafkaesque bureaucracy vaguely in the background. But, very quickly, Moran shows himself to be altogether different from a Kafka character: irritable and fussy, he sets out on a journey in which he has "only the vaguest notion of the work to be done" in a ridiculous pepper-and-salt suit, a faded boater without band, and carrying a massive black umbrella. In Beckett, even the instruments of vengeance are circus clowns. As Moran progresses on his journey in search of Molloy, his experience becomes more hallucinatory. There is a violent encounter with another man. Was it Molloy? We will never know. After a long and painful journey home, Molloy writes like a ruined man—or at least one who is now situated countless years away from what he was at the beginning.

Molloy is punctuated with the running refrain "I don't know" or "It's not certain"; and to emphasize the ignorance of the character—as well as the author—there is a continual alternation of sentences in which the later contradicts and undoes the earlier assertion. In the nineteenth century the realistic novelist claimed a godlike omniscience about his characters. They were perfectly transparent to his gaze, without a spot of opacity or darkness. Flaubert—to borrow the words of Joyce—was like a god indifferently surveying his creation while paring his fingernails. We are not sure, in this century, that we can command such understanding. This bafflement is not confined to experimental writers; you will also find it in so traditional a novelist as François Mauriac. Compare the latter's *Thérèse Desqueyroux* with Flaubert's *Madame Bovary.* Both novels have the same subject: a young woman of the provinces who gets in trouble with her marriage and her lovers. But where language itself in Flaubert, transparent and revelatory, will admit no matter recalcitrant to it, Mauriac rather throws up his hands in perplexity at the incomprehensible perversity of his heroine. Beckett, as we shall see, is to push this process of bafflement to its extreme—not because he is incapable of lucid writing but precisely because his mind is so lucid.

This process involves Beckett—in *Molloy* and all his fiction from that point on—in a peculiar problem: how to write precisely and indefinitely at once. Actions—like what happens on Moran's search for Molloy—must be indicated as sketchy and uncertain, hardly retained in the memory of the character who underwent them, and yet must not evaporate in precious wisps as in some of the narratives of the Symbolists. As in some modern paintings, the characters, done in a few strokes, must take solid hold within the canvas and yet seem to shimmer in and out of it. The problem is form and formlessness, substance and insubstantiality, Being and Nonbeing to be held together indissolubly.

Though Beckett had found his form in *Molloy,* it would have been impossible for him to rest with it or to have gone on repeating it. There could not have been a *Molloy II, Molloy III,* etc., as Trollope could go on repeating the same novel to the endless delight of his readers. We encounter here a phenomenon common enough in modern art—Stravinsky, Eliot, Picasso are other examples—where the work cannot be repeated, not out of some idiosyncratic restlessness of the author, but because the internal balance of forces within it is unstable and pushes towards a new resolution. The pretense of a single story holding the text together, though entirely satisfactory in this work, is too deceptive for Beckett to maintain in all honesty; and his next step is to scrap it in *Malone Dies* (1952).

Malone, more decrepit physically even than Molloy, cannot leave his bed, and while waiting to die, he will amuse himself by some stories. The fiction of fiction—that the stories are not really happening but made up—is here acknowledged rather than maintained. The stories are fragments, but marvelous. The Saposcat family, creeping and penurious, with their dutiful drip of a scholar son, Sapo; their lusty neighbors, the Lamberts, who slaughter their own pigs; Macmann, wrapped in his greatcoat, struggling against the elements. Only a few strokes are given, yet they haunt the canvas from which they seem about to vanish. Fragments and ruins of stories that cannot be told, that have perhaps no coherence—such will be the voices that henceforth haunt Beckett's people in both his plays and his fiction. The scene now shifts to an asylum (a remembrance perhaps of Murphy); the inmates go on a picnic, during which their keeper, Lemuel, kills them with an ax. The author, apparently delivered at last and by such violent means from his fantasies, is now ready to die.

But he does not die, and that is the maddening lament of *The Unnamable* (1953). Here the pretext of the fictional narrator is given up entirely, and the "I" of the author speaks. All those earlier characters—the Murphys, Molloys, and Malones—were merely figments of the author himself, and now it is of himself that he would speak. But who is this Self? Where is it to be found? "Je est un autre," said Rimbaud; the ego is a stranger. That intimate "I," which according to Kant accompanies all our representations of reality, whose voice haunts and murmurs alongside each experience, is not found as a simple subject-substance at the bottom of consciousness. The ego is in the world, an object for other people, living and created by *their* language. The real Self—what the Unnamable would speak about—cannot therefore be spoken about. Like a Laocoon, he writhes in the toils of language from which he cannot break free. He heaves and pants from one sentence to the next, as if struggling to clear his lungs altogether of language and be alone at last in that Silence where there are no more voices. Would the Self then, that phantom pursuing and pursued, be there when the babble of talk has gone? There is nothing to write about, nothing with which to write, and the author cannot go on—yet he must go on. It looks as if the writer-protagonist here had reached a dead end; but miraculously, in his very extremity, he has become a paradigm of the human condition itself, powerless but never quitting.

The three novels—*Molloy, Malone Dies, The Unnamable*—are spoken of as a trilogy, and Beckett himself has accepted the label. A trilogy, in the usual sense, continues the adventures of its characters from one novel into the next. There is nothing of that here. These three novels are a trilogy in another sense: the single story, if it can be called that, which they carry forward from one to the next is a continuous progress toward the dissolution of form. If we add *Murphy* as a fourth, then beginning from it the order of this progress becomes clearer, and a comparison with musical form is enlightening. The early *Murphy* gives us the usual diatonic of the novel, though punctuated by some very modern dissonances and orchestration; *Molloy* is polytonal; but with *Malone Dies* we have reached the stage of atonality, and this is carried so far forward in *The Unnamable* that we have the experience in reading it, as with some pieces of atonal music, of a pure progress in intensity—moving neither forward nor backward but sinking deeper and deeper into its beginning.

The most engaging of medieval mystics, Meister Eckhardt, in his sermon on the Sermon on the Mount comments upon the passage "Blessed are the poor in spirit, for they shall inherit the earth" by asking: Who, really, are the poor in spirit? What is it really to be poor in spirit? And he proceeds to answer: To be poor in spirit is "to possess nothing, to know nothing, and to will nothing." Beckett is far from having any truck with mystical theology, but the medieval description of spiritual impoverishment fits his characters perfectly: they possess nothing (hardly more than the rags they wear), know nothing ("It's not certain" rings like a refrain through all their disjointed soliloquies), and will nothing (the simplest acts, or what people sometimes think are the simplest acts, become impossible projects).

As for possessions, it is hard to say whether these human rejects even *have* their own bodies. The dissolution of form from *Molloy* to *The Unnamable* is also a progressive dissolution of their heroes' bodies. Molloy hasn't, as the common phrase puts it, a leg to stand on, but he hobbles around unkillably on crutches; Malone is worse off, since he cannot get out of bed; and the Unnamable, finally, corked in a bottle, is not sure at times whether he has a body left at all. Why then, it may be asked, do these characters hold such power and fascination over the reader? In the extremity of their nakedness there is something transcendently human about them, recalling Shakespeare's

> Poor naked wretches, wheresoe'er you are . . .

—as if this nakedness were the ultimate and the only fitting image to encompass all men.

Beckett's *via negativa* might, however, be more aptly compared with certain forms of Buddhism, which steer clear of the idea of God and even the reality of the soul. In saying this, of course, one has to guard against immediate misunderstanding. We have to issue the warning again and again that a work of art is not a compilation of ideas. What is involved in the present comparison is not at all the question whether Beckett derived ideas from Buddhist works, which in fact I do not know that he has read. We have here rather a progress in experience that the ancient Orient seems to have gone through centuries ago. Buddhist thinking, moreover, is intuitive and experiential, not abstract and logical. What makes certain forms of Buddhism peculiarly relevant to the modern encounter with Nihilism is that once indeed a large part of mankind did live with the Void, made their peace with it, and managed the life of society on that basis. The progress in Beckett's trilogy is not an intellectual contrivance for the sake of literary experiment. Let us remember Giacometti's statement that he did not want to make thin figures, he could not help himself. Beckett writes not what he chooses but what he can, out of a similar necessity. And this inner experience that drives him from *Molloy* through *The Unnamable* is what has been described by Buddhist philosophers as the deliberate relinquishing of the world of *nama-rupa*, name-form, the world of the tidy ego with its definite objects and articulate consciousness, in order to descend into the nameless flux out of which this poor ego, at once fictitious and tyrannical, has to be born again and again, like a bubble rising to the surface of a stream.

It might be argued that a work like this, which uses language in order to undo language, which suffers the spasms of words in the hopeless quest of silence, is self-contradictory. But perhaps life is too, and language, which is so close to it, shares this contradictory character. In any case, silence can be expressed only through language. Indeed, only through language does silence come to be at all. If there were no language, there might be an absence of sound waves in this universe but there would not be silence. For silence speaks to us only through language. And conversely, without such silence authentic language disappears. The staccato chatter of the loudspeaker neither knows nor invokes silence. Nor is this silence within language a mark of its deficiency. On the contrary, where it is most adequate language brings us into the silent presence of what it has uttered. No further words are needed, "the rest is silence." The limits of language do not lie at its borders like a wall that cannot be scaled. When Wittgenstein remarked, "Of that whereof we cannot speak, we must be silent," the witty retort of the positivist Neurath was for once correct: that if there were anything (in the sense of a definite something) about which to be silent, then we could speak of it. Silence inhabits language at its center, not its boundaries. With language and silence it is as with Being and Nonbeing—they *are* in their interpenetration of each other. *The Unnamable* seeks to convey this zone of silence that circulates behind and through every human life.

And whatever the arguments *a priori* against even its possibility, Beckett seems to me to have brought it off triumphantly. This novel, if it can be called that, completes the trilogy by bringing forward what remained upspoken in *Molloy* and *Malone Dies*. Of course, it takes time to get used to this jerky and stammering voice; but when one does, the book seems natural, simple and direct. Those who were fortunate enough to have heard Jack Macgowran's readings from Beckett will have recognized this simplicity. There miraculously on the stage before one's eyes was the single character who circulates below the different names—Molloy, Moran, Malone, call him what you will—but struggles to the surface to find his own voice only in this last novel. He is not remote from us, we are there in his reality every day of our lives. Needless to say, one does not bring it to the forefront of one's mind every day; and for some people it will always remain unrecognized even in the background. Some live in it and never know it, as Hemingway says. This is the reality inhabited by the narrator in Proust but not his characters, from whose interior silence—despite sixteen monumental volumes—he declared he could never depart. Here again, Beckett's line of development follows consistently from that earliest essay. He has chosen to enter that silence that Proust speaks of only from a distance. In so doing he must leave the reality of realism far behind. In the same essay Beckett had also approved Proust's excoriation of realistic art as a "miserable statement of line and surface," adding his own youthfully ebullient condemnation of "the penny-a-line vulgarity of a literature of notations." Over twenty years later he accomplishes his antirealistic vendetta. With *The Unnamable* he has pushed the novel the furthest yet from that purely external reality that the dogma of realism cherished.

III

Anyone who has followed the progress of this trilogy will understand why Beckett's plays cannot be lumped under the current rubric of Theater of the Absurd. This label itself, in the first place, is quite vague in its own conception. The three most prominent practitioners it is meant to include are Beckett, Genêt, and Ionesco, all of whom differ very much from one another. The cultivation of "absurdity" could be attributed to some of Ionesco, particularly where he is making deliberate use of nonsensical language. But since the use of this language is to serve a straightforward, at times almost didactic, purpose, how absurd is it? In fact, the label "Theater of the Absurd" covers a movement whose direction, however diverse the aims of the individual playwrights, is simply to get beyond the hobbling restrictions of realistic theater. But the word "absurd" here, as it impinges upon the popular mind, covertly subscribes to the preconceptions of realism. For does it not suggest to the ordinary playgoer that any liberty taken with the realistic canon must be trafficking with the absurd?

The vitality of this contemporary movement—which has now spread beyond Paris—is precisely that it wishes to restore the theater to the richness of its own resources after the impoverishment of the so-called realistic theater. The fact is that in the long history of the theater nineteenth-century realism—which tended in one way or another to be a social realism—was a heresy and an aberration. Such realism inevitably runs to the conviction that social conditions and social problems define the human essence. The theater built on this premise has nothing to do with Aeschylus, Sophocles, Shakespeare, Racine—not to mention the Nō drama or the Indonesian ballet. The depiction of conditions in the slums or among the miners in depressed areas is better done by journalism or the startling vividness of cinema documentaries. The so-called Theater of the Absurd seeks first of all to be theater and not something else.

Confronted by the cinema's overwhelming powers for visual realism and documentation, the contemporary theater has to struggle to rediscover its own roots in a manner not unlike that forced upon modern painting. Early in this century Matisse remarked: "When a camera can fix an accurate image of an object in the merest fraction of a second, it would be stupid for a painter to compete." The camera thus gave the painter the freedom to discover what painting is or might be. The theater is beginning to discover that it has resources of its own as powerful as those of the cinema. The basis of all its resources is that we are in the same room in the physical presence of the actors, and therefore the action going on there can involve us more directly. Moreover, there is an opportunity for a kind of direct theatrical *metaphor* that could not be so effective from a moving picture. Thus when Beckett, in *Endgame,* puts the two aged parents on stage in ashcans, he gives us the immediate and direct theatrical image of what the life of this old couple has become. The use of the buskin and enormous shoulder paddings in Genêt's *The Balcony* tells us immediately that these men are nothing but inflated uniforms, that their identity is the hypertrophy of their social function. Realistic theater never permitted such means of expression. A most powerful example of where the audience's co-presence in the same hall becomes extremely intense is that of the invisible guests in Ionesco's *The Chairs.* When well performed, the effect almost crackles through the hall: those nonexistent guests, like so many ghosts, seem to swarm all over the stage.

But the most powerful single resource of the theater is the elemental fact of speech itself, and the sheer drama inherent in the dialogue between one human being and another. For a film, dialogue is an adjunct, and can often be an incumbrance. Lengthy dialogue kills a picture. But drama is *language*, and everything else is an adjunct. It is here that realistic drama sold its birthright, and consented to restrict language to the incoherent mumblings of what was supposed to be ordinary language. The possibilities of language for form and stylization of phrase, for eloquence and poetry, simply disappeared. A collection of Broadway hits over the years can hardly be read without embarrassment, however much they may have been pulled off on stage by the brilliance of individual actors. Beckett's plays, on the contrary, are really written and they can be read. Their language is taut, controlled, austere—poetry without bathos.

But if the label "Theater of the Absurd" is unclear generally, there are also very particular reasons why it is inappropriate to Beckett. He himself has declined the description, remarking that absurdity implies a judgment and in his writings there is no judgment. This remark does not imply any Flaubertian claim for the absolute objectivity and detachment of the artist as, godlike, he surveys his own creation. With Beckett, the writer can no longer entertain such superhuman ambitions. The point is, rather, that when one has arrived at the state of being of the Unnamable one is beyond raising any question about the meaning or meaninglessness of life. If we hark back to Camus of *The Stranger* and *Sisyphus*, and the manner in which the question of the Absurd is posed there, we find that the background of Western theism, as well as its disappearance, is presupposed. Is the world ultimately intelligible or not? That is Camus' question. And assuming that it is not, or at least that it can never be for us humans, how then do we go about living with courage and lucidity within the flat horizon of our finitude? But Beckett

—and his characters—cannot rise to the level of such questions, which require a view of the whole, or pretension to such a view, that is impossible to them.

Or else they are beyond them. It may be not a deficiency but a superiority of mind that carries us beyond ideas and their claim to be absolute. There are no ideas to express, Beckett says somewhere, nothing to express them with, and yet one must go on expressing. Absurd? Perhaps, rather, it may be simply the matter-of-fact description of the state at which we must arrive for enlightenment to take place. That is a point beyond either Western theism or its simple-minded rejection. From that point the Buddha, questioned whether there was a God or not, replied by a silence, neither affirming nor denying. And at that point, of course, we do not come upon anything like a Philosophy, much less a Philosophy of the Absurd. "Philosophy leaves the world as it is," says Wittgenstein in one of his most deflating and simultaneously liberating aphorisms. All the turmoil of the mind, if we are lucky, merely brings us around to where we are. Let us recall Hesse's Siddhartha, who having escaped the bondage of words and ideas has come close to "the things themselves" that matter to him, the flowing water of his river, to his tree and his stone. The old Zen saying has it: "Before you have studied the philosophic doctrine, mountains are mountains and rivers are rivers; while you are studying it, mountains are no longer mountains and rivers no longer rivers; but when you have obtained enlightenment, mountains are once again mountains and rivers once again rivers." In Beckett's world, as Estragon reminds us, a carrot is a carrot. And the various objects with which his characters get entangled—bicycles, hats, greatcoats— are just bicycles, hats, greatcoats.

Accordingly, Beckett's plays, detached from the abstraction of the Theater of the Absurd, are properly seen as . . . Beckett's plays—and as such they speak entirely for themselves, and with a surgical sharpness of form, phrasing, and situation. After *Godot*, the plays have become more taut, incisive, more precisely specified for their medium, whether stage, radio, or a recent movie scenario. *Endgame* (1956) has almost the precision of a definition—a definition of human impotence under the weight of time fallen into fragments. Hamm, the master of the household, is both blind and unable to get up from his chair. Clov, the servant, cannot sit down. The two parents of Hamm, Nagg and Nell, are in ashcans on stage. Hamm wakes, their day begins; Nell and Nagg rise from their cans, tell a story, then go back down; at last Hamm covers his face with a cloth and goes to sleep.

Action has been suppressed here even more completely than in *Godot,* and there is even less semblance of any climax or development. The play is only one act, and its material looks unpromising; but in its starkness and brevity, it has a monumental scope and grandeur. Hamm himself is like a ruined Biblical king amid his desolate domain, which happens to be only this one room, just as some of Giacometti's figures, only a few inches high, can give the impression of an aloof and awesome grandeur. Beckett's characters stand transfixed and impaled by time as Giacometti's by space.

Time, in one of its aspects, plays so heavy a role in *Endgame* (even when, oddly enough, nothing happens in the play) that we have delayed up to now documenting the various manifestations of the temporal as it shows itself in Beckett. In line with the elemental character of Beckett's vision, time does not present itself in a contemplative luxury of various temporal perspectives à la Virginia Woolf. The plainest and most elementary way in which time shows itself is in all those withered and decaying bodies of his tramps. Let us remember, in this connection, that the oldest myth about time is that of Cronus devouring his children. And that Buddha, leaving his palace and discovering old age, sickness, and death, felt that here was something frightful for which heroic measures were called. The modern mind, behind its bulwark of medicine and sanitation, finds the physical grossness of decay in Beckett excessive and distasteful. But a visit to an up-to-date and expensive nursing home for the aged would daunt even the most sanguine extrovert: all those petrified mummies (and their numbers are increasing every year) kept alive by modern medicine are hardly evidence that our enlightenment allows us to escape the harshness of nature. We refuse to believe that old age and death are an awful fate that we have to accept, and as a result we become cowering neurotics living within the humanist's air-conditioned nightmare. Beckett's overinsistence upon the facts of physical decay might almost serve a therapeutic purpose.

Time, as the devourer, can strike with appalling swiftness. Pozzo, in the second act of *Godot,* asked when he went blind and Lucky dumb, suddenly roars:

Have you not done tormenting me with your accursed time! It's abominable! When! When! One day, is that not enough for you, one day he went dumb, one day I went blind, one day we'll go deaf, one day we were born, one day we shall die, the same day, the same second, is that not enough for you? (calmer.) They give birth astride of a grave, the light gleams an instant, then it's night once more.

This outburst is prepared by the speech in Act I where Pozzo speaks with Sophoclean irony (for darkness will later descend on him) of the sudden descent of night:

. . . An hour ago *(he looks at his watch, prosaic)* roughly *(lyrical)* after having poured forth ever since *(he hesitates, prosaic)* say ten o'clock in the morning *(lyrical)* tirelessly torrents of red and white light it begins to lose its effulgence, to grow pale *(gesture of the two hands lapsing by stages)* pale, ever a little paler, a little paler until *(dramatic pause, ample gesture of the two hands flung wide apart)* pppfff! finished! it comes to rest. But—*(hand raised in admonition)*—but behind this veil of gentleness and peace night is charging *(vibrantly)* and will burst upon us *(snaps his fingers)* pop! like that! *(his inspiration leaves him)* just when we least expect it. *(Silence. Gloomily.)* That's how it is on this bitch of an earth.

But this time can descend so swiftly that it changes into its opposite—the changeless. We are born and we die. When? The same day. In between time hangs heavy, falling apart into momentary atoms. *Endgame* invokes Zeno: "Moment upon moment, pattering down, like the millet grains of . . . that old Greek, and all life long you wait for that to mount up to a life." It is impossible for time to elapse, for half of that time would first have to elapse, and before that the half of the half, etc. etc. "Inches are infinities," Giacometti has remarked of space; but here time replaces space, and a single day is an eternity to get through. This is the *"temps énorme"* that haunts the protagonist of *Comment C'est* (1961) as he crawls on and on and on through the mud.

What is the unifying ground out of which these two manifestations of time emerge? They are both expressions of human powerlessness. On the one hand, man is helpless before the destroying rush of time; on the other, in his impotence to act he cannot bind time together, and it falls apart into tiny bits, like Zeno's grains of sand that can never add up to a heap.

As Beckett's plays continue, the form becomes tighter and the scope narrower until he ends with what he calls "dramaticules." Beckett is, no doubt, a narrow writer in the sense that he is always pursuing the same themes; but in making this judgment of narrowness one must not be hypnotized by the crude phenomenon of sheer bulk. He manages to say a great deal in a short space; and his gifts for poetry and characterization, however he may restrict them, are still potent in these shorter pieces. The aging Irish woman, Mrs. Rooney, in the radio play *All That Fall*, wheezing and chattering as she toils towards the railway station, could have come out of a play by Sean O'Casey. The old men, Holoway and Bolton, confronting each other in *Embers* (also a radio play), have the haunting quality of a good ghost tale. Winnie in *Happy Days*, buried onstage up to the waist and then up to the neck, is a portrait of

a woman as real, though in a very different way, as Joyce's Molly
Bloom. Beckett continues to make use of various framing props
—ashcans, recording tapes, characters buried to the waist or
planted in funerary urns—but these are not flashy gimmicks
that obviate the necessity of writing well. On the contrary, the
framing prop is really a stage metaphor, very expressive in
itself, permitting an extraordinary conciseness in the play but
also placing a heavy burden upon the writer. Once the woman
is placed immobile on stage buried to the waist, the author has
to carry the situation off, as Beckett does, by the sheer power
of his writing. In *Krapp's Last Tape* the use of the tape recorder
makes possible a powerful condensation of time by allowing the
protagonist's voice to speak to us directly from the past; but the
play has then to be sustained by the language itself, the fragmentary but measured lyricism with which the stabbing poignancy of lost love is evoked.

Nowhere are these framing props more effective than in *Play
(Pièce)*, which, despite its brevity, dissects the eternal triangle
more surgically than many a two-volumed novel. The three
characters—the man and the two women—are encased in large
urns that leave only their heads showing; a spotlight moves
from one to the other to prod them when it is their turn to
speak. In death they go on, like old phonograph records, with
the same stale hash of recriminations, hysteria, jealousies—the
same eternal tale of adultery being played on and on beyond
death. In comparison with the piercing detachment of Beckett's vision, Sartre's *No Exit* (which also locates its characters in
hell) begins to look like a contrived intellectual melodrama.
Desire is dead, and the insight that comes is that of death itself
—"Non che la speme, il desiderio è spento," as Beckett, quoting
Leopardi, already understood in his early essay on Proust.

The American reception of Beckett, which was slow but is
now gathering, is very instructive about our present spiritual
condition. The usual cries of "morbid" were raised; but really

the stone harder to swallow was a vision so stark and naked. We would prefer more complex works, clothed with the flowing draperies of rhetoric, and bedecked with the baubles of "ideas" that we can go on chattering about. Those who are in despair, Kierkegaard long ago told us, do not want to be reminded of it. However, in the midst of the modern intellectual clutter, this drive to pare our human condition down to its bare bones ought to be considered a very healthy phenomenon. At least we know where we stand; evasiveness becomes more difficult. No doubt, Beckett can find some revolting physical metaphors for our spiritual condition: the character in *Comment C'est*, crawling with his sack through the mud, quite naturally repelled the original reviewers of *Time* magazine and they denounced it as untrue and unwholesome. Yet this image would have been accepted by Dante as perfectly appropriate for this creature who says of himself that he had "lost his life up there in the light." That is not a small loss, if we remember the lines of Yeats:

> Now that my ladder's gone,
> I must lie down where all the ladders start,
> In the foul rag-and-bone shop of the heart.

Beckett has made his bed there; and his vitality, humor, and intense pathos serve to show that the cellar still crawls with a little life that, however you scratch it, is recalcitrant to death. He seems to inch laboriously toward a dead end, from which nevertheless he—and his characters—are always reborn irresistibly like so many phoenixes from their ashes.

POSTSCRIPT TO PART III

The essence of Western civilization is neurosis. This statement is probably outrageous in its bluntness, and gratuitously crude in the face of the many great and shining things the West has created. But let us entertain the proposition for a moment, if only as an exploratory metaphor, introducing what are needed qualifications as we go along. Hermann Hesse himself suggests something like this negative judgment on the West, since in the depths of his own sickness of spirit he had to turn to the East for the springs of renewal. True, in a later work, *Journey to the East*—a wild vaudeville of the imagination—he came to declare that this East was not a matter of physical geography but a country of the mind to which men of spirit everywhere belonged. Nevertheless, it was the East which freed him from his parochialism and provided the viewpoint by which he could seek the bridge between it and the West.

Recent anthropologists distinguish cultures as cool or hot. A cool culture, in its pursuit of stability, seeks to cool off the energies that would bring about such changes as might disrupt the social fabric itself. In doing so, it can be marvelously inventive in its rituals and myths, but always within a basic pattern which ensures that the individual will never feel himself to be an outsider and homeless in the group or in the world the group has created for itself. A hot culture, on the other hand, heats up all the forces that make for change, preferring dynamism to stability. In this pursuit, however, it may place extraordinary strains upon its individuals. Western civilization has been more dynamic and flexible than the East, but in the process has taken far more daring risks with the psychic well-being of its people.

The well-known secularization of life that has gone on since modern science began in the seventeenth century has been positively reckless in expending the inheritance of religion, myths, and traditions that provide some kind of psychological cushion and fulfillment for the individual. The progress of those three centuries has produced today a world in which, both in philosophical theory and in social fact, man feels himself homeless. The most searching philosopher of the period, Heidegger, in analyzing human existence has declared that man's fundamental Being in the world is a "not being at home" in it. That is a condition which easily induces neurosis, and the writers we have just examined show us that the strains of neurosis are everywhere in modern life. If, as Aristotle said, the essence of anything is to be judged by the end it produces, then we would have to say that Western civilization has been essentially headed toward neurosis, or driven itself in that direction.

Or let itself thoughtlessly be driven into that condition by recklessly abandoning its safeguards. For the present may be only a temporary and accidental drift, the interregnum between two worlds, as Matthew Arnold put it prophetically, the one dying and the other yet unborn; and in time the natural principles that tend toward limits and balance, as Camus hoped, will reassert themselves and create the conditions for a healthier psyche. Perhaps in the three writers we have just examined there may be some glimmering, faint no doubt, of where the new birth may come.

Sticking to the metaphor of neurosis, we note a distinct progression in intensity. Hesse presents us with characters (Steppenwolf is a good example) in the grip of neurotic conflict, but who are still struggling to open the door of their prison, and on the whole the prognosis is positive and hopeful. With Kafka the door has been closed, the neurotic state has clamped down fixed and immobile, like "a frozen sea," to use his own words, and one that no ax will ever break through. With Beckett we have reached a condition that might be described as post-neurosis. The term itself seems irrelevant to his mournful and hilarious tramps. A neurosis is a bourgeois luxury altogether beyond the horizon of their meager existence. If they have ever gone through any experience comparable to that, it is over and done with in that vast stretch of time before, and they have been defeated; and yet . . . such is the saving power of the negative, in this defeat there may be something of a victory.

In Steppenwolf the human and the animal contaminate each other. Haller refers continuously to the wild beast in himself that rages beneath the veneer of the civilized man. In fact, this animal does not belong to the wilds but to the strictly human zoo. The wolf of the steppes is not nearly so restless or gratuitously aggressive as his human counterpart. He is driven by hunger or the urge to mate, but when these drives are satisfied he is at rest, for the time being anyway. He is bounded and contained by his instincts, while man is the only creature who can be estranged from these boundaries. Groping for the worst words they could find, Hesse's generation spoke of the organized cruelty of trench warfare in the First World War as "bestial" or "inhuman." In fact, nothing could be further from the truth; no creature beside man is capable of such highly organized aggression carried on to such a protracted and stupid length. Here ideals and love of country become contaminated by the aggressive drives, and the latter in turn are twisted and deformed by being allied with abstract goals and the mistaken virtue of steadfastness, which only prolongs the destruction. War is that state in which the human and the animal in man contaminate each other; and the deranged parts that result are distinctly human, all too human, in their nature. Steppenwolf's sickness lies in the point beyond and between the human and the animal in him—the unrealized self that is not yet whole enough to embrace and give meaning to the two opposites. Meanwhile, instinct is deranged and human culture, which should adorn our existence, becomes a crucifying burden to bear. Freud's casebooks, which belong to the same period of the European spirit as Hesse's novels, are a somber documentation of this simultaneous derangement of the instincts and debasement of the spirit.

With Kafka and Beckett the religious impulse—in the one

case Judaism, in the other Christianity—comes closer to home and becomes more pressing. That might seem a surprising statement in view of the fact that Hesse is always dwelling on the sacred books of the East. Precisely. They are distant and precious treasures of human culture, to which the sensitive Occidental may have recourse in order to widen his own spiritual horizons. From the point of personal urgency, Hesse should have been involved rather with exhuming and reanimating the corpse of Protestantism in himself. The last thing one can say of Kafka is that the question of Judaism is for him a cultural matter. On the contrary, it is so personal that it sticks in him like a thorn in the flesh, which he cannot remove, which despite his tortuous head he can never remove, but which that same obstinate head can never let the body absorb into itself. There are some souls for whom the frustration of their religious yearnings casts a shadow over all other feelings. When Nietzsche declared "God is dead," he followed this with the audacious leap, "Therefore everything is permitted." We would have to express Kafka's reaction in a different way: "If God is dead, then it is no longer permitted to feel." If the heart is denied its ultimate longing, why was that longing ever given to it, and how can it ever muster feelings again for this absurd and empty world? The death of God can be suitably memorialized only in the extinction of all feeling—in an art that attains the ultimate flatness.

Beckett, at least, preserves his lyricism. His characters, denied everything else, at least are not denied that gift. They may be ripe for the muckheap, but they can keen over themselves, and they do so endlessly, humorously, mordantly, blasphemously, with the self-pity and self-accusation of Irish blather lifted to the level of poetry. In that lyrical flow life too flows back again, and a vision of impotence quite different from Kafka's takes shape. At a certain point the only way out of a neurotic conflict is the subsiding to a lower, or less ambitious, level of existence. We have no choice in the matter; the tension in maintaining the conflict within ourselves becomes too exhausting and painful to endure, and we are forced to give up our exaggerated claims on life. The painter cannot lift his brush, the writer cannot put words together and tries to escape from them altogether; there is nothing else to do—for the time being at any rate—but to submit to this wave that is rolling over us. It too is a force of nature, unfathomable from within us; and it may in time, who knows, bring renewal, but in a form our earlier ego-ridden state could not imagine. Perhaps we have only enough energy and interest to sit on a park bench in the sunlight. But a world may be discovered there that had been screened off from our previous high-strung and overambitious consciousness. There is no escaping the descent into the foul rag-and-bone shop of the heart—and there may be worse places.

Seen as ritual, this descent is a form of sacrifice. We have to cast our bread upon the waters if anything is to be restored to us. We may have to sacrifice our dearest and best, our pride of intellect or our vaunted will and its concentration upon its chosen goals, as Abraham was willing to give up Isaac and God gave up his only begotten Son, if we are to be reborn at all. In its simplest terms a neurosis, however intricate in its clinical details, is a case of overambition: we cherish conflicting drives that cannot be satisfied and reconciled at the same time. We reenact the drama of *hubris* that is the basic pattern of all Greek tragedy: the tragic hero has overextended himself and must succumb in order that the saving balance of things, at once cosmic and human, be preserved. However dissimilar our outward trappings, however more acceptable our social role and status, we have to enter into the condition of Beckett's waifs to take that step beyond the neurotic impasse. Only through humiliation does the stubborn human heart learn humility, and through it the saving sense of limits.

Do these humiliated tramps and their disjointed and fragmentary stories provide anything like a parable for our time? This civilization seems already to have overextended itself to the point where it produces anxiety and frustration all around us, and not only in its prophetic artists. Perhaps it will have to surrender some of its powerful ambitions in order to learn how and where it is really powerless. We know so much that we cease to know the primal things, which can be learned only in that foul rag-and-bone shop of the heart. There can be worse things than the experience of humiliation through which we learn humility. In Hesse the conflict of opposites is agonizing but still productive. In Kafka it has become so exhausting that paralysis and emptiness have set in. With Beckett the surrender has been made, the game long since declared not worth the candle, the ritual sacrifice performed. And yet his tramps, who can deny it, are in a better state spiritually, more substantially human, than Steppenwolf or Joseph K.

And so our argument comes to rest—an argument not intended to prove a simple conclusion but to exhibit a more or less complex state of mind and soul, in this case of Western civilization in our time.

Some witnesses have been called, their voices heard, and their testimony has woven variations around one theme: the threatening presence of Nihilism and the challenge of renewal for Western man. But, it will be said, these are only a few voices, and a highly selective list at that. What if we chose some healthier, happier artists, in whose work a familiar and stable world is accepted and trusted, and where Nihilism does not stand as the weird and unlikely guest at the door? Would not a very different picture of the time emerge?

The notion of "health" in an artist and writer is often an ambiguous one. Sometimes it is merely a ghost invoked by lazy minds who do not want their ordinary habits of perception to be disturbed and therefore insist that artists not be shocking by their novelty of manner or unpleasantness of matter. Still, there is some sense, highly personal and hard to define as it may be, in which we respond to writers as healthy or not. The reader who recoils from Kafka, declaring the author is sick, is perhaps not exhibiting the most patient and perfect aesthetic response, but he is on the other hand really reacting to what is there in the work and not substituting ideology like some more sophisticated critics. The objection should therefore be met, and we must, for the sake of balance, turn now to less modernist and distressing voices. But where find them?

First of all, there is England, traditional, conservative, and unshaken in its institutional life over these troubled years. If England's finest hour in this century was to stand up alone and steadfast against Hitler's armies, it had nevertheless prepared itself in other ways for this role of the island fortress. Culturally, it had been equally stubborn in resisting invasion from across the Channel. The avant-garde was a creature spawned on the Continent, and the British attitude was to let it die there. The new schools in painting and sculpture belonged to the French and were viewed at a safe distance and only very tardily. On the new movements in continental philosophy, Existentialism and Phenomenology, Cambridge and Oxford shut their time-honored doors. Atonal music was the voice of the troubled soul of Middle Europe, to which the Englishman, secure that "There will always be an England," need not listen. Hidebound insularity or the steadfast pursuit of one's own path? Either way it does not matter for our present purpose. If we are to refute the argument that has been taking shape through the preceding pages—if we are to escape from the twentieth century and the torments of modernism—where should we turn but to England and the English? Let us try.

Part IV

Counterexamples . . . Perhaps

9. Ou-boum or Bou-oum

. . . the Goblins . . .

In 1904, three years after the reign of Victoria had ended, one of its more eminent minds, Leslie Stephen, died, and his children, who were now orphaned, moved to a cheaper and then less fashionable quarter of London at 46 Gordon Square, Bloomsbury. Stephen was a notable enough figure for his death to be recalled even now, but the change of residence might pass unremembered except for two things: one of the beautiful Stephen girls, Virginia, later became famous under her married name of Woolf; and the son, Thoby Stephen, had been part of a small circle of interesting and talented friends a few years earlier at Cambridge. The friends had continued to see each other, and it was natural for them now to meet at this new address where, in the absence of elders, they could enjoy greater freedom and ease. Thus was born the Bloomsbury Circle, destined to be the most famous and distinguished intellectual group in England for the next three decades.

The promise of youthful talent was fulfilled. J. M. Keynes became the greatest economist in the world, Lytton Strachey the foremost biographer of the time; Roger Fry was England's leading authority on the fine arts, and Clive Bell a well-known writer on aesthetics. The group also included influential figures from the world of books and publishing, like Leonard Woolf, David Garnett, and Desmond MacCarthy.

But besides its profusion of talent, the circle had style, casual and unassuming, but elegantly graced by the presence of the beautiful Stephen daughters. At the time it was still a radical

281

and daring thing for women to share naturally and easily in the conversations of men. But emancipation was in the air, and no group was more emancipated intellectually than Bloomsbury. Victorian parents and grandparents lay behind them, and these young people were conscious of themselves as a new and very different generation. Intelligence, freedom from prejudice, good taste, something they called civilization—these were the things Bloomsbury valued. Reacting against the Victorians, they tended to pass by a good deal of the solid bourgeois and philistine nineteenth century, preferring the eighteenth as more rational, elegant, and aristocratic in its tastes. There were moments indeed when Bloomsbury rather fancied itself as a return to earth of one of the salons of eighteenth-century France.

But above all, Cambridge remained their spiritual center. There the circle of friends had first formed, and the spirit of the place continued to shine as their philosophical beacon. Toward the turn of the century something of a philosophical revolution had been accomplished at Cambridge by G. E. Moore and Bertrand Russell. Against the reigning Idealism, rooted in the religious view of things, Moore and Russell provided a more modest and secular philosophy, analytic and dialectical but not grubby: a form of Platonism that was stripped of Plato's passion and mysticism. Moore, in particular, became Bloomsbury's authority on questions of ethics and the good life. His work in that field seemed to offer all that an emancipated young mind of the time might require. Against vulgarity one was fortified by Moore's elaborate proofs that the good could never be defined by any natural quality. And against the possible quicksands of moral doubt there was the reassurance that the propositions of ethics—at least some of them—could be a priori and certain. And after passing through all his refutations of traditional theories, when one came to find out what positively made up a good life, Moore's ideals did not place any severe strain on oneself. What are the ultimately good things that make up the good life?

Why, intelligence and the pleasures of intellect, aesthetic appreciation, conversations with friends—in short, the ideal life as imagined by a Cambridge don, and as Bloomsbury was ready to pursue it.

Years later Keynes wondered how he and his friends could have been captured by so one-sided a philosophy. He had moved into the great world of money and international politics and found another reality there. In retrospect, Moore's views were seen to reflect "the extraordinarily sheltered and optimistic society that was to be found in Cambridge at the beginning of the century." Bloomsbury, borrowing this optimism, was strangely unprepared for the violence of the century to come. "We repudiated," Keynes laments, "all versions of the doctrine of original sin, of there being innate and irrational springs of wickedness in most men." But these doubts came a long time later, and in their earlier years no such thoughts had crossed their minds. The faith of Cambridge, which had formed their youth, seemed at the time like a blessed release from the moral cramp of Victorianism.

At the fringe of Bloomsbury stood E. M. Forster. Though close to some in the group, he was not of its inner circle. Though he had been born in London, his family roots traced back into the countryside, and facing the others he may have been conscious of this yeoman and rural ancestry in himself. What this difference between himself and the others was we may perhaps guess from the reaction of D. H. Lawrence, who detested the group for being too cerebral and rational. In his usual impetuous fashion Lawrence exclaimed that these Bloomsbury people made him think of "black beetles" that he wanted to step on. He made an exception, however, of Forster, whom he liked though the two were never in a position to become close friends. (Was it ever possible to become a friend of Lawrence's anyway?) Nevertheless, such differences as there may have been weighed less for Forster than his ties to the group. He adored Cambridge, where he had been happy for the first time in his life, and he cherished the enlightened aspirations of Bloomsbury. And these two—Cambridge and Bloomsbury—would seem to provide as sturdy a dike as we can find against the mutinous waves of modernism.

Besides, Forster's novels are traditional in form, and so stand out in resistance against the currents that we have been exploring. They make no bold experiments in technique; the virtues they celebrate are those of reason, humanism, and civilization. Why not take them as representative symptoms of our age rather than the more distressed and anxiety-ridden visions that we have hitherto been dealing with? Readers who are upset by the unfamiliar in art are often eager to clutch at the more traditional figures like Forster as proof after all that the less conventional artists are really funking_it, have lost their nerve amid the strains and stresses of life, and perhaps could not "write straight" in the first place. If your precious spirit of the age—so their argument might run if put in words—can permit one Forster, why can't other writers have the guts to be like him?

But perhaps matters are not so simple as the bluntness of this argument suggests, and certainly not that simple with Forster himself, who underneath his tranquil surface harbors some troubling depths.

In the first place, the spirit of an age is not a machine that automatically turns out figures cut to the same die. We have to think of it rather like a great and subtle current or wind, before which we must all bend, though we may tack about in different fashion depending upon our native equipment of sails and boat. Moreover, one thing that characterizes our time is its extraordinary and confused heterogeneity. Henry Adams, facing the future with melancholy uncertainty and seeking an image for our century to come, called it the Age of Multiplicity, to contrast it with the Age of Unity in the thirteenth century, the high point of the Middle Ages. Not only do we lack the overarching unity of a single religious faith, but we do not have the background of a common education or the shared inheritance of the classics that educated men once took for granted. There are not only two cultures, as C. P. Snow has told us, but literally dozens. A typical meeting of a university faculty today can sound like the clash of foreign tongues, each speaking from its own specialization with its particular assumptions, viewpoint, and very different body of information. Not only do scientists and humanists stand on different ground, but the scientists quarrel among themselves; sociologists may be at loggerheads with the economists, and psychologists with both; the schools of philosophers do not even condescend to try to understand each other; and even in mathematics, the universal language where unity of mind should be attained if anywhere, the quarrels among mathematicians provoked the great Poincaré to remark, "*Les hommes ne s'entendent pas parce qu'ils ne parlent pas la même langue.*" Our culture has brought down the tower of Babel from heaven to earth. The confusion causes suffering, for the failure of communication is always painful.

Yet all this heterogeneity does permit tranquil pockets here and there where the artist may follow his own line untouched by the current mode—a writer like Forster to pursue the conventional line of the novel, or a painter like Bonnard to celebrate the ancient rite of sensuous beauty undisturbed by modernism's clamor for the expressively ugly. Nevertheless, such quiet courses cannot be set without careful precautions about the general weather. If Forster has not sailed his craft into the eye of the hurricane, he always keeps an anxious eye upon it and lets us know very well whence the storm is blowing.

Forster's form is indeed traditional; and, even more, his tradition is an older one than the Naturalism on which the previous century, at least in France, set its intellectual seal. The English novel never succumbed to the Balzacian doctrine that fiction might become a surrogate form of social science and the novelist doggedly documenting his facts, a peer or colleague of the social scientist. More informal, diffuse and meandering, the English novel continued to retain its roots in the moralizing fiction of the eighteenth century. The contemporary novel was formed in large part in revolt against this leisurely tradition. Under the powerful influence of Flaubert novelists insisted upon tightness of form, carefully calculated structure, detachment, and objectivity. The young Henry James, for once in his life a rebel and an ideologist, denounced Victorian novels in a rather startling metaphor as "fluid puddings." No doubt, the English novel of the nineteenth century looks curiously old-fashioned beside the products of the Continent. It is always something of a shock to recall that Thackeray's *Vanity Fair* actually came out within a decade of *Madame Bovary* (1848 against 1857). Sauntering, casual, and wordy, Thackeray seems so old-fashioned and Flaubert so precise, analytic, and modern.

Yet, now that the revolt against the Victorian novel has had its day, we may be ready to admit that the device of commentary does permit a focus denied the novelist who aspires after an objectivity like the scientist's. The author can even let us know whether he likes or dislikes the character; and the responses of liking or disliking are usually what define our perceptions of people in life. The fact is—and this may come as a shock to some readers—Becky Sharp is real as a person in a way that Emma Bovary is not. True, we know some more intimate facts about Madame Bovary. We are inside her boredom, disgust, and troubled yearning, but she remains somehow vacuous at the center. She lives in the world's literature not so much as a person, but as an incarnation of "Bovarysme"—at once a set of attitudes and a social phenomenon.

The detachment of the writer may be of different kinds. We have already heard Samuel Beckett declare that there is no judgment in his writing. This is the writer at his last gasp, acknowledging the poverty of spirit that our time hides from itself, who knows that all stories have already been told and must disintegrate into fragments, and therefore who cannot pretend to set himself above his scanty material in order to

judge it. It is the detachment of humility. The Flaubertian detachment, on the other hand, is the writer's aspiration to be—
in the words of the younger James Joyce—invisible above and
behind his creation, surveying it like a god, indifferent, paring
his fingernails.

This ambition is audacious, but the audacity does in fact impose severe limitations upon the writer. He cannot make an
observation about his character like the one that Forster throws
out on Rickie in *The Longest Journey:* "Henceforth he deterio-
rates. . . . He remained conscientious and decent, but the
spiritual part of him proceeded to ruin." The word "spiritual"
sticks out oddly here. In talking about people in life we understand the word, though we may not use it, for this is the part
of the person that ultimately counts. But it is the part that falls
outside the ken of the Naturalistic writer. Strict objectivity con-
verts the person into an object, which analysis proceeds to divide into sets of drives, habits, and behavior, as if we were
dealing with a specimen in a laboratory. In the process the
spiritual center becomes lost or the very idea of it meaningless.
Despite his hatred of scientism, Flaubert's technique has its
philosophical roots in the Positivism of the nineteenth century.

Forster moralizes at the drop of a hat. Physical facts are not
pushed into the foreground, as in the American novelists. His
descriptions are more lyrical and blurred than cataloging and
precise. Physical actions, like a fight or scuffle, are dispatched
in a sentence or two in order to get to the talk or to the quick
moralizing paragraph, light, gracious, and probing. All quite in
the tradition of the middle-class English novel. But when we
turn to the content of this moralizing, how different Forster is
from his English predecessors! In Dickens, George Eliot, and
even the more lax and worldly Thackeray, good and bad stand
sharply arrayed against each other. Forster's vision, on the
other hand, is of good-and-bad together, one and inseparable.
Logic tells us that this cannot be so: good is good, and—if the
words mean anything at all—bad is the nongood, and never the

twain shall be asserted of the same thing upon pain of contradiction. But a priggish rationalism—despite Cambridge, despite
Bloomsbury—can never comprehend how the opposites penetrate each other in life. The Oriental is prepared by his culture
to understand this. Forster, out of his own moral experience and
insight, had arrived at the same understanding long before he
took passage to India.

True, on an abstract level, his values are unambiguous
enough, and they can even be neatly catalogued: individuality,
which has to be struggled for against convention and the herd,
and sometimes against one's own sluggish and cowardly shirk-
ing of self-understanding; decency and tolerance, but with
enough nerve to stand up against bullies; reasonableness, but a
reason that stands on good terms with imagination and instinct.
As values, these are unexceptionable. They are not only the
values which in the present state of things are the last hope of
preserving civilization, they are also what makes civilization
itself ultimately worthwhile. Unfortunately, they are easily pa-
rodied—by headmasters, officials of empire, and political orators—and therefore twisted out of sense. Unfortunately too, as
values, they are general, while the situations of life are always
individual and unique. The ideal is never actual. On the slopes
below its shining pinnacles lie muddle and existentialist anguish. Forster is neither a Pollyanna nor a Liberal orator because he knows that the best things in civilization, and indeed
civilization itself, are perched precariously over the abyss.
Around the clean well-lighted place the specters and goblins
will always lurk.

Do not be deceived because even when he tells us about
these goblins Forster can be most engaging and amusing. In
Howards End the Schlegels attend a concert. The music is
Beethoven's Fifth; the Andante has finished, and the family is
waiting for the Third Movement. Helen, the Romantic, tells
them here is the part where the goblins come; Tibby, a bit of
a prig and an aesthetic formalist, implores them to notice the

transitional passage on the drum. Then—but here we had best turn to Forster himself, who is one of the best writers at turning music into words:

The music started with a goblin walking quietly over the universe, from end to end. Others followed him. They were not aggressive creatures; it was not that that made them so terrible to Helen. They merely observed in passing that there was no such thing as splendour or heroism in the world. After the interlude of the elephants dancing, they returned and made the observation for the second time. Helen could not contradict them, for, once at all events, she had felt the same, and had seen the reliable walls of youth collapse. Panic and emptiness! Panic and emptiness! The goblins were right.

Her brother raised his finger: it was the transitional passage on the drum.

For, as if things were going too far, Beethoven took hold of the goblins and made them do what he wanted. He appeared in person. He gave them a little push, and they began to walk in major key instead of in minor, and then—he blew with his mouth and they were scattered! Gusts of splendour, gods and demi-gods contending with vast swords, colour and fragrance broadcast on the field of battle, magnificent victory, magnificent death! Oh, it all burst before the girl, and she even stretched out her gloved hands as if it was tangible. Any fate was titanic; any contest desirable; conqueror and conquered would alike be applauded by the angels of the utmost stars.

And the goblins—they had not really been there at all! They were only the phantoms of impulse and unbelief? One healthy human impulse would dispel them? Men like the Wilcoxes, or President Roosevelt, would say yes. Beethoven knew better. The goblins really had been there. They might return—and they did. It was as if the splendour of life might boil over and waste to steam and froth. In its dissolution one heard the terrible, ominous note, and a goblin, with increased malignity, walked quietly over the universe from end to end. Panic and emptiness! Panic and emptiness! Even the flaming ramparts of the world might fall.

Beethoven chose to make all right in the end. He built the ramparts up. He blew with his mouth for the second time, and again the goblins were scattered. He brought back the gusts of splendour, the heroism, the youth, the magnificence of life and death, and, amid the vast roarings of a superhuman joy, he led his Fifth Symphony to its conclusion. But the goblins were there. They could return. He had said so bravely, and that is why one can trust Beethoven when he says other things.

Panic and emptiness! And perhaps the worst we have to face is the panic of emptiness itself. Forster never sets his trumpets ringing at the summit of heaven; but allowing for the suitable differences, I think we can transcribe his words about Beethoven to apply to himself: because Forster knows that the goblins are always there, and that they can spring at any moment, we can trust him when he says other things.

I

The goblins may lurk in unexpected places, and the first that Forster encounters, surprisingly enough, is in Italy—a beautiful and seductive goblin, to be sure, but very unsettling to the British visitors with their middle-class money and their Protestant morality. The decent and proper British do not like to be reminded that the genteel fabric of what they call civilization is built upon the subsoil of our animal nature that can flare up at a moment in a kiss or a murder. The Englishman feels morally superior: his word is reliable in a way that the Italian's is not. Why then should he feel so uncomfortable in the latter's presence unless he were threatened by some inferiority of his own? However exact and exacting in his principles, the Englishman is muddled in his emotions; he suffers from an "undeveloped heart." His education may have done something for his head, but it has left his feelings quite puerile.

If Forster had no other point to make but this, he would still be among our more instructive moralists. The misunderstanding of the emotions—embedded in the popular language and elaborated in the technical works of philosophers and psychologists—is one of the more catastrophic parts of our culture. Passion is blind, we say; yes, but more often than not we will find the blind passion is one contaminated by some fanatical idea. And usually feelings are blind in those who are unused to live by them. On the other hand, would not the perfectly rational person without the appropriate feelings in a certain situation be among the blindest of human beings? We turn to the philosophers and are told that feelings are such things as "thrills, twinges, pangs, throbs, wrenches, itches, prickings, chills, glows, qualms, hankerings, curdlings, sinkings, tensions, gnawings and shocks." This is Cambridge speaking, in the person of Professor Gilbert Ryle, but a later and more plebeian Cambridge than the one Forster knew. What, one can't help wondering, is Professor Ryle feeling when he is not throbbing or wrenching or pricking or chilling? Is life just an absence of feeling between such spasms? We also recognize that our feelings may sometimes be muddled and sometimes clear, and the difference between the two is very important and sometimes not easily arrived at. Do I like or dislike a certain person? The answer may take me some time to come by. Twinges and throbs happen, and one is never less muddled or more clear than another; they are not the kind of thing that can be educated. But to the degree that our feelings can become clearer the heart can be educated. Usually life does the educating, and sometimes badly, because our culture does not take much of a hand at it. But if civilization had to choose between educating the feelings or the intellect, Forster holds that it would be wiser to take the first.

Fortunately, in Forster, Italy does triumph as the summons to life for some of the English. There they discover the emotions that had been almost strangled out of existence by the stodginess and pretense back home. But the awakening is also painful, it can bring dread and consternation, for it "may lead to a self-knowledge and to that king of terrors—Light." Some people are too frightened to meet that terror, and like Charlotte Bartlett, the tiresome spinster in *A Room with a View*, have closed the doors of life forever. To be open to life is more fearful than to sink back into the protective jail of convention and self-righteous moralizing. Even the lovely and charming heroine Lucy Honeychurch (though she is saved at the end) hovers over this precipice, at the bottom of which the denial of the body and its instincts is also a flight from self-knowledge.

In all of this Forster is in agreement with D. H. Lawrence. And though he does not, like Lawrence, roar, shout, and stamp to make himself heard, the message sounds just as persistently. Rural England will do as well as Italy as the background for the conflict between the atrophied forms of civilization and the life of the emotions. *The Longest Journey* is set in various places in England, but all ultimately revolve around Wiltshire and the Stonehenge country; and now the carrier of the spirit, because he dwells within the body and upon the earth, is the young countryman Stephen, half-brother to the crippled hero Rickie. Rough and unpolished, Stephen roams the countryside, sleeping out on the ground when he has a mind to and getting drunk on occasion at the local pub. He is an embarrassing problem for his civilized betters, who take out their embarrassment in their usual fashion by swindling him. But only through this unregenerate fellow does the unfortunate Rickie find his few moments of salvation before dismally losing them.

Rickie had made an unfortunate marriage, and we watch his spiritual deterioration under the pressures of an overbearing wife. But when he discovers Stephen is his illegitimate half-brother he revives enough to flout respectability and acknowledge him openly. Roaming with Stephen, he discovers the comradeship of the earth. (Stephen is whole and healthy, Rickie crippled; and let us remember that salvation, from its Latin root, means health.) But Rickie is still priggish, and his salvation precarious; and he is promptly disillusioned when his brother gets riotously drunk. In the one final gesture of heroism left him, he is killed rescuing Stephen from an onrushing train. Dying in utter despair, he tells his aunt that his revolt was wrong and she was right when she warned him: *"People don't matter, conventions do. Beware of the earth. We are not here for anything great. Only for the small things of convention."* If one wanted Forster's anti-motto, these words would do, since they express for him the final and absolute death of the spirit. For Rickie to die accepting them is a tragedy worse than his physical death. Forster does not share the spirit of violence of some other moderns, but his imagination is nevertheless capable of some very quietly brutal strokes.

This tragedy has been consummated against the background of the Stonehenge country, which Forster regards as the real center of England: "Here is the heart of our island: the Chilterns, the North Downs, the South Downs radiate hence. The fibres of England unite in Wiltshire, and did we condescend to worship her, here we would erect our national shrine." Indeed two shrines—the greatest monuments of British architecture—already confront each other across a few miles of this plain: the Salisbury cathedral and the ruins of Stonehenge. The one is the elaborate edifice of civilization, the other the work of prehistory, made by unknown men for unknown purposes, and which in its present disarray has the stark power of a piece of abstract sculpture. It tells a good deal about our time that some of its artists should prefer the latter to the former. Forster would not go anywhere near that far, but he does see the history of Britain as flowing backward to the primeval soil around this ruin. Before there were Saxons, Romans, and Normans, there were the mysterious builders of Stonehenge; and before them, there were the trees—ash and holly, yew and juniper—which modern civilization has been systematically cutting down.

In his long life Forster came at that turn of time when he could witness the forward wave of frantic urbanization. We who have come behind that wave can only speculate what its first shock was like for sensitive men and women. Forster saw the cities begin to march into the suburbs, the suburbs into the countryside, old houses razed, and their meadowlands and woods disappear into housing developments. His regret for the passing of so much loveliness is not the pique of a cantankerous and sentimental conservative. In his political views Forster was a liberal, and in fact a socialist of sorts, and always a stalwart partisan of democracy. People have to be housed, and therefore cities and suburbs must spread. Modern industry, which provides us with so many more goods for so many more people now alive, cannot be wiped out by fiat. The trouble with our social problems is that they run afoul of the inevitable good-and-bad which makes up human existence and which Forster never forgets. These first waves of urbanization were also the spearhead of an advancing tide that would inundate and wash away the world he had known.

In this uneasiness at industrial civilization Forster is, once again, on the same side as Lawrence, and accordingly the two will be conveniently filed under the pigeonhole of Romanticism. The label is not incorrect, but it may serve as an excuse for thoughtlessness. For the fact is that we today, a century later, still do not understand the Romantic movement in its real depth and greatness. It may seem odd to bring up the whole subject of Romanticism in connection with a mind like Forster's that is on one side so Augustan and rational; but precisely this clarity of his intelligence should help us to divest the subject of some of its usual confusions.

For the popular mind, Romanticism evokes a picture of ruined castles against a storm-tossed sky, of colored lights and incense, and, generally, irrational passions and impossible aspirations. For the highbrow, on the other hand, T. S. Eliot is supposed to have administered the *coup de grace* to Romanticism as a sloppy appeal to feeling and sensibility. No doubt, the Romantic impulse had declined into the blur of Edwardian and Georgian poetry, and Eliot was justified in restoring the claims of neoclassicism both to set standards for precision in the writing of verse and to fill a major place in the history of English literature. But as for the deeper vision that troubles a Blake, or

Wordsworth, or Hölderlin, that is something that Eliot seems never to have explored intellectually. Yet curiously enough it is this vision that is still poetically at work in *The Waste Land.* Eliot the ideologist is one thing, Eliot the poet another; and the poet belongs, as Blake would say, to the devil's party—in this case to the Romantics. For in *The Waste Land,* which still stands as the poem of our historical period, the blight upon the land is a blight upon man, and the death of the spirit is experienced as a death of nature, and vice versa.

And not only this poem, but the great part of modern literature, still stands within the orbit of questions that disturbed the Romantics. They were worried whether man was not about to take the fateful step of separating himself too far from nature. Not so long ago Marxist-minded critics could sneer at the Romantics as privileged gentlemen recoiling at the vulgarity of the Industrial Revolution. Today, when we are sunk in the morass of industrial pollution, we are almost ready to believe—in line with ancient wisdom—that poets can be prophets. That is confirmation on the more palpable level of external fact. The inner message of the Romantics may turn out to be even more prophetic, though there we have hardly begun to read them carefully. The first philosopher engaged in thinking through the Romantic vision is Heidegger, who reminds us always that his thought is only at its beginning. Blake, Wordsworth, and Hölderlin all had ecclesiastical ties of one kind or another; yet they drew their real spiritual sustenance from something outside the Church. They were the first generation to stand outside the Church in this way. Perhaps that is what provokes the antagonism of Eliot in his role of Anglican polemicist. However, another churchman, Cardinal Newman, took a very different and, I think, shrewder view of the matter. The Romantic poets, Newman argued, might be used as a spur to revive the spirit of the nation. For did not these poets seek to renew the primary feelings of human nature and thereby our sense of our ties with nature? And must not these be awakened if there were to be any feeling at all to flow through the channels of the Church? A people that has ceased to feel about nature will cease to feel about religion. Only through the renewal of wonder can man surrender to the sense of the sacred. "Poetically man dwells upon the earth," said Hölderlin. This statement is not a pretty "literary" aphorism, but literally true. The substance of man's life on earth is poetical, and if this poetry were to disappear altogether into the prose of science, we should have lost the meaning of life.

The conflict of feeling and reason may look like a minor worry when we set it beside the great social upheavals now going on in the world. Yet that indefatigable journalist Arthur Koestler tells us that the war between the "two brains"—the cerebral intelligence on the one hand, and on the other the central nervous system through which the emotions operate—is the gravest problem mankind now faces. Mr. Koestler has been through the mill and experienced most of the modern convulsions at first hand, so we ought to trust him to have his eye turned toward the real sources of trouble. And this division within human nature he thinks to be our most serious trouble because it is what lies behind all our wars and violence. Man's higher and lower brains move in tandem, and one may provoke the worst in the other: the aggressions of our tribal nature, for example, drive us to make war for abstractions. Mr. Koestler's hoped-for solution, however, is on the side of technical reason. Chemistry, he tells us, must come up some day with "harmonizers," which will put the two parts of us together in peace. Where Forster would educate the heart, Koestler would put it to sleep with pills.

On the one occasion when Forster's urbane and civilized voice is raised into something like a scream, it is the machine that provokes him. This happens in an early story, "The Machine Stops," which has become a classic in that gallery of horror known as science fiction. For a man not overly preoccupied with science, Forster is a very accurate prophet in 1911 of the technology that has already arrived or is on the way in: indirect lighting so perfected that one cannot tell the source of the light; television in every room so that the inhabitants never need leave their cells to communicate with each other (flesh-and-blood contact, like the body itself, has come to mean little for these people); universal air travel to any spot on the globe, so that one place is no different from another and there is no reason to travel. Air conditioning enables these people to live underground so that they never walk the earth or look up at the stars. They can see stars on their television screens, and this is enough for them—as it was for many New Yorkers a few years ago when they preferred to see an eclipse of the moon on TV rather than lean their heads out the windows and see the real thing.

Technology as the means of humanizing the world has here been brought to its peak in a thoroughly denaturalized world. Nowadays we talk a lot about "dehumanization," and more often than not a little carelessly. Since we have been involved through this book with the ambiguities of Humanism, it is necessary to insist on this point: Technology does not, strictly speaking, dehumanize the world since it seeks to replace nature with human artifacts. A completely humanized world would be one from which all natural objects would be banished. And if we did not like such an environment, it would be only because of some residue of nature left in ourselves. In Forster's story all of the service machines have to be controlled by one gigantic computer-like device, the form of forms, the Prime Mover in this completely air-conditioned world: the Machine. Only the Machine really lives, and the people have become dead corpuscles circulating in its veins. At last, however, the machine falters and breaks down. Amid universal panic and destruction some people reach the earth and see the stars. Forster tells us that this story was his personal response to some of the more heavenly utopias of H. G. Wells. Personal as the tone may be, the logic behind the story is unexceptionable, and carries a very pointed lesson for us now. So long as we think that the solution of the problems technology has brought must be purely technological, then we are involved in coordinating and subordinating machines to machines; and so are already on our way to building The Machine, any break in whose complex network could mean disaster.

Goblins? Yes, they inhabit Forster's world; and once we get used to them, our ears become attuned to those minor chords, never trumpeted at us but persistently there, that echo behind his calm and equable voice. Usually his novels move toward some reconciliation that attempts to put the broken pieces together. But however things may seem to move toward a final harmony, the notes of the negative—of defeat without redemption, or renunciation before unshakable human limitations— also sound, sometimes all the more disturbing for their quietness. We have already noticed, apropos of *The Longest Journey*, that in its own way Forster's imagination can be as brutal as any modern writer's. A more subtle and oblique stroke is dealt at the conclusion of *Howards End* (1910). Margaret Schlegel has married Mr. Wilcox, and the pair have settled down in Howards End, the old country house around which the inner life of the novel has turned. The Schlegels are sensitive and cultured; the Wilcoxes sturdy, energetic, and practical, but also insensitively hypocritical—victims of "the undeveloped heart" that, for Forster, is the shortcoming of the British middle class. The Schlegels provide the poetry, the Wilcoxes the prose, of existence, and here in the light of Forster's motto for the novel, "Only connect . . .," the poetry and the prose seem at last to have been joined.

But have they? Years before, the former Mrs. Wilcox had indicated just before her death that she wanted Margaret to have Howards End. Wilcox had set aside the request, persuading himself with very convenient if unconscious hypocrisy that this last testament was the rambling of a dying woman. Now, as both families are assembled at the end, a chance word from one of the Wilcoxes lets the forgotten cat out of the bag. Margaret questions her husband after the others have gone, and he acknowledges calmly—for he sees nothing wrong about it—that he ignored the dying request.

This brief exchange drops in near the very last page, and so casually that it might almost pass unnoticed. Both families, Schlegels and Wilcoxes, have gone through personal tragedy and should have emerged from the purifying catharsis with some deeper vision. But about his own behavior Wilcox, who has been dealt perhaps the harshest blows, remains as blind as ever. Decent and reliable as he thinks himself, he cannot see that he did a grave wrong to his dead and to his living wife. A shiver passes over Margaret: "Something shook her life in its inmost recesses." The hand of a dead woman has touched her life from beyond the grave. But this shiver is also a spasm of horror at her husband: on a point like this he and she will never communicate. Their marriage will no doubt become what convention calls a happy one, but its happiness will always be bound by this absolute limit beyond which they cannot really meet. So Margaret, the wiser one, accepting these limits and not even trying to explain, reassures him: "Nothing has been done wrong."

Another modern writer might have wrung his hands here and declaimed solemnly about the ultimate failure of communication between two human beings. But the point is just as devastating when it slides in so quietly. The isolation is as absolute as if Forster had employed the gross physical metaphor of a Samuel Beckett and enclosed the pair in separate jars or bottles on the stage. Perhaps because we have grown more obtuse since 1910 Beckett has to make his point more coarsely.

II

But the most unsettling goblins are to be encountered in India, for which the Italian ones are only a scanty preparation.

Much as Italians may upset British composure, Italy itself is a beautiful part of that classical Mediterranean civilization that the Englishman has to remember, however reluctantly, as the source of his own. But in India even the remotely familiar landmarks have gone. The presuppositions of life are so different that the Westerner begins to look at his own values from a different angle and wonder whether his own civilization may not be parochial and one-sided.

Between *Howards End* and his next—and as it turned out his last—novel, *A Passage to India* (1924), fourteen years intervene. They were not idle years; there were essays, sketches, reportage, in which we notice the mood often becoming more caustic and somber. But most of all there was the war, which for him and his generation marked the end of the world he had known. He would retain forever after as an image of the menace lurking below the tranquil surface of things the remembrance of a bright morning in August 1914, when, still lying in bed, he heard the milkman's voice come quietly up from below: "We've gone in." The aftermath of victory proved full of new confusions along with the old stupidities. The nations of Europe, he tells us, are in disarray, and time is running out. Across the Channel the French poet Valéry, whose sense of security had also been shaken to the core, intoned a warning and possibly a valedictory on the West: "We too are mortal." Less portentous, Forster's essays echo the same anxiety about a civilization that has gone shaky. Such is the background which he leaves behind to journey to the East for the scene and material of his last novel.

His journey to the East is very different from Hermann Hesse's. The latter seeks salvation by immersion in ancient Oriental wisdom. Forster does not try to lose himself in an alien civilization. Besides, India is too formless, vast, and incomprehensible by the norms of Western humanism. Forster is English to the core (though he has the extraordinary knack of walking around the Englishman to observe how he appears to other people), and English he must remain. The intellectual clarity of Cambridge and Bloomsbury do not prepare one for the mazes of Eastern metaphysics.

He is, however, much more of an observer than Hesse. Only ancient and legendary India appear in Hesse, for whom the journey to the East is ultimately a voyage of the mind; but Forster is very much aware that east of Suez there are millions of human beings whose ways are strange to us. That fact is enough to provoke his curiosity, which is strong. (In an essay on Proust, he has remarked that curiosity and despair are the hallmarks of the modern spirit.) It is also an ambiguous curiosity, springing from some deeper wells of the unconscious than his critical intelligence might acknowledge. India laps around his story, and seeps in through a hundred rills and inlets. He does not want to keep it out, of course, for the business of the novelist is to remain open to his material, but he lets in far more than we were led to expect at the beginning, and more perhaps than he had expected when he began to write the book.

He is not, at first, attracted by the Hindus. Professor Godbole is a mask so bland and remote that we feel there may be nothing, or at best merely a gray wisp of substance, behind the imperturbability. Forster prefers the Moslems as companions, for they are at least a little closer and more comprehensible to the Westerner. The Moslem doctor Aziz is a vivid and captivating young man, and in his quick feelings and rapid changes of mood, he is a distant cousin of the spontaneous Italians in Forster's earlier fiction. He is also a true Oriental, complex and aristocratic in spirit, and possibly the best portrait of a non-Westerner ever written by a European writer. The one human meeting place here between East and West is the friendship of this young doctor with Fielding, the British schoolmaster. The latter is in early middle age, hard-bitten but not jaundiced by experience, and with a lively and sympathetic curiosity about people, particularly the Indians. Decent and intelligent, Fielding is the good Englishman within the officious Anglo-Indian colony. But intelligence itself may be an obstacle to grasping the reality of India: "All that he had learned in England and Europe was an assistance to him, and helped him towards clarity, but clarity prevented him from experiencing something else." Is the author speaking of himself here? Of part of himself, yes, but the other part is the artist far more sensitive than his own clear-minded and likable schoolmaster. And even to the solid Fielding something happens through the exposure to India, for in the later pages we find him saying things that we could not imagine from him when he first appears.

The subtlest vehicle for Forster's vision, however, is the old lady, Mrs. Moore. The figure of the aged female as the possessor of some arcane wisdom beyond that of other mortals is not new in Forster's novels. The first Mrs. Wilcox in *Howards End,* hemmed in by her hard-headed and practical family, is in touch with some chthonic mystery that altogether exceeds their narrow grasp. But she fades into the background, a vague shadow who seems to have much more effect on the lives of those around her after her death. Mrs. Moore, on the contrary, steps forward into the light, though somewhat on the sidelines. Plot, be it remembered, is a subordinate element in Forster: "Oh dear, yes, the novel tells a story," he remarks in his *Aspects of the Novel,* confessing with a groan that the novelist has to carry this burden in order to say the things he wants to. Mrs. Moore is not at the center of the plot, nor does she launch the crucial actions; but all the plot flows past and around her, and what happens to her in the process is the story within the story of the novel.

She appears first as an idealistic but not particularly dogmatic Christian, who as she has grown older has found herself mentioning God in her conversation more often than formerly. On her first evening in India she takes a walk, enters a mosque, and makes a warm friend of Aziz, whom she has encountered there, by remarking casually, "God is here." Later that night, going to hang up her cloak, she finds the top of the peg occupied by a wasp. She does not disturb it:

There he clung, asleep, while jackals in the plain bayed their desires and mingled with the percussion of drums.

"Pretty dear," said Mrs. Moore to the wasp. He did not wake, but her voice floated out, to swell the night's uneasiness.

Back home in England the wasp would have been swatted. But in India it belongs to that vast circle of Being that includes without discrimination bats, rats, birds, insects, jackals—and man too, but not quite in the exclusive pew accorded to him by Christianity or Western humanism. Break this circle at any point and it closes together again. Man is only a part of it and not its master; at length he acquiesces, and learns to let Being be. Wasps too are creatures of God. Unknown to herself, she has taken her first steps beyond the tidy middle-class Christianity in which she was brought up.

These steps lead her at last not to serenity, but to a dreadful vision. To please his English friends Dr. Aziz has organized a trip to the Marabar Caves, which are famous for their echoes. The excursion ends in disaster: an English girl, distraught by heat and fatigue, falsely accuses Aziz of assault, and there follow his arrest, trial, riots, and civil commotion between the English authorities and the natives. The Marabar incident thus provides the fulcrum point of the outer plot, but also of the inner story, for something much more quiet and frightening happens to Mrs. Moore. She visits only the first cave: the crowd, smell, and the heat make her fight her way out. She will sit outside and let the others, who are younger, continue their exploration. But outside there is no rest: she is assailed by the echo she heard within the cave. Once again, Forster's aural imagination is splendid at transmuting sounds into words; but here the sounds are not musical, and not even the discords of atonality could mimic them, for they are noises beyond the contrivances of man:

There are some exquisite echoes in India, there is the whisper round the dome at Bijapur; there are the long, solid sentences that voyage round the air at Mandu, and return unbroken to their creator. The echo in a Marabar cave is not like these, it is entirely devoid of distinction. Whatever is said, the same monotonous noise replies, and quivers up and down the walls until it is absorbed into the roof. "Boum" is the sound, as far as the human alphabet can express it, or "bou-oum", or "ou-boum"—utterly dull. Hope, politeness, the blowing of a nose, the squeak of a boot, all produce "boum".

Now, resting on a camp chair, she hears the echo's meaning with her inner ear:

Coming at a moment when she chanced to be fatigued, it had managed to murmur, "Pathos, piety, courage—they exist, but are identical, and so is filth. Everything exists, nothing has value." If one had spoken vileness in that place, or quoted lofty poetry, the comment would have been the same—"ou-boum". If one had spoken with the tongues of angels and pleaded for all the unhappiness and misunderstanding in the world, past, present, and to come, for all the misery men must undergo, whatever their opinion and position, and however much they dodge or bluff—it would amount to the same, the serpent would descend and return to the ceiling. Devils are of the North, and poems can be written about them, but no one could romanticize the Marabar because it robbed infinity and eternity of their vastness, the only quality that accommodates them to mankind.

Her thoughts turn to religion as she had known it: ". . . poor little talkative Christianity, and she knew that all its divine word from 'Let there be Light' to 'It is finished' only amounted to 'boum'."

"Everything exists, nothing has value." Nihilism speaks here, not with the passionate tones of the Existentialist rebel or the social revolutionary, but with a voice more frightening because it is quieter. We usually think of visions as grand things, but there is no grandeur to what Mrs. Moore has heard in the cave. "She had come to that state where the horror of the universe and its smallness are both visible at the same time—the twilight of the double vision in which so many elderly people are involved." Could it be that the flamboyant gestures and Byronic attitudes of some Nihilists are an escape from the smallness of their final truth? Forster presses the point relentlessly: "The abyss may also be petty, the serpent of eternity made of maggots." Nor has her vision made Mrs. Moore a more attractive person to those around her. She has lost interest in whether her son marries or how Aziz's trial turns out; old and tired, she wants only her deck of cards for patience, and she asks of the young people merely that they ship her back home. She gets her wish, but never sees England again. She dies at sea and is buried in another India—the Indian Ocean this time. We are not told that she has heard any other voice before her death that would redeem the Marabar echo.

How far we have come from the goblins that pranced through the last movement of Beethoven's Fifth! Beethoven had captured them in the exquisite toils of Western harmony, and humanized them, and in the end that harmony must prevail and the major chords of triumph boom out. The Marabar echoes do not submit to any system of harmony. The earlier goblins told of panic and emptiness. But against those one can muster the shining virtue of courage and take arms; heroism is possible; and if the heroism fails, there is the grandeur of tragedy, the most sublime art of the West. But for ultimate Nihilism tragedy is impossible, since it depends on the illusion that man has value and his defeat is pitiable. The Marabar echoes, however, are a fact. What these sounds echo in human life is also a fact: not the whole of life or even, hopefully, its final upshot, but still a part that cannot be suppressed. No amount of sanitation can scrub it away. No social program will ever eliminate it completely. No philosophy will ever persuade us that it is merely the semblance of some greater good. But if India has never ceased to hear and live with the Marabar echo, it has also heard another note that life can strike, one almost as perplexing to Western ears, but which Forster too has been sensitive enough to catch.

Disaster has passed and Aziz is freed. But his friendship with Fielding becomes plagued by the inevitable misunderstandings between East and West. They are talking about poetry and religion, and Fielding now utters the words that we would never have expected from him earlier. Then he had shocked and puzzled Aziz and his Mohammedan friends by announcing that he was an atheist. For them religion is a matter of feeling, love of friends, family and Islam, and only a wicked or hostile man—and Fielding is neither—would declare that he does not believe in God. And only a silly man or pedant—which, again, Fielding is not—would think religious belief is a factual hypothesis on which we must have convincing evidence. Now, however, Fielding says that his ambition for Aziz, who dabbles in poetry, was that the latter should have become a religious poet. Aziz is puzzled by the inconsistency:

"Why, when you yourself are an atheist?"

"There is something in religion that may not be true, but has not yet been sung."

"Explain in detail."

"Something that the Hindus have perhaps found."

"Let them sing it."

"Hindus are unable to sing."

Forster himself goes on to sing something of it for them; and in one chapter (XXXIII) he spreads his wings and soars beyond what Cambridge and Bloomsbury would permit.

We are in Northern India, hundreds of miles from the Marabar Caves, and the occasion is a festival celebrating the birth of Krishna. Music blares from several sources—a "braying banging crooning melted into a single mass." Sweat and incense choke the air; children dart out and dance. Everything is muddle, a frustration of form and reason as the Westerner understands these. The opposites embrace and are one: music and noise, incense and sweat, the sublime and the ridiculous. The holy of holies produces not solemnity but a holiday mood. The celebrants throw red powder at each other, let butter slide down their noses and into their mouths, prance around with infants in their arms as so many separate incarnations of the God. Good taste is sacrificed, but the ceremony achieves— Forster tells us—what Christianity has shirked: the inclusion of merriment and joy. Amid all this fun the God is born, and the joy of this birth must be not for man alone but for everything in the universe, "birds, caves, railways, and the stars." Salvation must be universal and democratic. All matter and all spirit must participate in it. "Everything exists, nothing has value," whispered the Marabar. To which the festival of Krishna answers: "Everything exists and everything has value."

The Marabar echoes and the gay tumult of Krishna's birth— these are the opposite and necessary poles of the religious vision. Neither can eliminate the other. Nihilism can never be refuted or banished, but hopefully it can be incorporated into some further vision. That is why the great religions, even when they speak of the light and ecstasy, also present us with a picture of human life so unsparing that it makes progressives blanch.

Forster stands outside this vision. He is sensitive to it, he can take note that it is there, and he can even, as we have seen, beautifully record parts of it; but he cannot enter into it. The Christianity of vicars and maiden aunts that he had been exposed to in his youth had done its permanent damage. "Poor talkative Christianity"—that was all he knew of it. A civilization had let its God die amid preoccupations of commerce, industrial progress, corsets, and antimacassars; and Mrs. Grundy and Mrs. Parker presided over the demise. The historical task that presented itself to Forster's generation was to escape from this cramp and desiccation, and its representative book was Lytton Strachey's *Eminent Victorians,* in which the religion of grandparents and parents was portrayed as priggish, fantastical, or fanatic—or all three at once.

It is a marvel that Forster has been able to go so far in meeting the transcendental spirit of the Orient. There is in fact a feeling of catharsis that one takes away from this novel about India. The author has been at or at least near the boundaries of life, and has come back purged of illusions and more detached. The maturity of middle age has set in. Compared with his earlier books, things and people are seen more in the round and consequently a little more deflated, and yet, miraculously, there is no loss of vigor. Still, cathartic as this experience of India may have been, it seems to have left Forster all the more deeply perplexed by the Europe of the 1920s.

He was not to write another novel after *A Passage to India*. He had heard the Marabar whisper, and henceforth he could not indulge himself in the illusions of fiction. That is the dramatic way of putting it, and it might very well be the long-run truth of the matter. But the tapestry of creation is woven out of so many threads from the artist's personal life that it is pointless to speculate which one went wrong to create the snarl. Forster himself commented dryly: "My world had vanished and I could not write of it anymore." The middle classes (which were his subject matter) continued to exist in England until 1939 at least, but it is a mistake to identify a writer's world simply with his economic class. The world we live in is a more total and internal matter of which external arrangements of society form only a part. Some sense of security, known before 1914, had vanished from England. Cambridge would persist always as a remembered ideal (and in the last years of his life he moved there). But those shining promises of intelligence and the good life which it told of in the early years of the century had been driven back into the academic cloister by the rough currents of the age. Forster has not explained in detail why his world had vanished; we can gather only bits and pieces from his later essays. It remains a mystery why an author at the height of his powers should give up writing the kind of thing he does most beautifully.

But it may not be pointless to speculate what a novel of his would be like if it had taken its point of departure from the vision of the Marabar Caves. He has told us about that vision, as it struck one old English lady, but he has not shown us the vision itself as it might emanate darkly from the center of a whole literary work. Perhaps that cannot be done. The work we have examined that comes closest, Faulkner's *The Sound and the Fury*, is involved in the paradoxical struggle of simultaneously digesting and rejecting its material: every small connecting link in its intricate structure is a stroke of meaning against the meaninglessness that is ultimately to be expressed. But if the Marabar cannot be at the center, then at least a little closer to it, as the explicit tone of the whole? Such a work, however we try to imagine it, would go against the grain of Forster's temperament and talent. He could not write with that high-strung tension of Faulkner that brings us to the edge of desperation. Nor would he have been capable of the physical coarseness of Joyce that in the Nighttown episode of *Ulysses* can drag his characters into the no man's land between the animal and human. The hallmarks of Forster's genius—and they are the limits that are also his power—are modesty and moderation, which forbid the spirit of excess to which other moderns are driven. He is too civilized to transgress, even in the name of art, the limits that his sense of civilization imposes.

But what of that hypercivilized yet subtly more destructive spiritual violence of a Proust?[1] Forster considered him the representative modern writer because Proust's great novel is an "epic of curiosity and despair," and these are the qualities that most characterize our age. The two go together, for Proust as for us, and the curiosity leads to despair. Restless to know ourselves, we throw away tradition and limits, and the results are not always comforting. Ultimately Proust's becomes a mon-

1. Proust is not given separate treatment in this book, but he is in the background throughout.

strous and demoniacal world, in which nobody is spared, and even the adored and adorable grandmother who had sustained the hero through childhood and youth is at last revealed as a flushed and stupefied old woman. Time, the sovereign reality, disfigures our bodies and deforms our characters, and where time leaves off, Proust's relentlessly analytic curiosity takes over and pulverizes the remnants into dust. The complex rituals of civilization are preserved, but in fact they only enhance the horror like elaborately formal steps in a danse macabre.

Forster is no more capable of this spiritual excess than of the physical violence of Faulkner. He has a healthy curiosity, yes, but his modest and self-effacing talents must keep this in balance like everything else. And what of despair? We are told a good deal, perhaps too much, about Proust's despair and its sources. But what do we know of Forster's? The Marabar passage could not be contrived merely by a skillful juggling of words; somewhere or other in his life its author must have touched the bottom depths. But Forster falls back on British reserve and the classical sense of limits. Even the Marabar echoes must be kept in their place in the balance of things.

Here again, the amiable surface is deceptive. His tone seems always so cozy and intimate, he seems so to be taking us altogether into his confidence. He has rebuked writers like Joseph Conrad and T. S. Eliot for being too forbidding and setting barriers between themselves and the reader. But he himself is not quite so confiding as he seems, and on some matters he drops a discreet silence. Of Eliot, particularly, Forster has remarked that he is among those writers who have seen something terrible in life, hint at it repeatedly in their writings, but do not tell us plainly what it is. The observation might apply to Forster himself: he tells us that the terror is there, but he prefers to keep it at a respectful distance.

In this respect he suggests comparison with the poet Robert Frost. For decades Frost's poetry had kindled little warmth in the avant-garde. The homeliness of his language and the simplicity of his traditional forms seemed to place him outside the adventurous and exploring spirit of modernism, and the poems had been recited so often in schoolrooms that they seemed to be made up of commonplaces that we had already heard. Time taught us to read him differently, and to learn that the poet does not have to howl in order to acknowledge the Furies. Of the first and last things of the human spirit the poet may speak softly, even with reserve, provided he speaks distinctly. Spiritual excess and the audacity of violence should be allowable to, as indeed they can only be carried off by, a few very exceptional geniuses. Today when so many minor talents are shouting from the roofs at the top of their lungs the terrible thing in life they have seen (which often turns out quite trite on examination), we may begin to appreciate the quieter voices that keep something secret. Frost's beautiful lines about himself might very well be spoken of Forster:

> As I came to the edge of the woods,
> Thrush music—hark!
> Now if it was dusk outside,
> Inside it was dark. . . .
>
> Far in the pillared dark
> Thrush music went—
> Almost like a call to come in
> To the dark and lament.
>
> But no, I was out for stars:
> I would not come in.
> I mean not even if asked,
> And I hadn't been.

It is enough if the writer has told us the darkness is there so that henceforth we shall never be altogether unprepared if we should stumble into it. He need not, unasked, plunge himself and us into the brambles and underbrush where not only the straight way, but any way at all, may be lost. There will be others enough to do that.

10. Myth or the Museum?

Exuberance is beauty.

—BLAKE

I have the mind of a grocer's clerk.

—JOYCE

James Joyce as a possible counterexample within the folds of modern art! Even to suggest the possibility might be taken by some fervent Joyceans as an act of *lèse majesté* against the figure who was for a whole generation a hero of the avant-garde and has now been enshrined, in the current phrase, as one of "the sacred untouchables" of the modern movement. At least Forster is conventional in form and language, but Joyce is among the boldest and wildest innovators in both. Yet in a deeper sense he may be far more traditional than the Englishman. And before we reject the proposal as willful paradox, perhaps we had better listen to some words from the Master himself.

Joyce was not always happy with his adulators, and in one candid and sarcastic remark to his young friend Nino Frank in the later Paris years he managed to say a great deal about them and about himself: "Ce serait bien drôle que je fasse un petit roman mondain à la Bourget. . . . Ils seraient bien attrapés, hein?" He was enough of a rogue that, given the time, he might have turned out a tidy social novel in the conventional manner of Paul Bourget for no other purpose than to catch his interpreters out. The exegetes would certainly have been put out of work. The criticism of Joyce does tend to become exegesis, and

312

often the interpreter gets buried under the exegete. Joyce conspired with this tendency, being ingenious enough to provide intricacies sufficient to feed even the most Talmudic appetite. At the same time he was uneasy that underneath the vast debris of exegesis the simple and ordinary and elemental things he was trying to say would get lost. In this jibe of a casual moment he has put his finger on the heart of his own mystery—the discrepancy between the complexity of his means and the simplicity of his substance—which we have to explore now. In the process we may learn that Joyce, despite all appearances, is really not captured by the easy formulas of modernism though he brings us back in the end to something most problematic and troubling in the modern condition.

We were lucky, years ago as very young people, to have read *Ulysses* while it was still banned and the book had to be finished in a few days to be returned to its jealously possessive owner. Without benefit of commentaries, and without the dubious luxury to crawl through the text at a snail's pace hunting out allusions and parsing for symbols, we were nevertheless drawn forward by the enormous energy and vitality of Joyce's creation. Quagmires of obscurity may have lurked after that first reading, but they could wait for explication; they did not stand in the way of the overall impression of power that the book asserted over all such hindrances. How different the fashion in which students now encounter *Ulysses!* The book may be allotted to a separate course of a whole semester; the chapters assigned one by one, minutely dissected, and the mountainous secondary literature explored. Scholarship may be advanced, but something of life goes out of the whole process. Instead of swallowing the book hot and raw, as in the end it has to be, it is tediously added up as a sum of intricate parts. The enormous bulk of Joycean criticism has had the effect of vastly exaggerating the difficulties of *Ulysses.* No doubt, it bristles with difficulties for the minute scholar; but we are talking now of reading it not as a scholarly chore but as a work of art. The plain fact is that *Ulysses* is a novel and can be read as such. That is, it can be read as a single story—the massive progress of a day through time—and the parts of this narrative can be held together in a single grasp by the reader's imagination. For, years after that first reading, with the commentaries read, the allusions and symbols long since ferreted out, and the intricate cross references plotted, is it not the power of that first impression we come back to? The robustness, energy, and vitality of Joyce's genius persist after all the technical eccentricities and innovations have been taken in stride.

Robustness, energy, exuberance—these are not the qualities we think of as distinctive of the modernist movement. They are, however, the qualities that lead one to compare Joyce with older writers like Rabelais. Surely there could hardly be a figure more antithetical to the moderns than the towering humorist of the Renaissance, bursting with blood and guts, who gave unbridled expression to the Humanism of his period. In the course of three centuries that energetic Humanism of the Renaissance was to become wracked with anxieties. In comparison with its robustness the modern spirit—whatever its other profundities—strikes us as thin and exiguous. For his mordant and coarse vigor, for the destructive and self-destructive quality of his imagination, Joyce has been compared with Swift; for his willful and ebullient eccentricity with Sterne. And as for language itself, in *Ulysses* English attains a richness of surfeit that it had not known since the Elizabethans. Such comparisons must of course be taken for what they are worth; Joyce is Joyce, and therefore not to be captured under any preestablished likeness. But the fact that we are led to make such comparisons should be sign enough that Joyce sticks out oddly among the moderns.

In the 1930s, when he was vigorously polemicizing for Christianity, T. S. Eliot made out a case for Joyce as a traditional and Catholic writer. At the time the judgment looked as if it might have been sectarian in its motives; but these polemic interests aside, Eliot's critical judgment seems to me to be right. To be sure, Joyce is a rebel against the Church, but the nature of his rebellion is such that it still encloses his sensibility and imagination within the Catholic framework. The provincialism of Ireland, as it turned out, was an advantage to Joyce the creator in several ways. First, there was the obvious resource of the richness and earthiness of Irish speech. Beyond that, rebellion against the Church still had a meaning for a young man in Ireland, while in another country it would have already been old hat, as indeed it is a generation later for the Irishman Samuel Beckett. The result is that Beckett stands in a void, in which the wisps of Christianity float back like troubled memories. The two tramps in *Godot* remember maps of the Holy Land and Christ on the cross between two thieves. Joyce, rebel that he is, never stands in that void.

Somewhat the same quality of resistance and containment followed Joyce's revolt against Dublin and Ireland. If one compares his relationship with Dublin to Kafka's with Prague, how little, or at least differently, alienated Joyce seems! Kafka flitted through the streets of Prague like a ghost; Joyce was a positive presence in Dublin, as the city is an overwhelming presence in his book. Even when physically absent from it, he lived in imagination within it. While working on *Ulysses*, he wanted news and gossip of the town and he wrote his Aunt Josephine to send him "any old drivel you can think of." And in his last work he has wrapped himself in the gigantic cocoon of Dublin as the symbolic place of all places, anywhere and anytime, consummating his lifelong love-hate dialogue with his native city.

There is a difference between the two types of outsider, as we have already learned from Camus. Meursault, the Absurd Man, drifts passively at the edge of things, watching them always from the distance he has created between himself and them. In his second phase, however, Camus found that the rebel had a more positive being. His revolt has reestablished him within the ordinary day-to-day life of humanity. He is no longer at the margins of existence, but plunged inescapably into the center of things. Joyce had only a minimal interest in politics, and political rebellion as such does not come within his ken. But in his artistic and spiritual rebellion against Ireland and the Church he persists within the framework of both. It is perhaps the absence of alienation, in this deeper sense, that accounts for the amazing fact that the whole question of Nihilism—which we have seen to be the persistent affliction of the modern spirit —does not enter into his work. And to be untouched by this fundamental anxiety of modernism is the respect in which he is perhaps most crucially *anti-moderne*. Of course, Stephen Dedalus does declare at one point that the church is founded "like the world, macro- and microcosm, upon the void." But this is the exclamation of a single character at a single point in the story and neither defines nor exhausts Stephen's attitude toward life. Or take the most "negative" passage Joyce has written—the long and desiccating catechism of the "Ithaca" scene, when tired Bloom and Dedalus reach home in the empty hours of the early morning. Here the rational mind relentlessly dismembers its world into fragments; but this bleak hour subsides into the chthonic surge of Molly Bloom's final soliloquy, which envelops and sweeps away the tired self-inquisition of the male intellect. For Joyce the negative is but one moment within the flow of life, never the point of view outside of life from which we might spin out a philosophy of the whole.

But surely, it will be argued, Joyce is such an innovator in the matter of technique that his work must be seen as a break with tradition. That is the way textbooks on the novel usually pigeonhole him. But let us look a little more closely at the uses to which Joyce puts his novel techniques.

One of these techniques is the famous "stream of consciousness," which was, however, a method that Joyce did not invent but borrowed, and toward which he maintained a rather casual attitude. "It was really a device," he remarked, "by which I could march my eighteen episodes like troops over a bridge." The fact is that Joyce's treatment of consciousness is profoundly traditional in nature. It once used to be the fashion to lump Joyce and Proust together as the great exponents of "the psychological novel" (whatever that may mean), but here comparison is in fact enlightening just because the two are at different poles in their understanding of consciousness itself. Proust, as a Frenchman, belongs to the tradition of Descartes, for whom consciousness is made up of mental states that exist within a private mind. The novelist, like an analytic chemist or magical alchemist, seeks to distill complex states down into their residual atoms and molecules. Each private mind is a sphere hermetically sealed within itself. Though it may reflect the world without, it does so always with one distortion or another, and from always outside and never within that world. The more rarefied and precious the state of mind the more inexhaustible is Proust in dissecting it. In this aspect of his genius he is an heir of the Symbolism of the 1890s with its yearning for exquisite and extraordinary moments of consciousness that escape the banality of the world. Samuel Beckett has observed that Proust's world is botanical, since his characters, like so many gorgeous flowers, wear their sexuality in the open. To pursue the metaphor further, we should have to say that it is a very special botanical world at that—a labyrinthine hothouse filled with luxurious and exotic hybrid blooms, the air heavy with rank perfume. This is a world sick at its core and on its way to death. Its characters are sophisticated members or hangers-on of the *haut monde.* By contrast, Joyce's people, if one could even imagine them straggling by chance into one of the salons of the Faubourg St. Germain, would look dreadfully gauche and out of place. They would hardly be exquisite or neurotic enough to be admitted.

Joyce's treatment of consciousness is based on an altogether different philosophical premise from Proust's. Stephen Dedalus' is a very complex mind, one of the most complex on the intellectual side in all of fiction, but let us walk with him awhile on the noonday beach while he soliloquizes gazing out over Dublin Bay. We are immediately met by difficulties, for this young man has read much and retained most of it. Within a few lines there are allusions to Aristotle's theory of light, Böhme's *Signature of Things*, and Bishop Berkeley's views on space. But though these references may puzzle us at first, they do not lead us back into the labyrinth of a private prison, à la Proust, but directly into that world of shifting signs outside with which Stephen, like the mythical Proteus, is struggling to cope. Joyce does not stand outside Stephen's consciousness and seek to decompose it into its elements like a rare chemical substance. On the contrary, we are directly within Stephen's mind, and being within it we are already beyond it within the world: "seaspawn and seawrack, the nearing tide, that rusty boot"—all there within that noonday light in which Pan sleeps.

Consciousness here is a pure transparency, not a mental substance. It is the consciousness of Heidegger, not of Descartes. For consciousness, as Heidegger has told us, is simply our mode of being in the world. On this point, we must remember that Heidegger was seeking to escape from the Cartesian prison back to the open and accessible world of the Greeks, and Aristotle had already long ago grasped this fundamental fact of consciousness. "The soul is in a certain way all things," he says in his *Psychology*, a book which young Joyce in his first exile had read at night in the Bibliothèque Nationale at Paris. The so-called stream of consciousness is really the stream of the world as it lights up within an open present for each character, always and everywhere—more obviously in the cases of Leopold and Molly Bloom, more poetically and complexly with Stephen—engaging their concern with supremely mundane matters of fact. The whole art of *Ulysses* is not intended to lose its point of view on any occasion within any private mind, but to make sure that each consciousness is embedded within that single Day, which—with all its seediness, banality, raucous humor, and flashes of beauty—revolves before us like a cosmic cycle that is eternally present.

Which, of course, brings us directly to the question of time, where again Joyce seems to take his place among the ranks of the modernists. *Ulysses* is, as everyone must know by now, the story of one day in Dublin, June 16, 1904, covering less than twenty-four hours. But the whole life of the characters, and not merely for that fragment of time, is spread before us. The most trivial and random things can trigger memories of the past, even of people now dead, and these past events are presented directly and without transition as if they were immediately present. Through the interior monologue of his characters Joyce can thus shift his temporal perspective from present to past abruptly and as he chooses. Here then, it would seem, is that "multi-layered treatment" of time that Erich Auerbach rightly takes to be one of the most significant discoveries by novelists in this century.

Virginia Woolf's *To the Lighthouse* also tells a story that covers a short duration, in this case two days, though they are days widely separated in time, and by moving freely back and forth from present to past, she conveys the sense of almost a dozen lives. However, her experiment with time is vastly more fluid, subjective, and relativistic (almost in Einstein's sense) than Joyce's, and to such an extent that we are sometimes puzzled at first reading to know the precise temporal point at which we stand. With Joyce, on the other hand, the framework of that single day is never in doubt, and the past that emerges is always embedded within that monumental presence.

The fact is that despite all talk of temporal perspectives Joyce's imagination is peculiarly and deliberately static. The eighteen episodes of *Ulysses* are, as it were, carved out of single blocks, and their development proceeds as much by way of thematic elaboration as by simple temporal progression. Joyce pursued this ideal of artistic stasis from his earliest days. He began his apprenticeship in youth by writing down "Epiphanies," brief sketches in which things encountered in the ordinary life around him, a house or a street or a person, would stand forth in one momentary illumination and be revealed as what they are. These epiphanies led to the short stories in *Dubliners*, which present ordinary people fixed in a particular moment or situation, and whose aesthetic effect Ezra Pound described as "a beautiful waiting." This first book provides the imaginative mold within which Joyce still operates in his later more massive works. *Ulysses* is the gigantic elaboration of what was originally intended as one of the stories for *Dubliners* ("Mr. Hunter's Day in Dublin," with the forever to be unknown Mr. Hunter, a Protestant, giving way to the Jew Bloom). In an even more ambitious attempt, *Finnegans Wake* seeks to condense all history into one mythical and timeless epiphany, the whole compass of the work being present at any point of its development ("When a part so ptee does duty for the holos we soon grow to used of an allforabit").

Joyce, who always held fast to every scrap of experience or thought, never abandoned the theory of artistic vision presented by Stephen Dedalus in the *Portrait* as a moment of "luminous silent stasis" when the mind, aglow like "a fading coal," lets the Being of the things it encounters stand forth and shine in their own essence. The aim of the artist is to pierce through the fluidity of becoming with its crooked and distorting perspectives to uncover the luminous stasis of Being. The view is not a modernist one, unless we identify it with the later Heidegger, who in this respect is decidedly traditional; and indeed Joyce's source was his reading of Aristotle and Aquinas.

Yet there is movement and there is time in *Ulysses*. The single episodes may stand fixed, but from one to another the Day itself moves, the light thickens and wanes, and the earth keeps on turning. If I were forced to choose the single protagonist of the book, I think I would pick this Day itself within whose cosmic cycle all the individual lives of these Dubliners are held fast. What Joyce has done is to make this movement of time be carried by language itself: the radiant language of morning that passes into the heavier and denser language of afternoon until it reaches the tired self-destroying catechism of night that in turn must give way to the final throbbing soliloquy of Molly Bloom, who, spinning in her own thoughts, evokes the earth spinning silently on its axis to bring in another dawn. Here is time indeed, subtle and all-pervasive, but it has nothing to do with the time of subjective perspectives, of Berkeley, Einstein, or Virginia Woolf. Philosophically, it belongs to a simple straightforward Realism: classical and Aristotelian time, which is the "measure of before and after" by the cosmic movements of sun and earth.

But time—as we have repeatedly seen in earlier pages—infects every crevice of reality. As each of us understands time in some fashion or other so do we understand reality, and consequently so does the novelist understand the life of his characters in time. In Mrs. Woolf's novel, to go back to our last comparison, the sheer fluidity of time with its shifting perspectives creates a certain gossamer insubstantiality about the characters, as if they were woven of the wind. Auerbach has observed on this with admirable precision:

. . . The speakers no longer seem to be human beings at all but spirits between heaven and earth, nameless spirits capable of penetrating the depths of the human soul, capable too of knowing something about it, but not of attaining clarity as to what is in process there, with the result that what they report has a doubtful ring, comparable in a way to those "Certain airs detached from the body of the wind," which in a later passage move about the house at night, "questioning and wondering." . . .

No one is certain of anything here; it is all mere supposition, glances cast by one person upon another whose enigma he cannot solve.

The modern novelist does not assume that divine or quasi-divine omniscience of his nineteenth-century brother, which would see into every nook and cranny of its characters' beings.

Instead, characters are presented with a depth of mystery and an edge of vagueness as if human personality itself were not a kind of thing that could be totally comprehended. Again, Auerbach provides the useful and precise historical generalization:

> The author at times achieves the intended effect by representing herself to be someone who doubts, wonders, hesitates, as though the truth about her characters were not better known to her than to her readers. . . . This attitude differs entirely from that of authors who interpret the actions, situations, and characters of their personages with objective assurance, as was the general practice in earlier times. Goethe or Keller, Dickens or Meredith, Balzac or Zola told us out of their certain knowledge what their characters did, what they felt and thought while doing it, and how their actions and thoughts were to be interpreted. They knew everything about their characters.

Why when we know generally so much more than the nineteenth century should our novelists be so much less sure of their characters? The Existentialism of Sartre provides one answer to this question. The basic premise of Sartre's philosophy is a radical distinction between things and persons. A thing is just what it is, no more and no less. That bowl on the table before me is a bowl and nothing else, the paper beside it is paper, and lying beside that is a pen; each is external to the other, precisely circumscribed by its own boundaries, and each is just what it is and not something else—or, as the philosopher puts it, in each of these things essence and existence coincide exactly with each other. We, however, are persons, not things, and our being is not so easily circumscribed. Indeed, Sartre takes this as the definition of being human: man, he tells us, is the being who is what he is not, and who is not what he is.

At first reading this looks like blatant paradox, but it is in fact but a condensed summary of the obvious experience of memory and anticipation as these pervade our life. My past is not something external to me, but an intimate presence heavy and pregnant within me. Yet that past is *no longer*—something that is no more and yet that I somehow persist in being. Similarly, however much I may cast off vain hope and strive to live in the present, there must be some minimal anticipation merely to carry out the daily business of life; and that future anticipated is a time that is *not yet*, and hence once again, to the degree that my present opens into that future, I am now what I am not. Moreover, memory and anticipation are not mere fleeting occurrences of the moment, and hence peripheral to what I am now. On the contrary, they are woven into the warp and woof of our being to the degree that we are human and must find whatever meaning we can for ourselves and our life by binding the time that is not, the past and future, into the time that is, the present. Thus the novelist who presents us with too definite and clear-cut characters would be philosophically inadequate, since he would be offering us an oversimplification instead of that concrete reality in which we are and are not, perpetually weaving our being between the shifting horizons of time backward and forward.

And then, Sartre reminds us, there is also the fundamental fact of human freedom. If we are just what we are, then we are stuck with it and cannot change. If we are free, however, we can not only alter the things around us but even transform ourselves. We can be what we are not. But for that future self, which I am not now, to be an effective summons to me it must already have sent its roots down into the self that I am now. In the call to freedom I am that self that is to be but is not yet. The great traditional novels of realism, in this view, do not render this unique reality of human freedom; the immortal characters that detach themselves from those pages are not human beings like you or me, struggling between being and not-being within the slippery folds of time and possibility, but so many flies imprisoned in amber for all eternity.

When he descends to analyzing particular motives and emotions, Sartre puts his principle to fiendish use. Down there in the human arena everything turns into duplicity and ambiguity; men and women in their relationships are simultaneously cheats and dupes both of themselves and of the other, perpetually not being what they are and being what they are not—with a vengeance. Such pessimism is perhaps to be expected from the French with their ingrained distrust of any human sincerity—a theme which they have explored in their literature from Montaigne to Gide. Sartre's philosophy itself, however, is really optimistic in outlook. For if our character does not have the clear-cut identity of a thing, we may be confused and uncertain about it but at least we are not chained to it in servitude. With other modern novelists, however, this device of uncertain and vague characterization usually expresses, as in Virginia Woolf, a sadness before life and its fleeting insubstantiality. In Samuel Beckett it conveys the collapse of human pretensions altogether. Beckett, of course, pushes this uncertainty much further than Mrs. Woolf. We are sometimes left uncertain not only of the time and place but of the nature of the action itself. Moran sets out to search for Molloy and eliminate him. Sometime in his journey he encounters and has some kind of blows with a man. Was this man Molloy? And did Moran kill him? We do not know. And on his journey back home, may it not be that Moran has in fact become identical with Molloy? Here the uncertainty is pushed to its metaphysical limit. An empty and desolate prospect for some readers. But perhaps we need a reminder as drastic as this that with all his dazzling advances in science and technology man is more confused than ever about his own identity. He certainly seems to know less who he is and where he is going than the nineteenth century did.

None of these motifs is present in Joyce, for the simple reason that he does not belong with this modern school at all but with the older writers, like Dickens, Balzac, or Zola, who in Auerbach's phrase, "knew everything about their characters." The difficulties in *Ulysses* are matters of reference, oblique and incidental, multiplied sometimes to the point of trying our patience but always for the very good purpose of making the texture of the narrative as dense and lifelike as possible, so that in reading the book we seem to step into the actual city where we may sometimes hear people talking about other people whom we have not met but whose mention is perfectly natural and understandable in the speaker's mouth. Who was the J. A. Jackson who won the half-mile bicycle race in College Green that day? We shall never know; nor do we care, unless we are pedants. It is the kind of fact that Dubliners might have been interested in and taken notice of in passing. Our ignorance of Jackson's identity casts no air of mystery over this item.

Joyce's basic conception of his characters is never indefinite and uncertain. Ambiguities and inconsistences they may have, but these are ordinary and understandable ones. And when all the labyrinths of the text have faded away for us, the characters remain whole and intact before our imagination—flagrantly violating Sartre's definition of human reality, for they are just what they are. They never threaten to dissolve into airs and echoes, into the haunting lyricism of a vanishing occasion, like Virginia Woolf's people. Solidly and substantially there, they walk the streets of Dublin forever, monumentally present like the great figures out of classic fiction.

Why was the traditional character of Joyce's work not immediately recognized? Looking back from the vantage point of the present, we find it hard to understand some of the earlier responses to *Ulysses*. Irving Babbitt, for example, found the book depraved and Leopold Bloom, in particular, "a monster of sensuality." Today this seems an unaccountably harsh judgment on the humble man who, despite all the indignities heaped on him, remains gentle and charitable throughout the day, so that opening the book again we feel we are meeting an old friend and not a freak. Babbitt, of course, was a product of old-fashioned New England puritanism, and would naturally be scandalized by Joyce's sexual frankness. But even a more cosmopolitan and less rigid reader like E. M. Forster recoiled before the book and found it to be "a monster with glittering scales and crawling with vermin." Forster's own exquisite talent had been shaped by the standards of Georgian England and Bloomsbury, for which the coarseness and exuberance of Joyce's novel was much too strong meat.

But Joyce's scatology, like his sexual frankness, seems to us today to be neither excessive nor deranged, and in the end completely justified within the scheme of the whole work. The trouble for these earlier readers was that persistent paradox in Joyce himself—the discrepancy between the complexity of his surface and the simplicity of his substance. The surface was puzzling and bizarre, and therefore Joyce must be a disruptive and menacing figure. Even in a reader like Jung, whose professional experience had prepared him for acceptance of the sexual and scatological material, the enormously detailed texture of the book proved heavy going, and on his first encounter with it he spoke of *Ulysses* as "a gigantic tapeworm that seemed to grow by feeding upon itself." Nevertheless, he persevered beyond the surface to find the substance, and ended as an admirer ready to recommend the work as "a Bible for the white-skinned races," since Joyce, as he thought, with a kind of Oriental acceptance had brought the contraries—fair and foul, beautiful and sordid, sublime and pathetic—into a whole and unified vision.

The history of the reception of *Ulysses* shows us how much and how rapidly things have changed in this century. We have changed so much, and Joyce himself has been part of that change; yet even in this matter of his influence his modernism is ambiguous and doubtful. When we think of the flood of sexual writing on which he helped to open the dike—the awkward self-consciousness or adolescent exhibitionism that now pours from the stage or movies—we doubt that he would approve of it. Certainly, his own use of sexual motifs was never in the spirit of exhibitionism or sensationalism but out of a stubborn fidelity to the wholeness of experience. We were a generation whose youth was formed by Joyce, and we loved his audacity, but in middle age we come back to him for more middle-aged virtues —particularly his almost transcendental preoccupation with the ordinary. "I have the mind of a grocer's clerk," he said of himself—a statement which no Joycean should ever forget. Joyce in fact places us between two worlds of taste and two worlds in time, to neither of which we can belong: between those earlier readers who saw in him only a menacing and destructive force, and the generation now coming up which succumbs to all manner of adolescent furies in the name of free expression. But then, for prudent Odysseus—as for prudent Bloom—it is always hardest to walk the middle path.

I

Yet Joyce, no more than Forster, can escape this modern age. No man, says Hegel, can step clear of his time any more than he can leap over his own shadow. Despite the traditional cast of his mind, despite the energy, exuberance, and humor that never let him slide into the abyss of Nihilism, Joyce turns out nevertheless to be a representative figure who speaks from the depths of this time of need, though not in a way that is commonly recognized or that he himself might have liked. What is his "message" about ourselves and our time? And, first of all, does he have a message at all? For that we must turn from *Ulysses* to his culminating work, *Finnegans Wake.*

Shortly after *Ulysses* appeared, T. S. Eliot was taking tea with Virginia Woolf and the two naturally fell to talking about the book. Eliot, she reported later, was for the first time in her experience of him "rapt" and "enthusiastic." For the prim and restrained young man that Eliot then was, and in the chastening presence of a lady and a more established figure like Mrs. Woolf, this enthusiasm was indeed extraordinary. "How could anyone write again after achieving the immense prodigy of the last chapter?" Mrs. Woolf found the chapter "underbred"—which is exactly how her own Mrs. Dalloway or Mrs. Ramsay would have felt about Molly Bloom. But Eliot too had his reservations: he insisted that Joyce had killed the nineteenth century, exposed the futility of all styles, and destroyed his own future. There was nothing left for him to write a book about. Then perhaps under the influence of Bloomsbury itself, among whom the great Russian novelists were just then being discovered and boomed, Eliot added that Joyce's book gave no new insight into human nature as Tolstoy's *War and Peace* did. "Bloom tells one nothing."

What could Eliot possibly have meant? Surely he was not asking for didactic art, about which he has been elsewhere very caustic. Presumably he meant the absence of some moralizing point of view, a principle on which F. R. Leavis of Cambridge was later to make some hair-raising reevaluations of the English novelists. The great novelist, we are told, is one who has a "point of view"—and most important of all, a moral point of view. Tolstoy has it, and Joyce (like Shakespeare perhaps?) does not. Well, the writer must have a moral point of view; he could not put pen to paper otherwise. But he does better sometimes the more unconscious it is while he writes. And the example of Tolstoy is an ambiguous one, since there are in fact two Tolstoys, the moralist and the novelist, and the power of the latter transcends the partial points of view in which his characters may be temporarily caught up. Pierre in *War and Peace* goes through a great deal of soul-searching about the meaning of life, but is then caught up in the organic sweep of it that is wider and deeper than any human point of view; and in the end we see him, older and married now to Natasha, at a point where his earlier questions have been swept away but never answered. It is in representing that vast sweep of life, rather than in his moralizing, that Tolstoy's uncanny power as a novelist lies. And what about Shakespeare? A few years later Eliot bridled when some Humanist followers depreciated Shakespeare in relation to Goethe because the latter "interpreted" life while Shakespeare only "mirrored" it. If Shakespeare has a point of view, it is pretty well hidden, but Eliot merely snapped back that a good mirror might be worth any number of interpretations.

Curiously, neither Eliot nor Mrs. Woolf (he perhaps because she was present) stopped to ask whether Molly Bloom teaches one anything, and to wonder what the point of this woman is to whom after all Joyce has given the last word in his novel. What would Molly have thought of Tolstoy's Pierre or Bolkonsky or Levin—of all these earnest young existentialists struggling for a truth that will be authentically their own and in which they will at last "stand face to face with life itself"? Such as she is, she already stands there, or at least at a point beyond their question, where in fact it would seem to her like the game of young men, pretty dears, playing with words like toys.

"Joyce had destroyed his own future"—so Eliot thought at the time, though he was later to change his mind. But for many readers this cloud of suspicion still hangs over Joyce's last work: he had carried experimentation so far in *Ulysses* that he had nowhere else to go—except into the bizarre eccentricities of *Finnegans Wake*. The writer who felt that his mastery of language permitted him to do anything he pleased with it surrendered to a self-indulgent play upon words. In *Ulysses* he had written the story of one day, and now—out of some arbitrary and abstract sense of symmetry—he would write the story of one night. These views represent this last step in Joyce's development as the result of conscious contrivance or pat decision, born out of the desperation of a writer who has exhausted his material. In fact, however, Joyce could no more have contrived this last step than he could have resisted it if he had willed to. He had opened a door on the unconscious, and he had to go further beyond the threshold. Now his own unconscious—like the flowing river he celebrates in the *Wake*—swept him into the open sea. The true inevitability of a work of art lies in this authentic happening out of the unconscious. "When they started coming," we remember Giacometti saying, "I had not the least intention of doing those thin men." This inevitability of Joyce's development, moreover, is not merely an event within his personal biography but a happening for this time of need, which in fact brings to light what may be one of its more hidden needs.

To understand it at all we have to take a brief glimpse back at the realistic novel and the premise on which it was founded. Though many forces went into the shaping of this great literary form, its most basic premise was the modern historical consciousness with its belief in the sovereign reality of history. In the historical arena the individual works out his human destiny for good or ill. Mythical times might dream and allow the present to go on repeating the past. But we believe in change and progress, and the historical consciousness tells us that the present is never a mere repetition of the past but in its uniqueness is fraught with all manner of profound and problematic possibilities that can be the subject of great and serious art. When Stendhal added the subtitle "Chronicle of the Year 1830" to the title page of *The Red and the Black*, he was departing from the practice of older novels that might begin with a typically indifferent phrase, "In the year 18—— in the town of G——", where the particular year or locale does not carry any weight for the events that the narrative will unfold. In *Ulysses* the precision of the dating is carried further: not only do events take place in a particular year, 1904, in a particular city, but on a particular day of that year, June 16, 1904, and at definite and particular hours of the day. We now know that Joyce, digging into old newspapers as well as his memories, did not surrender completely to literal documentation but transposed people and events as he saw fit. Still, nothing in the work is out of line with the date, and the texture of the whole aims to convey the impression that these were the events that did actually happen on that particular day.

Yet even at this stage Joyce's imagination could not be confined by the sheer particularities of history. He has to embed his realistic facts within a legendary framework: his eighteen chapters are planned as parallels—some more and some less far-fetched—to eighteen episodes in the *Odyssey*. Stephen Dedalus and Leopold Bloom, moving through their day in Dublin, repeat the archetypal patterns of Homeric legend. Of course, every realistic writer is caught up in this tension between the particular and the universal. If he pushes his documentation too far, without some universal dramatic or narrative patterns, his story crumbles into shards of facts. Myth has been defined—in the words St. Augustine used as a criterion for valid Church doctrine—as what holds everywhere and at all times, *ubique ac omni tempore*. The myth is Joyce's means of universalizing his minutely particular material and his parochial locale. In *Ulysses* the myth is a scaffolding in the background, hidden and remote for some readers; but in the last work it has advanced so far to the foreground that the whole of history is now to be embedded within the framework of myth. In this eternal dialogue between myth and history (which has become once again one of the intellectual themes of our time) Joyce ends by giving the last word to the myth.

Exasperating in its difficulties as *Finnegans Wake* is, the logic with which Joyce goes about his myth building is simplicity itself and follows the traditional lines of the primitive mythmaker. Already in *Ulysses* he had moved toward making Bloom, an ordinary type, into an Everyman, and now he begins from the point where he had left off: his hero is HCE—the initials for Here Comes Everybody. (In his realistic embodiment, which tends to get lost, as it should, in the intricacies of the dream, he is an unimportant Dublin tavernkeeper, about whom we can dig out just about as many facts as we would know if he were a character in one of the short stories of *Dubliners*.) Primeval man must have his woman, and in the primitive fashion that does not separate the human from the natural she appears as Anna Livia Plurabelle (abbreviated throughout as ALP), the incarnation of the river Liffey that flows through

Dublin. This primal pair ("the He and the She of it") must, as in all primitive myths, beget offspring, and so we have the original family: twin sons and a daughter.

The brothers must be two and twins because man himself is dual in nature, and they embody the eternal opposites of the human psyche: one the introvert, scapegrace, and outcast; the other the extrovert, public figure, and man of action. The daughter, younger and more beautiful than her mother, is the eternal other woman toward whom the male heart everlastingly strays. Why are there not two daughters as there are two sons? The duality of the woman—who more than man is the creature of nature—would seem to be sufficiently represented by the natural difference of age and youth. After all, men fall in love with another woman only to seek the same in a younger form. After Isolde of Ireland, Tristan fell in love again with another Isolde in Brittany; and Swift went from Esther to Esther. All told, then, a compact and reasonable family of five, to which cast Joyce adds two supporting characters, the menials of the household, an old woman and man who do the chores about the place. That brings the total of this cosmic household to seven, which just happens to be the number of the days of the week or the seven colors of the rainbow or any other significant collection of seven that Joyce and his reader can think of. And so the fantastic whirl of association can be set going to baffle some and intrigue other readers. But that can wait for a bit; what we have to keep in mind at the moment is the simplicity of the basic structure.

This family structure, in one of its aspects or another, is to be impressed upon us on every page. All human history, in fact, is the recurrent embodiment of the primal family and its interrelationships. The warring brothers can be Cain and Abel, Napoleon and Wellington, Brutus and Cassius, the Pope of Rome and St. Laurence O'Toole—or, going beyond the human realm, the Ant and the Grasshopper of Aesop's fable.

Joyce borrowed the general scheme of his work from Vico,

the odd, extraordinary Italian philosopher of the eighteenth century. The choice was not the result of any deep intellectual pondering by Joyce on the philosophy of history. He had read Vico as a youth, loved his baroque and exuberant Italian, and since he was one of those on whom nothing is ever lost, the memory of this then obscure Italian clung to him. But it was a lucky and a prophetic hit on Joyce's part: Vico's reputation is now booming and he is considered one of the most original minds ever to have dealt with the philosophy of history. His originality, however, consisted in tilting the balance more away from history to what we would nowadays call anthropology. Instead of taking the essence of history as something expressed in the chronologies of military and diplomatic events, Vico sought the essential story of a people as it was embedded in its language, customs, laws, and rituals. This is exactly the procedure of the anthropologist today. The emphasis here (and this suited Joyce's temperament perfectly) is put upon the daily round of human existence, and not on the exceptional, unique, and unrepeatable event. Moreover, Vico took the family as the basic social structure, and this too exactly fitted Joyce's own vision of things. Accordingly, the narrative of the *Wake*—if the term "narrative" may still be employed at all—is not about a series of events succeeding each other in time, but is rather— to borrow the language of contemporary anthropology—the elaboration of a structure.[1] That these events themselves—in their variable and flickering, crowded and nonsequential multiplicity—recede in importance before the pervasive kinship structure is a measure of how far Joyce the mythmaker has gone in truly inserting himself into the point of view of the primitive.

1. The illusion of a hidden narrative is fostered by some commentaries like the *Skeleton Key* of Campbell and Robinson and Anthony Burgess' *Shorter Wake*. These are very useful books, but they do mislead some readers into hunting for a tiny nugget of plot beneath Joyce's shifting and variable surface. Something is happening in the *Wake*, but it is not a narrative sequence of the usual kind. In a sense, everything has already happened. The past of history has already been absorbed into the perpetual present of myth.

History includes everything, even autobiography, and Joyce can inject the events of his life and himself as a character into the book. For what is supposed to be a universal history of sorts the *Wake* is, oddly enough, the most personal of Joyce's works. Such allusions are perhaps fair game since the reader who becomes interested enough to struggle with the book is likely to be drawn into the author's own cocoon and learn something about his life. Thus the warring brother pair appear as Shem and Shaun, who in one of their manifestations are Joyce himself and his brother Stanislaus: Shem (James) is the scapegrace writer, and Shaun (Stanislaus) the more sober and moralizing citizen. (Even after they had long since gone separate ways, and Joyce was no longer cadging off him, he could not be quite fair to his younger sibling.) But Joyce does not quite stop at such relatively accessible references; everything is taken as fair game for his omnivorous memory, and every bit of local bric-a-brac, however special or out of the way it may be, gets wedged into this enormous compendium. "He was in his bardic memory low," he says of Shem-Joyce. He can neither invent epic plots nor even remember the ones of the past except in fragments. But what matter if all the grand stories of history are themselves merely fragmentary and imperfect illustrations, endlessly recurring, of the old primal family structure. Shem-Joyce must follow his own course and "treasure up any fragment of trek-talk that came his way." In the world of the true myth there is nothing meaningless, analogies and correspondences abound everywhere, and anything may be connected with anything else. Civilization, Lévi-Strauss tells us, recklessly expends its ideas, while the savage mind hoards every crumb of meaning.

Joyce indeed might seem to be following the conclusions of the most recent anthropology, which of course did not exist at the time he was writing the *Wake*. Lévi-Strauss has described the mythmaking of the primitive as a kind of *bricolage*. The word is hard to translate: the *bricoleur*, to put it roughly, is a jack-of-all-trades and a kind of handyman who builds structures,

sometimes quite elaborate ones, out of whatever heterogene-
ous materials lie at hand. The engineer-contractor, on the other
hand, belongs to technological civilization: he builds his structures out of prefabricated parts cut to numbered specifications
—and the results turn out all to look the same. A myth, however, always seems different in the retelling. For the primitive
mythmaker builds his story (which is to illustrate at once a
cosmic and a social structure) out of whatever odds and ends
come to hand: scraps of tribal ritual and memory, animal lore,
totemic classifications—any old drivel his Aunt Josephine can
tell him. Joyce is the complete *bricoleur* in *Finnegans Wake*. All
the trash of our culture is to be put to use—advertising slogans,
radio blurbs, argot, clichés, proverbs, puns, music hall ballads,
popular songs, the backstairs gossip of history as well as the local
gossip of Dublin. All this garbage is poured into his "wholemole
millwheeling cyclometer." A civilization about to bury itself
under the debris of its own immediacy is to be redeemed, and
the way, as in some present schemes for saving us from our
hopelessly befouled environment, is by recycling human
wastes.

By contrast, other attempts to build myths in this century
have been all too obviously the work of a very selective and
literary sensibility. Yeats, Lawrence, Graves, and in his way
Eliot—the list is a formidable one in modern letters, yet none
is as much in the genuine spirit of the primitive as Joyce. Yeats
made his cloak "out of old embroideries," mainly from astrology
and the sayings of some visionary mystics, but the vulgar
materials of common life that get into his poetry hardly get into
the hermetic system of *A Vision*. For Robert Graves, as for
Joyce, the mythical figure is the Woman: after the male gods,
and particularly Apollo as the god of Reason, came to rule the
Olympian roost, civilization has been straying further and further from the Goddess until in modern times it has degraded
women to the role of "auxiliary state personnel." But Graves's
Goddess is ultimately a Romantic figure—pale and blue-eyed,

la belle dame sans merci, the eternal Other Woman but never the wife. The primitive mind could not accept as archetypical the woman who is not also a wife and mother. Molly Bloom and Anna Livia are cut from less ethereal stuff than Graves's bewitching Goddess. D. H. Lawrence went to Mexico seeking to pin down his own inchoate myth in some of the old images from Aztec culture. But *The Plumed Serpent* is a sad and disappointing book. Lawrence himself was a tired and sick man at the time, and he was dispirited by the direct contact with primitive Mexico. The life of the Indians turned out to be too coarse, somber, and inert, without the radiance he had expected from a people who had escaped industrialization. He could not take the dark with the light in primitive culture.

Eliot—in *The Waste Land* at least—is closer to Joyce in bringing the vulgarities of modern life into the picture, and he is also something of a *bricoleur* putting together the odds and ends of memory to prop a falling world: "These fragments I have shored against my ruins." Unfortunately, the ruins remain ruins; the poem finds that no myth will work and therefore the land and its people have come under a blight. *The Waste Land* succeeds in being the myth of the mythless man. Subsequently, Eliot was to become a bitter critic of these efforts to concoct a new myth for our time. Why try to build a private myth when there was already a public one in existence, Christianity, into whose fashioning had gone the experience and thought of whole peoples over the centuries? The advice was entirely sensible and prudent, but few literary men have seen fit to follow Eliot's example. Christianity, it would seem, no longer has the power to release the life-giving waters—at least for its artists.

II

But why myth? Surely it is one of the most compelling phenomena of our time that so many of its most gifted writers (and we have spoken above only of those writing in English) should have gone in such passionate hunt for the myth. In 1792 the revolutionary Assembly in Paris proposed that in the calendar they were forming that year be established as Year I, thus ushering in a new era of rationalism for the whole of mankind. The proposal has not lasted, the old dating still holds, which ought to tell us something about the psychic inertia of human nature. What would those ardent and even fanatical rationalists think if they could come back and glimpse Western civilization, supposedly after a century and a half of what should have been further progress, not only still embroiled with the tatters of myth but actively trying to renew them? And notice we are not talking about a glimpse of the mythical in nature but of the deliberate effort to build myths. Faulkner, for example, was captured by the god (or goddess) present in the Mississippi earth, at once lavish and exacting as it holds humans in the rhythm of its seasons. But he does not set out to build a highly structured myth out of this vision. The fact that so many of our better writers—and otherwise too so different in their individual temperament—have been engaged in such a conscious quest can hardly be taken as a mark of personal eccentricity or aberration. These efforts come out of some deeper hunger of our time.

Science does not give us the unity of experience that we need and want. It dismembers and fragments, and goes on dismembering and fragmenting, because that is its job. Nor can we find this unification in philosophy, which in any case has ceased to attempt it since Hegel. And even if a philosophy were to put such a unity before us, it would not be enough: we are concrete creatures of flesh and blood, and we want the concreteness of the symbol in order to hold our experience together. Here the imagination enters as the vivifying bond between the abstractions of the intellect and the diffuse particularities of sensation. The image vibrates with meanings, inexhaustibly so, but at the same time has the vividness of actual experience. And since we are temporal beings, we need images that also develop in time —hence stories.

The stories must tell of the most universal and at the same time intimate matters we all live through, but never fully comprehend. The myth thus speaks of the unknown, both in the cosmos and in ourselves. It stands on the edge of that darkness, both within and without, that we shall never escape. Why then do we need myths? Because despite all our progress, and our vaunted accumulation of knowledge, we are still children in the dark who have to make up stories so that we will not be so alone, that the darkness itself may become more familiar and friendly, and the poor shreds and patches of our life be pieced together.

The men of the Enlightenment (to be specific let us think of the French Assembly of 1792) dreamed of the emancipation of reason from myth. For them indeed that was the very meaning of history. With consciousness thus emancipated, history would become the realm in which man at last found his freedom to create himself in his own chosen image. Man aspires to be God —Sartre was not extreme in putting it this way, for what is this dream of History but the wish that man stand in place of the Creator and be able to re-create his own being totally, if he so chooses? As an Existentialist, of course, Sartre believed that the project was doomed to failure on strictly metaphysical grounds. We now have more factual and mundane reasons for placing limits on this godlike aspiration. Our industrial progress has brought us to a desperate crisis of the environment. We have reached the point where we are beginning at last to recognize that, whatever our technological level, we are still tied to this planet, with its shallow crust of soil and thin envelope of air, as precariously as the Australian aborigine. We seem about to wreak just as much violence on the inner environment of our human nature. Some of our worst troubles come from our inability to live with the archetypical patterns of life—youth and age, parents and children, man and woman. So we have the "generation gap," and the battle of the sexes threatens to degenerate into neurotic warfare. A primitive who could observe us carefully would be amazed that a culture so clever in other ways could make such a botch of the basic patterns of life. The emancipation from myth leaves us neurotic.

Let the reader at this point glance back at the sculpture by Henry Moore that we looked at earlier. It is a good picture to go with the *Wake*. This body which seeks to know itself as issuing from and belonging to the earth speaks from the same archetypical depths as Joyce's work. Both provide compensatory images for the emancipated consciousness of our time.

A third of our life is spent in sleep—a good deal more time than the usual novel accords it. In an amusing and enlightening bit of arithmetic on the time spent by fictional characters in the various pursuits of life, E. M. Forster observed that they hardly eat and sleep but spend all their time in human relationships—a fact which in itself indicates that the realistic novel is a contrivance of singular artifice. Now something strange happens when we fall asleep: the centuries of history and progress fall away; in sleep the civilized man and the aborigine are one. Thus the writer who would deal with a sleeping character is placed in a curious relation to history: he is, so to speak, beyond it—in prehistory and post-history at once. That is not a point of view that encourages the belief in progress. Yet even the philosophers of progress were convinced that history must move beyond itself. After all, if we progress and progress, life eventually must be so changed that anything like human history as we now know it would disappear. The ultimate goal of History was to land us in post-history, whether this be the classless society or some other ideal state. Well, with *Finnegans Wake* we have already arrived at post-history, but it does not at all look like the dream of the utopians. We have turned full circle back to the inescapable bonds of the natural life: sleep and waking and the daily round. Here is a mock-universal History (which in effect destroys history) of 638 intricate and difficult pages that deals simply with a man and woman in bed—not in the fashion of the

Swedish movies but simply sleeping; and the final fugal movement at the end is the massive slow approach of dawn that will
summon the pair back into their daytime labors. We ourselves
descend there every night, and—so far as we know—the man
of the future, whatever he will be like, will have to descend into
that same old matrix.

Finnegans Wake probes for the natural man beneath the
cultural man. In the process culture itself seems inevitably to
get devalued. Seventeen languages and their literatures are
ransacked to provide Joyce with the words and tags that he
plays with as if they were so many toys. The solemn formulas
of culture become the subject of fun and games. In this mockery
of culture, of course, he is not alone. One of the pervasive, and
most significant, characteristics of our time is that its own high
culture has become questionable, and in some cases even alien,
to itself. Erich Auerbach observes of European fiction between
the two world wars: "There is hatred of culture and civilization,
brought out by means of the subtlest stylistic devices that culture and civilization have developed, and often a radical and
fanatical urge to destroy."

The revolt takes many different turns. The Germans in the
1920s called it *Kulturbolschewismus:* modernism in art seemed
as destructive of the traditional forms of culture as Communism
aimed to be of existing social institutions. The Dadaists drew a
mustache on the *Mona Lisa.* That was a revolt of high spirits,
a gesture to celebrate one's spontaneity and freedom from the
shackles of tradition. Elsewhere, however, the revolt takes on
a more somber tone. Steppenwolf (we have seen) treasures the
precious heritage of Mozart, but it is also something of a burden
that he carries, and he must take care not to let his reverence
for tradition become petrified into a rigid barrier against life
itself. With Samuel Beckett the revolt becomes an ordeal: all of
human culture, language included, seems impertinent before
the facts of decay and death. Lucky in *Godot,* ordered to think,
gives out an incoherent burst of words full of the shards and

fragments of human learning that he can no longer bind together to make sense.

The difference between ourselves and the previous century
here is one of the astounding facts of modern history that we
have scarcely begun to understand. The nineteenth-century
writer too had begun to feel menaced by this question of culture, but for an entirely different reason. Democracy and the
extension of literacy had widened the class of the literate, but
their literacy was not of a very high order. The phenomenon of
"the two audiences"—highbrow and lowbrow—appeared for
the first time. The serious writer began to feel alienated from
the growing mass of the bourgeois audience; but the reason he
despised this class was just that it was vulgar and crass, while
what he valued in himself was that he was the self-chosen
guardian and carrier of the precious heritage of high culture.[2]

Right now Pop art and Pop literature are the wake of this
wave washing up on our shores. Some of this art is interesting
and some very dull, and its motives seem to be as varied as its
performance. On one side it is prompted by a certain democratic acceptance of our life today. If most people see more tin
cans than flowers, why not paint the tin cans? If the refuse of
our civilization spreads all around us, and is what most of us are
looking at nearly all the time, why should the artist pretend to
look past it in order to see something different and more beautiful? There is also the motive toward relaxation on the part of the
artist. Why get up tight in order to try to produce a masterpiece
when the very idea of a masterpiece is one of the relics of a
defunct tradition? Why take oneself so solemnly as even to try
for a masterpiece? Hang loose and let it all hang out! And as

2. Flaubert's *Bouvard et Pecuchet* is something of an anticipation, but then
almost unconsciously, of the writer's revolt against culture today. The work was
intended as a satire on two crass bourgeois who set out to educate themselves.
Its aim and scope were thus set within the limits of the realistic novel. But such
is Flaubert's pessimistic fury about man and his hatred of his age that he breaks
through this realistic mold and gives us a pair of clowns reducing all human
learning to drivel and nonsense.

always life has proceeded to imitate art, and the artist's revolt against culture has passed into a revolt by youth against all tradition. Anyone who had followed carefully the discontent in the arts fifty and forty years ago could have predicted that something was bound to give way and we would have the present breakdown. Political and economic issues do not get to the heart of youth's dissent. These issues are the occasions on which discontent spills over into revolt, but the underlying malaise is more diffuse than any specific social grievance: the culture as a whole no longer attracts the young or satisfies them. Its rituals no longer fire the imagination or kindle enough energy to carry on in the duller ruts and routines of life. The magic relics of culture, like a broken churinga of a primitive, no longer wield their potency.

Joyce is prophetically at the center of all this ferment, but he himself is far removed from it. The *Wake* uses all the trash of Pop culture that Joyce could get his hand or ear on, but the impromptu spirit of Pop art is utterly alien to a work that consumed seventeen years of exhausting labor in minute and meticulous elaboration. The idea of a writer sitting down not to write a masterpiece would have been simply unthinkable to him. Joyce wears a jester's cap and bells, but he is still a traditionalist who delights in every relic of culture that provides him material for fun and pun. There is neither hatred nor cynicism in his destruction of culture. The reduction may be thoroughgoing, but his comedy and humor are irrepressible and rise to the surface. Here is Shem, the nay-saying writer, described as Joyce himself writing the *Wake:*

Sniffer of carrion, premature gravedigger, seeker of the nest of evil in the bosom of a good word, you, who sleep at our vigil and fast for our feast, you with your dislocated reason, have cutely foretold, a jophet in your own absence, by blind poring upon your many scalds and burns and blisters, impetiginous sore and pustules, by the auspices of that raven cloud, your shade, and by the auguries of rooks in parlament, death with every disaster, the dynamitisation of colleagues, the reducing of records to ashes, the levelling of all customs by blazes, the return of a lot of sweetempered gunpowdered didst unto dudst. . . .

Yet the fierceness of all this destruction only generates its own life-giving fun:

. . . but it never stphruck your mudhead's obtundity . . . that the more carrots you chop, the more turnips you slit, the more murphies you peel, the more onions you cry over, the more bullbeef you butch, the more mutton you crackerhack, the more potherbs you pound, the fiercer the fire and the longer your spoon and the harder you gruel with more grease to your elbow the merrier fumes your new Irish stew.

The third of Vico's three cycles is the age of democratic disintegration, when there is a universal breakdown of tradition and authority. Joyce covers all three cycles, and all at once; yet there is a movement toward the last cycle, where in fact we seem to be in the last section before the epilogue of dawn. Joyce never stepped outside the book in order to locate it historically in any of these cycles. However, from the manner of its writing, the fact that it falls into the lingo of modernity when it wants to impart the presence of the third cycle makes it possible to say that this book itself is an event within that last age of man. But Joyce has added a Viconian *ricorso*, the turn of cycle when, after the chaos of anarchy, a time of renewal comes. This comic genius is an inveterate optimist: "Yes I will yes," he says with Molly Bloom. Breakdown is breakthrough—toward a new dawn. Perhaps our age is about to begin where *Finnegans Wake* ends. Joyce has been a good prophet in so many other ways that we can hope he will turn out to be right here.

III

And now the question which the exegete may shirk but which cannot at last be evaded: Does *Finnegans Wake* really succeed? I think it would be too much to ask that one man could do what a whole culture could not do for itself and make the myth live again.

The trouble is that the discrepancy in Joyce between the simplicity of his substance and the complexity of his surface, which was present in *Ulysses*, reaches its peak in the *Wake*. Joyce aims to get at the most elemental things in life, but the means he employs toward this end inevitably get in the way of it. He is mired in the debris of the culture that he would redeem. The artist in this century—as we have repeatedly seen in our earlier pages—has been engaged in a struggle to reacquire his ties to the earth. Before a world grown so imposingly complex, in its technical and social organization as well as in the mountainous mass of its systematized information, the artist may seem a feeble creature, but he dares to exist by reasserting the primal and elemental things that mankind may be on the way to forgetting. Joyce attempts to carry this process further perhaps than any other writer. He plunges us into the life-giving waters of sleep to find there the primordial figures in the human drama—the Man, the Woman, the Children. But the self-consciousness of the modern mind pursues him into those depths.

In the search for the universal he chooses the strategy of becoming encyclopedic, and the apparatus of scholarship begins to smack more of the library and museum of Alexandria than of the mythmaking of the early Greek bards. The pedantry that mocks itself is still pedantic. The myths are trotted out with a jesting self-consciousness until we feel that it is not the myth itself we are encountering here but a museum of comparative mythologies. The primitive, in its true sense, is the primal, and the validity of Primitivism is a search for the primary. At the core of Joyce's book lies the conflict between Alexandrianism and Primitivism, which has appeared before in human history but more than ever has become central to our age; and Joyce is like one of the creatures of opposites in the *Wake*, driven in two contrary directions at once and forced to hold on to each side in self-conscious irony. The paradox of *Finnegans Wake* is that while it aims to tell the story of Everyman and thus appeal to the most elemental emotions, it is written in a language that draws out the hidden pedant in all of us.

This blanket accusation has to be qualified, and first of all by conceding that there are partial triumphs and partial rewards in this book to justify ten lesser works. If energy is delight, as Blake said, and exuberance is beauty, then there are delightful and beautiful things here that surpass anything in *Ulysses.* Indeed, there are passages so breath-taking that one feels almost guilty about carping at the book as a whole. There are also other passages so exasperating and dragging and heavy-handed that one could wonder how a writer of Joyce's gifts could have put his hand to them at all except that he had to build an enormous scaffolding for his diffuse material that he was later unable to tear down. But Joyce is not to be judged by such partial triumphs or partial lapses; he demands to be measured by a standard commensurate with his own Himalayan ambitions for the work, and that means at the least that we must ask whether it succeeds as an aesthetic unity.

It is not the difficulties as such to which one objects. Difficult works we have long since grown used to; and those who love Joyce would be willing to grant him carte blanche in building his Daedalian labyrinths. It is the nature of these difficulties that is questionable. Do they hinder or enrich the grasp of this work as an aesthetic whole?

Let us take a specific case, and for this purpose the first sentence will do. Since the book is circular in pattern, the last sentence, or sentence fragment, flows back into the first, and we begin there: "A way a lone a last a loved a long the." The woman-river is flowing out into the sea, into death—but also into rebirth in the first sentence: "riverrun, past Eve and Adam's, from swerve of shore to bend of bay, brings us by a commodius vicus of recirculation back to Howth Castle and Environs." If we follow the course of the Liffey River we pass by the church of Adam and Eve's (a church in Dublin, and also our first parents from whose fall history began, and here in Joyce's book we are at the beginning of history again), and through the commodious town of Dublin (vicus is also a road or lane) until on the outskirts of town we come to Howth Castle. The initials HCE are the male, from whom the historical cycle will begin once again. A clear and concise proem to the whole work. The word "riverrun" with its flow of liquid consonants seems only a happy coinage for the course of the stream. But it is something more, for Joyce, following Keats's advice, loads every rift with ore. *Riverranno* is the third person plural of the Italian verb "to come back, return," and more often than not in conversation the final syllable is dropped, *riverran*. They will return—yes, the whole kit and kaboodle of history, the man and his wife and the warring brothers and the seductive daughter. For anyone who knows Italian the effect is immediate and ringing.

Why seize on this small detail? The commentators, the ones I have read anyway, haven't noticed this little item, and were I tempted into the field of scholarly belligerence I might declare they haven't understood the first word of the book. Some obscure practical instinct in Joyce must have let him know the competitive pugnacity of pundits would keep this puzzling book from dropping into limbo. For an impractical man he had a curious left-handed practicality, and was not only able to push his difficult books before the public but also to promote the works of friends like the then unknown Italo Svevo. He had a good deal of the Shaun character in him, much more than his brother Stanislaus, a shy and retiring professor, on whom he pins the worldly label. There will always be readers of *Finnegans Wake* as long as there are people who love puzzles and men are competitive enough to quarrel about their solutions. But just here is the danger: it becomes easy to confuse one's pleasure at solving a puzzle with the delight in art as such. The commentator sticks in his thumb and pulls out a plum and in time that satisfaction may be enough to replace his appetite for the beautiful. One of the most learned experts in the *Wake* whom I know is a man otherwise insensitive and unconcerned with art.

But there is a second and more serious point about this first word. For someone who knows and speaks Italian the effect is immediate. One hears the "they will return" in "riverrun" with the ear; one does not arrive at it by inference. But how about the languages and allusions I do not know? Well, there is always a convenient trot. But that knowledge will then remain something secondhand and remote, relatively inert and dead mental baggage rather than the immediate and living word. Joyce himself borrowed single words from languages he did not know, like Chinese, and the child of his imagination was alive and unified enough for him to work them in where he pleased. But is this procedure sufficient to objectify that living whole before the reader, or—what is the same thing—bring the reader inside the vision where Joyce himself stands?

The unity of a work of art can never be a concept, said Kant; it must be grasped as an immediate intuition of the imagination. No scheme of ideas, no general plan or design, is sufficient by itself to produce that incarnate unity that is a work of art. We know the scheme of the *Wake* and enough of Joyce's devices, but is that knowledge sufficient to hold it together before our imagination as a single living whole? The commentators do not address themselves to that question; it is enough for them to pull out their single plums of decipherment. But Joyce himself was aware of it and has said some revealing words on the subject. In 1932 T. S. Eliot offered to print some sections of *Ulysses* in a *Criterion Miscellany* he was planning. The offer would have been a help to Joyce, for the book was then banned in both England and America, and Eliot's was a publishing house of great prestige. But Joyce objected to the fragmentation of a work which he felt must be absorbed as a whole. However, he had already allowed sections of the *Wake* to be printed, and he felt called upon to explain the difference in a letter to Eliot: *"Ulysses* is a book with a beginning middle and end and should be presented as such. The case is quite different with *Work in Progress* [the provisional title of the *Wake* at that time] which has neither beginning nor end."

Ulysses takes place in the daytime world and has the unity and continuity, such as it is, of that world. However many its tedious and obstructing passages, these eventually fall into place and are carried along in the movement of that day that sticks as a single whole forever in our imagination. There is no such comparable movement to give structure to *Finnegans Wake.*

It is a mistake to think that as Joyce gave us the stream of consciousness in the *Ulysses,* so here in the *Wake* he is giving us the stream of the unconscious. The question "Who is the dreamer in *Wake?"* which still goes the round of the critics is completely beside the point. It was started perhaps by an essay of Edmund Wilson, who sees the whole of the *Wake* as "The Dream of H. C. Earwicker," so that he is even forced to the absurd extreme of saying that when we hear the voice of the woman in the book it is the husband dreaming that she is talking! Joyce is bound by no such realistic restrictions. He is creating a dream-language and through this language a dream-world in which we are to see whatever it is that is happening. This dream world, like an actual dream, is filled with blurred shapes, figures of ambiguous identity shifting and coalescing, and also abrupt and violent *non sequiturs.* How could Joyce ever hope to unify such impossible material, and moreover in a book which by his own deliberate intention was to have no beginning, middle, or end? The devices he adopts for unification seem abstract or mechanical or both, and hardly the work the imagination requires. Tirelessly he weaves the initials of the man and the woman into nearly every page, but are those initials sufficient to call forth the embodied presence of the people themselves?

Perhaps the characters in a dream must be disembodied. There is in any case a vast difference between the characterization in *Ulysses* and that in the *Wake*. The characters of *Ulysses* walk out of the book and stay with us. A reader may forget great tracts of that novel and yet the characters still remain alive in his imagination, and that in itself is one ground for its aesthetic unity. But the personages in the *Wake* are not characters but archetypes. And as archetypes they have a vague and numinous existence. Like gods, they are not people but presences. In parts of the *Wake* they come to furious and ebullient life, but they never walk out of the sacred precinct of the text into the world. In the famous Anna Livia Plurabelle chapter the goddess is bewitchingly present and alive, but does she live beyond the enchantment of the language and do you carry any definite features or identity away with you? The vague if potent reality of the archetypes makes them directly unamenable to literature. That is why the dreams told to us by another person often seem to us flat and inconsequential; what is alive and potent to him, because he is experiencing it as a living presence, is incommunicable outside the fabric of the dream itself. One must admire the scrupulous fidelity with which Joyce has adhered to the nature of his dream material even if it should eventually bring about artistic failure.

In the period of Alexandria old age had overtaken the Greeks, and the great song—as Yeats has said of us today—was no more. The myth no longer lived in them with fire enough to make them bards. Unable to be poets, they became scholars, scientists, grammarians, philologists, and—that tribe which multiplying so feverishly today seems more than anything else to link us with the Alexandrians—anthologists. Nevertheless, they still hungered for the myth and cultivated it in their own fashion. They researched the myth, made elaborate symbolic and analogical interpretations of Homer, and even anthologized the myths in collections. But the more they labored at these scholarly tasks, the further the myth receded from them.

Now Joyce is one of the primary imaginations, of such irrepressible energy and vitality and with such a strong hold on the commonplace that he would seem to be the last of modern writers to be pinned with the label of Alexandrian. Yet he cannot escape this age in which he lives, and in seeking to embody the myth once again he must do so self-consciously and at a distance through all the heavy apparatus of mock scholarship. And because the myth does not for us live an open and acknowledged life in the daytime world, he must let it recede from us into the formless world of night and sleep. Perhaps that is the only place where myth will be able henceforth to live. Perhaps the myth has permanently passed out of history, and henceforth the human mind is embarked on the rational stage of its evolution. Would that be altogether progress, or might it instead represent a degree of detachment from the unconscious that is full of dangers? Perhaps this age is still so unsure of itself that it is unable to know and admit the myths it lives by. Not even when they erupt unconsciously in the fanaticism and fury of ideologies.

Questions, questions that this overwhelming and baffling book hurls us into and that our time is not yet ready to answer. In any case, the monstrous and splendid failure that is *Finnegans Wake* leaves us with a sobering judgment on our present condition: modern man is able to make contact with his myths only when he is asleep and dreaming. That *is* something to think about.

Conclusion

11.Discontented Civilization

The method is not only a symptom of confusion and
helplessness, not only a mirror of the decline of a world.
Most of the novels which employ this multiple-reflection
of consciousness leave the reader with an impression of
hopelessness. There is often something confusing,
something hazy about them, something hostile to the
reality which they represent. We not infrequently find a
turning away from the practical will to live, or delight
in portraying it under its most brutal forms. . . .

>—ERICH AUERBACH
> on the fiction between the two world wars

We have modified our environment so radically that we
must now modify ourselves in order to exist in this new
environment.

>—NORBERT WIENER

Every time is in need, but each time experiences its need in
a way peculiar to itself.

Two recent movies may help us gather together the varied
threads woven throughout this book. The two stand as far apart
as could be: the first a documentary, *Sky Above Mud Below,*
which deals with savages of New Guinea; the second a science
fiction fantasy, *2001: A Space Odyssey,* that projects us into the
near and far future of our technological civilization. For all I
know, the two will have already been forgotten by the time
these words see print, so quickly do the ephemeral products of
this new art become obsolete. A stroke of chance, however,

makes them stick fast together in my mind. Being an irregular moviegoer has its advantages, one of which is that you sometimes see reruns in odd and exciting juxtapositions with each other. Having missed these two films when they first appeared, I was lucky enough to see the reruns on two successive days; and counterpoised thus one against the other, they stand fixed in my memory almost as if they had been run off on two facing screens. They make a strong enough contrast in their own right, for the two tell a startling and instructive story about the difference between primitive and civilized life. And though chance may have brought them together to our attention, there seems to be historical appropriateness in ending our excursion into the novel by turning to two instances of that more immediate, obvious, and sensational art of the film that seems to be replacing it.

These New Guinea natives are not physically attractive like the magnificent specimens found among some African tribes. There is nothing here to attract even the most romantic soul to want to return to this primitive condition. Their home in the jungle is gloomy, their shyness seems sullen, and as the camera closes in on them, there is that shock—which the fledgling fieldworker in anthropology so often experiences—of something alien, coarse, and repulsive. The shock wears off with repeated exposure. In time the fieldworker, when he has come to feel the human substance beneath the cultural oddities, can say with the commentator in this documentary, "After a while they seem just like us." And in one particular passage the ugliness of these savages seems to fall from them and they become transformed in our eyes.

The natives are to cut down a giant tree. Their purpose is to house in it the souls of their warriors who have just fallen in battle and then wash out this enormous bole into the sea so that the dead spirits will no longer plague them. The magician-priest first climbs the tree, sprinkling it with a white powder as an anointment. Then amid a great gabble and clucking the tribesmen set about cutting and hacking. Once felled, the tree has to be dragged at enormous effort over a difficult and rough terrain into the men's lodgings in the village. There it will be worked over for days and carved into two smaller planks, which are then lashed together like an outrigger and headed out to sea.

Unfortunately the camera cannot follow the carving as it goes on in the men's hut, for those precincts have now become taboo for the outsider. But there is one dazzling shot in which we catch a brief glimpse of the finished product as it is being launched into the ocean. For one brilliant moment these planks, now intricately carved and shaped, flash before our museum-weary eyes as works of art more beautiful perhaps than any now being done in Western civilization.

Consider the extraordinary cluster of human needs that are here faced, satisfied, and kept in delicate balance. The dead are mourned; they are offered a propitiatory gift that will at the same time keep them from having too oppressive a weight upon the living. So the dead are revered but also kept in their place. The relationship between the living and the dead is a continuous transaction in which the balance between the two, like the balance of nature itself, has always to be maintained. At the same time the whole process finds aesthetic expression in a beautiful work of art. Grief is alleviated, the simultaneous fear and awe of the dead kept alive but within bounds, and the human need for beauty fulfilled—all within one single compact ritual.

Does our modern civilization have anything to set beside this ritual? Our funeral rites seem pallid and passive by comparison. The Catholic mass for the dead is still built on the communion of the living and the dead, which is exactly the idea behind the New Guinea ritual. But few participants at the mass think of this communion as true *communitas,* which derives its deepest significance from the primitive meaning of barter and exchange, a transaction in which something has to be paid on both sides.

No, the religious need to preserve the balance between the sense of life and death hardly finds satisfaction in any open and public rite today. Have needs like this really disappeared from the human animal, or have they gone underground and lie buried inside us to lead a stunted and malignant life of their own?

And then, we are no longer doers and makers in the business of our rituals. Art is no longer an enterprise shared by all the people of the tribe. The primitive does not consign his art to a separate sphere of the aesthetic, but carries it on as part of his religious structure, which in turn is indistinguishable from the totality of his social life. Perhaps in disjoining these—art, religion, social usage—we have set the three to wander through an empty land like homeless ghosts that we, unlike the New Guinea natives, fail to placate. "We have put art on a reservation," anthropologist Lévi-Strauss has remarked, thus establishing a significant parallel between our assignment of art to a peripheral place in our own society and our confinement of primitive peoples to marginal lands which are unfavorable to the conditions of their life. And just as primitive peoples restricted to their reservations become demoralized and lose grip on their inherited forms, so art in some quarters today seems to have lost confidence in its own traditional rituals.

If it is the same human animal as those New Guinea natives that we encounter in *2001*, we would hardly guess so at first. Here two astronauts are voyaging in a gigantic spaceship toward a remote planet. They are accompanied by a computer whose functioning skills are so complete that he has become a kind of individual in his own right and is addressed as Hal. At once quasi-human and superhuman, Hal not only has operational powers that surpass those of his two human companions, but he soon shows himself to be the most complex and interesting character in the film. He has become so human, in fact, that he falls prey to the baser motives of mankind. He begins to plot against the two astronauts and actually does destroy one. The other escapes at great risk and manages at last to dispatch Hal by systematically ripping out his wires. As Hal succumbs, he gives way to a bathetic adolescent and then infantile wail of emotions. It would seem that you can program exceptional skills into a computer only at the risk—as sometimes happens with exceptionally gifted humans—of leaving it prone to neurosis.

The film, toward the end especially, mystified most audiences; and Arthur Clarke, who collaborated with the director Stanley Kubrick both on the screenplay and as scientific adviser, wrote the novel *2001* apparently to clear up the ideas behind the mystification. (This practice, which is becoming more common, of writing the movie script first and the book afterward, is another symptom of the historical fate that now threatens the novel: to become an adjunct of film.) The novel blurs quite a bit toward the end too, but the shape of its ideas is generally discernible. The astronauts, it turns out, were on a journey to a distant planet that is an outpost of a civilization far more advanced than ours. Millions of years ago these superior beings had planted a big black slab on the moon to serve as a warning device in case any civilization, like our own, should develop to a point where it was able to reach that satellite. Its discovery by us earthlings had set off this cosmic voyage to find, if possible, the center of this civilization.

Mr. Clarke's fantasy of the lines along which this civilization had developed shows us that science fictionists cannot escape a compulsion toward metaphysics even while they have to express it in a style conducive to their own habit of thinking in terms of gadgets. These superior creatures have constructed computers infinitely more skillful than ours, and what should be the next step, then, but to divest themselves of their bodies, and pass into their own machines! If the computer can think and experience in patterns infinitely richer and swifter than one's own, why not let it take the place of one's own inferior brain? And since the device is also able to receive and scan impulses from anywhere in the universe, to enter it is to become one with the mind of the cosmos. Clarke, an inveterate and hard-headed despiser of philosophers, seems to stammer in amazement as he finds himself caught up—one suspects greatly to his surprise—in the ancient dreams some philosophers have harbored about "Spirit . . . and even beyond." "If there was anything beyond *that,* its name could only be God." The sole astronaut who has survived the treachery of Hal is absorbed into the black megalith and is reborn a child of the cosmos, a particle of the universal mind.

There is something gratifying in seeing a fanatic of technology like Clarke become converted to the mysticism of Father Teilhard de Chardin. His conversion would be more satisfying, however, if this advance toward the spiritual were understood as something more and other than an increased skill with computers and information machines. And we notice too that obsessive habit of technological utopians, to which E. M. Forster has called our attention in "The Machine Stops," to debase the poor archaic vessel of the body until here, in this most advanced technological phase, it is simply shed like an inefficient and worthless husk.

The film does not handle these ideas; and indeed it cannot, for movies cannot think without losing all their power of immediacy. But the director has expressive means of his own, among them the major device of type casting. The actors are all chosen for their notable lack of any individuating trait or quirk, like the bland and anonymous faces in advertising or on television. Against this background of anonymity no wonder the most complex and interesting character is Hal, the computer. He at least has an internal conflict while one cannot imagine the humans, who are nothing but smooth masks, ever capable of that degree of inwardness. A tendency in that direction seems already present in our space programs. Pilots are carefully screened for the evidence of their adjustment all along life's way; they are properly married, have the proper number of children, have always fitted in with the team, etc. etc. Evi-

dently, persons with any quirk of individuation might be un-
steady in handling the intricate gadgets of space technology
over long stretches, and in a crisis might blow up. Perhaps it will
be our way of aiding natural selection by breeding only those
who can cope with the machine. Dr. Norbert Wiener has told
us that "we have modified our environment so radically that we
must now modify ourselves in order to exist in this new environment." One way, apparently, is to turn out human beings who
are more like machines—like the machines of the present, that
is, for in the meantime those machines of the future will become more complex, and even potentially neurotic. The film
suggests the future danger that as we produce humans less
neurotic we may do so at the expense of programming our
human neuroses into machines. It may not be so easy to follow
Dr. Wiener's suave injunction.

Kubrick spreads this bland anonymity of space throughout
the film. On the satellite station above the earth there is a
Howard Johnson's, which suggests a good name generally for
what space will be like when colonized by man—Howard Johnson's in the Sky. Synthetic food pastes squeezed from tubes,
credit cards for interplanetary travel, and all the television
channels from earth you could want—it is all there, not only
Howard Johnson's but a Hilton in the skies.

Kubrick seems to me much shrewder here than a writer like
Norman Mailer, who turns himself frantically inside out to find
some ultraprofound significance in man's first landing on the
moon. Of course, nearly everyone was caught up in that rush
to historical speculation, including the President himself, who
rather recklessly declared it to be the most important day in
human history, thereby scandalizing his spiritual director Billy
Graham by forgetting so easily the birth of Christ. The significance of that first landing on the moon, it seems to me, was
answered by the third voyage, when people were already bored
by the whole routine. The characteristic of modern history, as
Nietzsche foretold, is that everything becomes absorbed into

"the endless recurrence of the same." One fundamental fact about man, Heidegger says, is his tendency to lose himself in facts and their banality. The extension of ourselves into outer space, as Kubrick shows, is only more of the same, and can hardly tell us much about our own meaning. Time and again we are given shots of the long cylinder of the ship sliding through empty space until in our boredom at the repetitive image we begin to find space itself very boring. To try to measure man's significance against the vastness of space leaves us only with the thought of the insignificance of vast space.

Between the violently contrasting images left by these two films one would hope not to have to choose. But the reader will probably have perceived that, if forced, my preference would incline toward archaic man. At least one knows where one stands with him. His possibilities and his limits are relatively clear to us. One is not sure what one can expect from the man of the future. Of course, those savages of New Guinea cannot be made glamorous, and though in some of their less attractive features they are sadly "just like us," we could not, even if we willed, go back there. Yet, limited as their lives may be in other ways, they do have the consolations of art as an organic part of life and a religion solidly embedded in their social rituals. What would art be for the men of the far future? Some diversions would be needed to fill the blank monotony of space voyages extending over months and perhaps years at times when these technicians are not busy reading their instruments or pushing buttons.

Kubrick's film has to keep busy with the action and cannot show us this slower and more reflective life in space, but in the book the astronaut who is left alone after his companion and the computer Hal have been murdered tries to pass the long stretch of time by dialing plays and music from earth. (Pascal felt frightened by the silence of infinite space, but it does not seem more cheering to learn here that the space of the future, far from being silent, will be crackling and chattering with electronic noise.) The great classic plays of Shakespeare or Ibsen bore him because they seem so remote and their problems could be "resolved by a little common sense." The music too becomes remote, though some of it does have a soothing effect. Art in the future, evidently, would become what some positivistic theories already make of it—part of the department of emotional engineering, useful as a kind of pill to manipulate our feelings. Architects would still be needed to build those comfortable Howard Johnson rest stations in interplanetary space; but beyond that, one finds it hard to think where one could fit art into the world of 2001. The confrontation of these two films reinforces our earlier speculation that art is perhaps a product of the archaic part of our nature and may retain its vitality only as it draws its sustenance there and only as long as we ourselves maintain some tie to that part of us.

I

Even apart from these menacing glimpses of the future, our present civilization seems to leave its artists uneasy. That is certainly the impression from glancing back at the material we have traversed. But is that perhaps the bias of our selection? I think not; and for corroboration we may turn back to our earlier guide, Erich Auerbach, who was in a unique position to be a reliable witness. He had been brought up in the older humanities, and thus already had a formed and mature taste when he encountered the first wave of modernism at a time when it was erupting in all its novelty amid a Europe in turmoil after World War I.

There is no doubt of the shock the encounter left: for Auerbach this new literature was an assault upon the nerves. He found in it confusion and helplessness, the mirror of the decline of the world. (It was to be the decline of his world in a narrower sense, for the rise of the Nazis destroyed the German culture he had loved and ultimately drove him from the country.) The European novels produced in the twenties left him with the impression of "something confusing, something hazy, something hostile to the reality they represent." And he even detected something of a death wish in them—"a turning away from the practical will to live, or delight in portraying it under its most brutal forms." That is the response of traditional sensibility to the onslaught of the modern. We should not discountenance it therefore. It is certainly one side of the truth—and a side to which we, for whom modernism is long since a part of our past, are sometimes too inured. One has to conclude that by and large our civilization has not made its writers and artists happy.

That was also the conclusion of Sigmund Freud about the assorted bourgeois whom he had met as patients. The title of our chapter is borrowed of course from his *Civilization and Its Discontents,* which is at once the simplest of his books and the least tied to the peculiarities of his own system so that its judgment upon modern civilization can be taken independently of the Freudian philosophy as a whole. In this little book in fact Freud was summing up the experience of a lifetime spent on the distressing intimacies of the consulting room. For some reason it seems necessary today to stress that Freud did not invent his cases. He invented explanations of them (which are not always convincing), but the cases themselves happened, they were among the phenomena of the period, and we have been trying to sketch a phenomenology of this century. His conclusion from witnessing all that anguish was simple and clear: among the burdens that culture imposes upon us is a certain repression of instinct, but modern civilization does not offer us the enhancements—as religion once did—to make this repression bearable. And so the tension breaks out everywhere in neurosis.

Freud thus locates our modern trouble in the area of the instincts. That is where we too have found it in the writers and artists we have looked at. Of course, he does fit the instincts into his own rather narrow scheme. There are two of them, sex and aggression, and each is understood simply as a drive that seeks immediate discharge. For a man who considered his contribution to psychology to be in the understanding of the instincts Freud had a rather grim view of them: on the whole they are threatening, and the only thing to do with them is to control them so far as possible by the conscious ego, with the assistance of that sometimes tyrannous policeman, the moral conscience or superego. He does not favor the view that the instincts might have some wisdom of their own, or that they might have wider scope than immediate sexual or aggressive discharge. If we are to generalize about the instincts in man, we ought to look at the primitive in whom these play a more preponderant role. Our example of the New Guinea natives would suggest that the range of the instinctual is wider and richer than Freud imagined. What about the instincts for beauty, order, for a ritual that establishes some harmony between our visible life and the invisible realities that haunt it? Here modern civilization leaves us unfulfilled, and therefore frustrated in the further reaches of our being.

The example of Freud leads us to raise again the old question about the relation of civilization to happiness. Civilization did not arise to make men happier but to heighten their tensions. This was the suspicion that first dawned on the French explorers to the South Sea Islands in the eighteenth century, and from their reports it entered into the thought of Rousseau. But quite apart from any taint of romantic nostalgia, it stirs again from the findings of modern anthropology. To begin with, civilization widens the gap between man and man. Primitive groups have their pecking order, and the chiefs enjoy status and advantages over other individuals, but all still remain close to each other within the round of their daily labors. The invention of literacy served to entrench a class system by deepening the division between those who possess the instruments of culture and those who do not. This increasing distance between man and man is the external social accompaniment to the widening of the extremes within human consciousness itself. Civilization was the necessary instrument for the psychological development of mankind out of the womb of the unconscious and the umbilical closeness to nature. That was our historical destiny, on which it is impossible for us now to turn back. It does not seem to have been intended to make us happier. We enjoy a higher level of consciousness at the expense of greater tensions within ourselves. Hitherto that burden was accepted because the values of civilization seemed unquestionable. We might not be as happy as some South Sea islanders, but they did not have the glory of a Michelangelo or Shakespeare. The discontent that now creeps through modern culture is the self-doubt of a civilization that has lost faith in its own value.

This doubt has even shaken our confidence in progress, which was once an unquestionable article of faith. A few decades ago the distrust of technology was an avant-garde position. Today that distrust has become so widespread that it has become banal. One hesitates to add to it, and in fact one feels pushed toward defending technology. It is, after all, the most adventurous, creative, and original part of our culture. There can hardly be any more striking symptom of loss of heart than when a civilization begins to doubt what it does best.

The optimists believe there has been progress, the pessimists do not; but yawning beneath both pessimism and optimism there is the gaping question whether the idea of progress itself has any definite and verifiable meaning. We were seated on a veranda one summer evening watching the sun set over Cape Cod Bay. Our host was a distinguished scientist whose hobby this vacation was watching and grading sunsets. "I'd rate this one as about 7.6," he remarked to get us into the game (his scale was zero to ten), and we all began watching with him. It was a quiet and demure sunset, rather nunlike—as nuns once were supposed to be. Then in a moment it began to change; some long streamers of light shot up through the clouds and what had been gray and quiet now became ruddy and vermilion and orange. "Ah, things are picking up," our host exclaimed, "I'd give that now an 8.6." Then the dispute broke out. Was that earlier sunset (of just a few minutes before) really inferior? Did it not have an altogether different quality from the sunset that had succeeded it, and shouldn't it be judged in terms of its own specific qualities? Hadn't something been lost—that exquisite and soft grayness—in its becoming more spectacular? And from there the discussion passed on to whether and in what sense qualities are measurable at all.

The measurement of any specific quality always involves some arbitrary procedure. We can isolate heat and measure it along the numerical scale of a thermometer. But qualities in life are not so easily isolated. A concrete quality is usually not a single quality but a cluster of qualities within qualities. The quality of a wine is an example of such a cluster. We do pretend to measure the quality of wines very precisely along the numerical scale of prices. Wine merchants will quarrel over the relative price of two wines down to the last centime. But with all due respect to the art of wine tasting, and the prodigies of discrimination some experts are capable of, one must recognize that the measurement by price calls into play any number of extraneous factors like scarcity and demand as well as snobbishness. And then the quality is modified in turn by all the qualities in the life situation into which it must fit. The most expensive burgundy does not do as well at a light luncheon as a good clear chianti.

Sunsets and wines are simple things beside the quality of life in a civilization. Here we are far less able to isolate one quality from its attendant circumstances. Every culture is a concrete totality whose aspects are interrelated within the whole. Change one aspect and you must change others. Gain something here and you must lose something there. How could we ever hope to range civilizations neatly along some objective linear scale? Where would we rank the Athenian Greeks in comparison with us? Or, to come closer to home, the Navaho culture with our own loud and vociferous civilization that has almost trampled it under? Anthropologists tell us that the Navaho was an unusually "happy" culture with great psychological resilience and depth—qualities that we can hardly claim for our own uneasy and restless times. Once we press such questions it becomes less and less certain that the idea of progress itself has an exact and determinable meaning. That it may not would be a conclusion more depressing for some people than historical pessimism itself. Among other things, this doubt casts a rather somber light on those revolutions which deliberately sacrificed millions of human lives in the name of progress.

Technology became confused with progress, I suspect, because here was a crutch for the faith, here an advance could be quantitatively measurable. Machines can certainly be rated one over the other in exact figures. The automobile today, for example, is superior in speed and performance to the automobile of fifty years ago, and certainly to the horse and buggy. The figures indeed can be made to look very precise and impressive: speed, horsepower, compression ratio, bore, stroke, RPMs, etc., etc. Unfortunately, the figures tell us nothing about the qualitative effects of the machine when it fits into the human world. And here, once again, nothing fails quite like success. Industrial society seems to defeat itself by its own prodigious powers. We have been so successful at mass-producing so many automobiles and creating wealth enough for so many people to own a car and ride in one that cross-town traffic in Manhattan now is slower than in the days of the horse and carriage.

Nature abhors a vacuum, ran the old adage. It seems truer that she does not like the straight line, least of all progress along a straight line. Technology, which was supposed to master nature, is itself caught up in the natural process of checks and balances, of push that creates its counter-pull, of the innumerable interplay of opposites that makes up the ecological balance.

One of the fairest dreams of technology was that it would produce the really Affluent Society. The affluence it creates, however, is heavily mortgaged to the damage it inflicts upon the environment. Willy-nilly man stumbles against limits, and if he strides over one, he finds himself confronting three or four others that he has created and that he had not foreseen when he took the first step. Camus was right when he foresaw that this problem of limits would be the central moral challenge to our civilization. We will in the end be able to correct the balance with nature only by cutting the level of our consumption, which means of course a return to a more frugal and limited ideal than gross affluence. However far we push out in a straight line into space, here on this earth at least we will have to continue our part in an old Greek play, where the frenzy of excess is punished by the Furies and even the gods themselves have to comply with the demands of cosmic balance.

But in pure science? Here surely there has been and can continue to be an unambiguous progress that is not contaminated by dangerous side effects as with technology. Recently one scientist predicted cheerfully that "in 1980 we shall know ten times as much as we did in 1970." Probably; for every discovery seems to make possible ten further ones, and the number of scientists now at work, it has been estimated, is greater than that of all scientists who ever lived before. Such snowballing of numbers must snowball into results.

Yet with all that new information will we be ten times wiser? Every new discovery upsets the balance of common sense for a while. The new find distorts our vision because it seems to offer the key to everything, as the great Descartes eagerly grasped after the newly discovered pituitary gland as the solution to the puzzle of mind and matter. The sciences might become ten times more fragmented, and they might have ten times less the sense of their own unity and meaning than they have today. We know a thousand, perhaps a million times more than Aristotle did, yet his vision of nature and of man within it

—of the human world as embedded within the natural world— could be by its very ignorance more comprehensive and satisfying than ours.

Still ten to one is formidable odds, and we ought to go along with this ratio a little more positively. Imagine a man in a certain spot from which there is only one road out. He takes the road and finds it leads to a dead end. Multiply the one by ten, and he now has ten exits at his disposal. Each, as he tries it, turns out to be a dead end (for scientific explanation can go only so far). Of course, he can keep busier going from road to road, and that may be some improvement, but it is not one I am able to get very excited about.

Or, let us make the metaphor a little more specific while still preserving the ten-to-one ratio: imagine a hospital that has one wing where the most advanced medicine is carried on. A decade hence the same hospital should have ten wings, each housing its own very developed specialty. Human mortality would have become a vastly more intricate and technical matter even than it is today. The patient, or rather his doctors, would have the luxury of choosing in which of the ten he is to die. In the end, however, he dies—and dies alone.

The Enlightenment that held before us a vision of unlimited progress could deliver on this promise only if death were eliminated. Perhaps science will someday make good that promise and the engineering of individual immortality will become a reality. Arthur Clarke indeed predicts we should have it sometime not long after the year 2000, but even he doubts that it will be a good thing. Swift found the *struldbrugs*, those shriveled immortals, the most wretched of all the imaginary peoples that Gulliver encountered. And his picture of them might turn out a good prophecy of the universal and miserable stagnation that would result from scientific immortality. Death and sex, after all, appeared together at a certain stage in evolution. Below that level the simpler organisms are asexual, and though they can be destroyed by physical or chemical means they are not mortal in the sense that death is a part of their normal life cycle. Sexual reproduction, birth, and death were nature's means of securing a renewal of life along with its genetic enrichment. One biologist has remarked that the greatest invention of nature was death. If science were to abolish the death of the individual that would be the supreme adventure in man's warfare upon nature. And perhaps his most disastrous.

II

Marxism does not know these doubts of progress, since it was formed in the ideology of the Enlightenment, which it has never abandoned. Where progress has not been made in the modern world the obstruction has come through the ineptness and evil of Capitalism, a system whose moment in history has long since passed. Indeed, from the austere Marxist point of view all the anxieties of spirit that we have noticed in the artists of our time are but the symptoms of bourgeois society in its sickness and decadence.

This view is not easily disposed of. It would be foolish to underrate the ideas—the official ones, that is, for what the artists in those countries may secretly feel is another matter—of the half of the world that is set over against ours. At every step in this book I have been aware of that shadow in the background and of how different our troubles of the spirit would look from there. It would almost seem like an impertinent luxury to speak of a time of need without addressing oneself to those material needs that still lie heavy over the bulk of mankind. The poor exist, all over the world and in ever increasing numbers—that is a reality from which Marxism still derives its immense historical dynamism, and particularly in the most underdeveloped regions. American intellectuals who had witnessed the god that failed and therefore felt that we had seen the last of Marxism in the 1930s were in fact lulled by the illusions of our affluence. The United States as an island of affluence has a fragile existence in a world where it is surrounded by poverty. Do not these economic and social needs make up the real need of our time, the gauge by which all the luxuries of literature and art have eventually to be measured?

Still, one has to be selective. To have dealt with our materials on these terms would have required a different book, and different philosophical premises. Reality—to remember Hegel—is wherever it appears, and one must take it up there where it appears to one. Besides, Marxist societies are not likely to escape forever the tribulations of the spirit that have afflicted Western writers and artists in our time. In the early days of the Khrushchev thaw, before it had turned out to be only a temporary defrosting, the *New York Times* reported about a public meeting in Moscow at which a young man stood up and said, "If only somebody would give us something in which we could believe." He was not talking about a new model of tractors or a new five-year plan in which they might be employed. His name was not given, he was not arrested—at the time anyway. He remains one of those unknown voices out of history that haunt one's mind as his question must eventually haunt Marxist society. For when such a society has attained stability, when the bellies are fed and there is no enemy class within against which they may stoke the furnaces of hatred and no external foe to unite them in a nationalistic frenzy, in the midst of that calm then the strange and unwelcome guest of Nihilism may appear at the door with his request, "Give us something in which to believe." Then begins its time of need, and the literature out of our night of the bourgeois world in its decline will have simply rehearsed the paths through which that society will have to travel.

III

Existentialism, at least, cannot hide its encounter with Nihilism. It is born out of and against that shadow. As the other philosophy of our time (at least as far as the public at large is concerned), it speaks from the opposite quarter of the spiritual compass from Marxism. It is troubled in a way that Marxism is not, but modern artists are. It offers us another and very different understanding of the discontent of our civilization, which is closer to the spirit of our art.

The Existentialist theme has really been quite simple and persistent throughout modern culture. Since it was first sounded by Pascal in the seventeenth century it has continued with many variations but always with the same message: the uneasiness of modern man arises from a rupture between himself and nature that leaves him homeless within the universe. Pascal looked out with dismay upon the world that the New Science projected: infinite in extent, mechanical in its operations, without purpose itself and therefore indifferent to the purposes of this creature, man, that had somehow arisen in its midst. "The silence of these infinite spaces frightens me." The universe does not answer our call. Henceforth, man must be seen in the light or darkness of this cosmic alienation. He is an orphan of unknown destiny cast up on the doorstep of the universe.

Pascal had his Christian faith by which to make the leap beyond this cosmic forlornness. When this faith is gone the burden becomes heavier, until with Nietzsche it is almost unbearable. Against the backdrop of this meaningless universe man has now to create his own meaning as a risk and a gamble. Nihilism is a historic fate that mankind must live through in order to transcend. In the end nothing can justify our existence except the will and energy and daring to create of it an intoxicating spectacle. As Nietzsche of all philosophers suffered the problem of Nihilism in its extremity, so his answer is also the most extreme. Yet all the Existentialists of this century, however varied the stripe and shade of their individual persuasion, have philosophized in his shadow.

With all the ink spilt on Existentialism in recent years one significant and rather dramatic little incident has scarcely been noticed. Yet the two personages involved were the principal contemporary figures, Heidegger and Sartre, and the incident compressed within itself the crucial issues that are at stake in this philosophy (and also lie behind our present book). "Confrontation" would be too strong a word in this case, for the two principals crossed each other's bows without collision, signaling discreetly and at a distance, and one of the parties (Sartre) seems never to have been able to make out the signals of the other. Yet an encounter of minds, tangential and quiet as it may be, is never without its drama, and Heidegger has memorialized the occasion in one of his most important essays, "Letter on Humanism" (1948). Since we have had occasion to make some slanting remarks on Humanism in our previous pages, here is a chance to gather those observations into philosophic coherence—and also to notice once again the curious ambiguities of that complex attitude known as Humanism.

At the time Heidegger was under a cloud. After the Allied victory he had been suspended from teaching because of his sympathies with Nazism in its early years, and had not yet been reinstated. Sartre, on the other hand, was riding high on the boom of Existentialism as the movement of the moment in postwar Paris. Since Existentialism, with its constant harping upon anxiety, might not be palatable fare for the general public, Sartre adopted a very clever ploy: it might be sold as a new humanism. Whereas traditional Humanism always had some comforting glow about it, for in fact it always secretly rested on the assumption of the continued existence of the religious institutions around it, this would be a new kind of humanism, more daring and adventurous, willing to accept the heroic and absurd lot of man's existence in a universe that, as Pascal had said, "knows him not." Hence his title, "Existentialism: A New Humanism," originally of a lecture but then turned into a famous essay.

Heidegger had been in some sense the father of all this, but the father had changed a good deal in the meantime. His earlier *Being and Time*—which had been one of Sartre's chief sources, though Sartre took from it only what suited his own temperament—remains still one of the most striking philosophical productions of the century. In it Heidegger had drawn a somber and powerful picture of man, solitary and alone, building projects against the backdrop of Nothing, and always within the inescapable grip of time. But though the work made him famous almost overnight, it did not leave him satisfied. "I did not find what I was looking for there," he is reported to have said, and turned instead to the study of poetry, and particularly the Romantic poet Hölderlin.

The choice of this poet by this philosopher was perhaps inevitable. Hölderlin was the poet of the same native region (Suabia), and he sought to poetize out of communion with the gods and sages of ancient Greece. Here was another sense of Being different from the tension of modernism. In the utterance of the poem Being is not the affair of the human will engaged in its resolute death-bound project, but comes as the illumining gift bestowed by whatever god, Heracles, Dionysus, or Christ, to whom the poet is servant. That was the source of Heidegger's well-known "reversal," which he has spent his later years adumbrating, and it is from this point of view he takes note of the Sartrian brand of Humanism.

It is also the only occasion on which Heidegger has commented on a contemporary thinker at length. For such an encounter most philosophers would bring out all the machine guns of debate. But Heidegger approaches his subject more obliquely; he is more evocative than declarative—a style that is proper to his later message. Still, there is something of a debater's sharpness with which he singles out, and repeats, the most telling sentence from Sartre: *"Ici nous sommes sur un plan où il y a seulement des hommes."* Man's fate on this planet is an affair of men to be settled among men themselves. On that strictly human level history at last attains authenticity. How existential and heroic this attitude! But let us listen to Sartre's statement again: "On that level there are only men." A more prosaic and literal-minded reader might be tempted to exclaim, "What, no cats and dogs!" Frivolous perhaps, but let us see whether this frivolity has its own insight before we become too solemn. Konrad Lorenz explains the depth of man's tie with his dog as the secret longing to reestablish our bond with "that unconscious omniscience we call nature." Or we can recall the eloquent words of Sartre's friend and critic Lévi-Strauss about those blessed moments of release when we can gain some sense of the "essence of life beyond thought and beyond society" through our encounters with the nonhuman world—"in the wink of an eye, heavy with patience, serenity and mutual forgiveness, that sometimes through an involuntary understanding, one can exchange with a cat." Such experiences would be unknown to Sartrian man, who does indeed stand alone and knows no bond with nature and no kinship with other animate beings outside the human world. Taken literally, his statement makes us think of that city of the future prophesied by Baudelaire in which even trees and shrubs would be replaced by glittering metallic decorations made by man himself.

Heidegger of course would not stoop to arguing about cats and dogs. His means for getting at the same point are more solemn and austere. He sees Sartre's position against the whole history of Western philosophy, and particularly the culmination of that history within the last three centuries. The establishment of modern science in the seventeenth century was the consequence of a change in man's being. He begins to see himself more as the active master of nature. Bacon expresses this new project in the most vivid and drastic way: the advancement of science will come, he tells us, only when we put nature to the rack to answer our questions rather than passively follow its lead.

And indeed the great strides of modern science have been accomplished through the imposition of certain deliberately chosen models upon nature. It is we then who choose these models, and our active will is thus central to the whole process. In philosophy after Kant the will becomes more and more the center of human reality. Nietzsche is the last in this line who works out this metaphysics of the will, and therefore the metaphysics of modern civilization, to its ultimate conclusion. This will is a will to mastery over nature—and therefore a will to power. But power is not a quiescent state at which the will seeks to arrive in order to rest there. Power is the active exercise of power. The will therefore wills itself as the will to power ceaselessly willing itself. The will to will! Here is all the willfulness we could want. Here is the metaphysical frenzy which lies at the basis of the famous "dynamism" of modern civilization, which has transformed the planet and thrust the whole of mankind into a new era of history, and which in the discontent of our own period perhaps has come at last to doubt itself.

It is also the metaphysics that hides behind modern Humanism. So long as it seeks to detach man from nature, to make him the master of Being rather than its guardian, every Humanism —whether it call itself Existentialist or Marxist, and sometimes Sartre seems to want both labels to the extent even of showing that the early Marx was really an Existentialist—is haunted by that ultimate specter of the human will willing itself in the void. Sartre may very well quote Marx admiringly to the effect that "the root is man"—that man himself lies at the center of all his social and historical problems. But if the root is man, Heidegger would ask, in what then is man himself rooted? The history of our time shows that this is not an idle question. For what does our age present us with but the spectacle of metaphysical rootlessness on all sides and in so many disguises?

Beyond this point Heidegger cannot take us. He can trace the sources of this philosophy of the will, diagnose its ultimate presuppositions, and warn us of its ulterior consequences; but he himself cannot produce that sense of Being for a new era that would replace the present. And this is not a mere matter of personal inadequacies. True, his later writings seem to carry indirectness to an extreme and are full of hints, murmurs, and suggestions, as if his philosophic words themselves were an instance of that "waiting," which he tells us is all that we can do in this time. But this halting tone also issues from the logic of the historical situation itself. If the philosophy of the will leads to an alienation from Being, then we cannot secure that tie again by a sheer act of will. Willfulness is not replaced but reinforced by another act of will. If the more man seeks to wrestle Being totally to his purposes the more it recedes, then he can secure his tie to it once again only by learning to "let be." The new god or gods that need to be born will come neither at our command nor by our contrivance. They will come, if at all, as an authentic "happening" out of the depths.

To learn to let be is to learn to wait. The thinker, Heidegger tells us, must learn to wait, and if necessary to wait a whole lifetime. When he had seen a performance of Beckett's *Waiting for Godot,* he was very much moved and remarked, "The man must have read Heidegger." The claim of precedence might strike us as amusingly egotistic if it did not also imply a confession of humility. For in recognizing his kinship with Beckett, Heidegger is in fact acknowledging that the whole of his philosophy, complex and erudite as it may be, nevertheless stands humanly speaking in the same spiritual condition as the two tramps in *Godot.*

IV

To wait is to be in transition toward something else. The young now chant that this is the dawning of the Age of Aquarius, as if the whole world and its future were easily passing into their hands. Privately, when one talks with them, they are not nearly so confident. For older people more entrenched in the past, the rapidity of transition becomes so dizzy that it creates confusion and anguish. We practice a kind of colonialism toward history analogous to the geographical colonialism of the last century. As the earlier imperialists trampled over the various cultures they encountered in space, we are caught up in a process that does the same thing within the dimension of time. As we stride over the past we uproot it and jettison it. This anguish of transition has been expressed nowhere in modern letters more incisively than by Hesse in *Steppenwolf.*

He [the Steppenwolf] said to me once when we were talking of the so-called horrors of the Middle Age: "These horrors were really nonexistent. A man of the Middle Ages would detest the whole of our present-day life as something far more than horrible, far more than barbarous. Every age, every culture, every custom and tradition has its own weakness and its own strength, its beauties and ugliness; accepts certain sufferings as matters of course, puts up patiently with certain evils. Human life is reduced to real suffering, to hell, only when two ages, two cultures and religions overlap. . . . Now there are times when a whole generation is caught in this way between two ages, two modes of life, with the consequence that it loses all power to understand itself and has no standard, no security, no simple acquiescence. Naturally, everyone does not feel this equally strongly.

Hesse speaks out of the immediate mood of Europe in confusion and dismay after World War I, but the terms of his diagnosis still apply. Our mood is more diffuse, nameless, and pervasive, but the anxiety of transition is still there.

Between what and what are we then the transition? That is the question that we find harder to answer.

Art (which we have taken throughout as the key to the inner life of the period) may supply us some clue. Here at least all the marks of transition are plainly before our eyes. Here too things move so fast that the whole of the Modern movement has already become, complete and intact in itself, a part of the past. Looking back now at the writers and artists we have talked about in this book, we have the impression of a force that, however close to us in years, has already spent its power. From the point of view of the young and what they now read, from the point of view of what is now being presented to them or that they themselves are presenting on the screens and stages and in the galleries of New York, the whole Modernist movement, in its scope and ambition, has already receded into the classicism of the museum. That isn't where the action is anymore. A long wave of the Western spirit, gathering far back, began to crest in the second decade of this century and crashed in a brilliant scattering of spray in the 1920s. What was valuable in the works of the following decades still flowed from the wash of that immense wave, but the flood has now become a trickle. For the moment we are in the trough between the wave that is spent and the new surge that has not yet come. In this meantime we are now going through a period of pop culture in which the high ambitions that the Modern movement—in spite of its ironies and iconoclasms—still harbored for art will be given up.

T. S. Eliot once justified the spirit of experimentation in modern art in a single, very sharp aphorism: "It would be as pointless for an artist to repeat what already has been done as for a scientist to discover a truth that has already been known." In the present state of the arts this remark does not ring quite so convincingly as it once did. The artist does not seek to produce something new, but something convincing. If he achieves something valid, it will be new, in any case; for the restless "life of forms," which makes up the real history of art, never stands still.

Art in this century (as we have seen) has undergone a more or less systematic destruction of forms; and validly so, for it has produced some valid works in that destructive process. But with the door once opened, experimentation can become frivolous and meaningless—and thus one more unconscious voice of Nihilism. A few years back French critics spoke of the "need to break the back of the novel." Well, the novel's back has been broken by this time, and it is a question whether the patient in its wheelchair will survive. The present dominance of the cinema (particularly among the young) raises the question whether literature as a whole, and indeed literacy itself, will continue to enjoy its once preeminent position. The moving visual image, instantaneous in its impact, may become the dominant medium of communication, as McLuhan has suggested, and thus replace the printed word, which after all has prevailed in human history only through the last four centuries.

Kierkegaard described anxiety as "a sympathetic antipathy and an antipathetic sympathy." We are fascinated by the possibility that we nevertheless dread even while we pursue its lure —and eventually the negative aspects of the thing, the most to be dreaded, become the most intoxicating. That is the kind of anxiety that can operate in artistic experiment. An artist can pursue experimentation to the point where though he may still be enriching the resources of the medium he is in fact fascinated by the threat to the art itself. Two decades ago it was avant-garde and shocking to talk about "easel painting"—the painting perceived as a framed window on space—as a form that was historically finished and incapable of resurrection. Nowadays that talk is old hat, as if it merely ratified a *fait accompli*.

Certainly, a good deal of what is done now (after the collapse of Abstract Expressionism) makes a different claim upon the space around it from any painting of the past. Those very large, flat, mainly empty or merely repetitive areas of paint have changed the status of painting to an impersonal adjunct of modern architecture, which itself aspires toward a functional impersonality. We do not look at these paintings as individual works in themselves, but rather out of the side of our eyes, as it were, as they create some splash of color in a large hall or foyer. The official confirmation of this new role for painting was given when Frank Lloyd Wright was commissioned to design the Guggenheim Museum. Wright was well known not to like painting and painters, and he proceeded to prove his point by making his building a monument to the obsolescence of the painter's art. The whole construction is designed to subordinate the paintings to the single spectacle of the long ramp that curves downward around the main hall from roof to ground floor. The spectacle of this hall is imposing, but the effect is to deflate the importance of any single painting that might be exhibited. For the paintings usually shown at the Guggenheim Annuals that might be an advantage, but how would the masterpieces of the Metropolitan and Frick Museums—they are only a few blocks away, and the experiment could easily be made—look if they were hung here? It would be a collision between two different epochs of the human spirit, and each would lie in uneasy tension with the other.

In music, finally, the transition has become so steep and accelerated that it seems to have brought the whole house down on our heads. Imagine the music of the last three centuries selectively condensed into one long-playing record. It is a wonder nobody has yet made such a record, for it would be a most startling summation of Western history. The gracious concords of polyphony give way to the intricate harmonies of diatonic music, where dissonances may sound but always (as in the world of theology) find ultimate reconciliation. Fragmentation sets in; tonality turns into cacophonous polytonality, which in turn gives way to the homeless voice of atonality. The haphazard dance of atoms in the music of chance becomes the engineering of casual noise as six radios are played at once—until in the end there are only great chunks of silence with occasional squeaks of sound like radar blips. A rather startling sequence! It is as if Mozart were to break down and stammer in the incoherent fragments of Samuel Beckett's Lucky and then at last become silent.

Yet where in this process could one possibly have called a halt? That is a question with which the aesthetic conservative does not really grapple. To arrest this history at any point would have killed that particular style through sheer repetition. The medium itself seems to push toward these further possibilities. We seem torn between the Scylla of aesthetic stagnation and the Charybdis of empty experimentation. Consequently, the lot of the serious avant-garde artist becomes more difficult.

Perhaps it was this giddy prospect of musical history that led the composer Arthur Honegger some years ago to blurt out the pained question: "Have we indeed lost the arts?"

Well, not quite—or at least, not yet. However much it has been pushed to the margins of our social life, however much we may have—in the words of Lévi-Strauss—placed art on a reservation, it still hangs on by the skin of its teeth. Yet that survival has exacted a heavy price from the artists themselves. It required nothing less than a destruction of forms in order to make a prodigious return to the sources of art itself back beyond the bourgeois phase of its history, which we now recognize to be that of Realism.[1] Modern artists have dared to enter once again that world of the imagination, more encompassing than the boundaries of realism, where their works struggle to live beside Easter Island and Stonehenge as well as Ingres and Courbet. Beyond the glut of documentary journalism, literature survives only where language and the word retain the primordial resonance they had in the sagas and myths of early man. In music, the most publicly explosive work of the century was Stravinsky's *Sacre*. In retrospect the technical innovation of that work seems hardly so shocking, but such innovation was not the composer's primary intention. He said at the time that he wanted to create music that would draw upon the wellspring of primitive life for its vitality.

The sculptor Noguchi once privately remarked: "The work that haunts my imagination the most, and the one to which I would like my own to aspire is—Stonehenge." Notice that this chosen image is not Phidias, not Michelangelo, not Donatello, not Rodin. To help find what he seeks he has to go back beyond the canon of classical Humanist and civilized art to the mystery

---

1. The fact that Social Realism is still the officially sanctioned art in the Soviet Union is one more indication how a society, originally radical in its intentions, can become conservative in practice, and how much its ideology clings to the nineteenth century.

of the prehistoric. Why such a need? Because this choice of a model cuts, in several different directions, across all the neat compartmentalizations by which our civilization has managed to divide the primal unity of experience. Stonehenge, we now believe, was a monument to the sun (or sun-god), but at the same time a practical instrument to regulate the calendar by measuring the risings and settings of sun, moon, and stars. It was thus at once a structure in the service of both religion and science. Through the wear of time and weather, and the random depredations of later men, Stonehenge has now become— at least in the mind of this modern artist—a great work of sculpture. Thus man, nature, and history have all conspired together to produce an object that is at once artificial and natural, utilitarian and aesthetic, unifying within itself all the divisions in Being that we have set up between beauty and use, man and nature. One can easily see then why this ruin should haunt a modern sculptor's imagination. Art, to continue to be what it is, has to effect a radical return to its own source in the unity of Being that, against all the centrifugal whirl of modern life, remains still the artist's perpetual center of departure and return.

Art would call us back to that primal source. Primal, primordial, primitive. The words ring different changes upon the same meaning, but the last particularly suggests something that has already passed away in time and now belongs only to the world of the anthropologist. So we come back, here at the end, to those primitive figures from the documentary film with which we began this chapter. Let us take one parting glance at them.

We are an age in transition; we seem to be sure of that, we have been told it often enough, but we are still uncertain between what and what we are the transition. Difficult enough to keep confidence in a civilization that is in passage, harder still when we do not know into what it may be passing. To know where the road leads might lessen anxieties. We could make our arrangements, alter our attitudes, or at least look for the nearest exit. Not that there aren't enough hypotheses around. For example, we are living through the fag end of capitalist society, and other economic and social arrangements are bound to take its place. Or we may cast our history along different lines: we are in transition from a Christian to a post-Christian society, though in point of fact we seem to have been floundering half in and half out of the latter for some time. And so on. The possibilities are not lacking, there are probably too many of them. But even vistas as broad as this do not satisfy our furthest speculations. Perhaps something else is going on behind our back, some deeper issue is emerging beneath those convulsions. Our modern disasters, like the atomic bomb, and our modern knowledge compel our imagination toward more sweeping perspectives. The first because it reminds us how easily all of human life, not this or that transient social arrangement, might vanish from the cosmos; the second because it has long since taught us to see man and his history against the whole evolutionary sweep of life on this planet. Knowledge and disasters—strange how the two go side by side if not hand in hand, just as in the Garden of Eden. Still, we must follow their lead and let imagination dwell once again on those extremities that our age invokes: those polar opposites from anthropology and from science fiction—the New Guinea savage out of the rain forests of the primeval past and the anonymous space man out of a future that has at long last become dimly apprehensible to us. Between what and what are we the transition? That is the question we have been asking. May it be that in the glaring contrast between these two figures we have our answer?

Epilogue

We end then with a question. A nice gesture it would seem, to beg off with the words of that tired French historian who out of his skeptical fatigue declared, *"Je ne propose rien, j'expose."* No such grand gesture is permitted us; we cannot claim his arrogance of detachment, as if one could stand outside one's age to expose it. No, we end with a question as we began with one, as we have sought to persist in that question throughout. As for proposals, they will not be lacking. They will be needed too. But first might it not be better to abide with the questionable character of our modern situation a little longer, a little more persistently and a little more submissively, before we rush off into one or another of all the proposed ideologies of salvation? Let us at least grasp the question before we invent our answers.

Still, it may seem a little too pat to end with so banal a contrast. The primitive and the space man—what could be more obvious, and how can these bedfellows so violently yoked together be a symbol unique for our own age? Was not man at every point on the long corridor of history in slow transition from his savage state? Perhaps, but previous ages had not brought these contraries within their near horizon. They could not be haunted by the image of the space man because their technology had not come close enough to making his possibility actual. We are the first, after all, who have exited from the womb of the earth's gravity into the void of space, and we have to worry about what it will be like to leave home and mother. On the other hand, we have brought the primitive closer to us in our understanding. Modern anthropology has amassed more knowledge of primitive man than was possessed by all the civilized centuries before us. Our knowledge has not helped him, though; his ranks are thinning. The more he knows us and we know him, the more his numbers decline and his culture becomes diluted. The appearance of space man seems secretly timed with the disappearance of archaic man. Primitive peoples are in fact dying off or being drawn into the orbit of civilization so rapidly that in a few years there will be no more left. When they are all gone, when there are no more savages, noble or ignoble does not matter, will human history at last, assuming there are still humans, have left its primitive stage finally behind it?

Perhaps not. Even as we prepare to push off into space we are not sure how much of archaic man we may still be carrying within us. Biologically we are still the same species as that New Guinea savage. Brothers? We would not like to think so. Our consciousness has become so different from his that we must be different. *Cogitamus ergo sumus.* But beneath that surface of consciousness how many layers of that archaic creature do we still harbor? Another branch of our modern science makes us wonder. There is irony for you: one part of our knowledge provides us with the instruments to get free of the earth, while another part tells us how much, deep down, we are formed of the muck and slime of that same earth from which we can never be quit. So for our first parents in the garden of Eden the forked tongue of knowledge whispered its ambiguities.

Banal and obvious these cinematic images of space man and savage may be, but they express the ultimate division in our time of need. They have other incarnations. We have already met them, in less banal and obvious form, in the two sculptures of an earlier chapter: the blank head by Giacometti and the half-eroded, half-inchoate body by Henry Moore. That body sinks back to the earth, claimed by the same ties that hold the New Guinea primitive within his rain forests. On the other hand, as our imagination follows the astronaut into space, as he recedes farther and farther from us, his features become less

determinate until his face assumes the emptiness that Giacometti has carved. Farther into space, farther into Nothing. The
two sets of images report the same clash and the same challenge, the war of the opposites within us that we cannot escape
without becoming less than ourselves. "I should turn away from
it all," Samuel Beckett intones, "away from the body, away from
the head, let them work it out between them, let them cease,
I can't, it's I would have to cease."

The mere leap into space by itself does not signify. It is only
more of the same, and as one isolated event in the long history
of technology probably less important than the first internal
combustion machine. It is as a symbol that it captures the imagination, a symbol of a departure from the earth in which we are
all swept along. Earlier civilizations still hugged, whether they
knew it or not, that primitive forebear to their bosom and
preserved his ways. Their knowledge did not depart too far
from the world of the senses which he had first set in order.
Their myths repeated the patterns of his. Their religions refined
or elaborated or unconsciously echoed his. For most aspects of
the civilized religions the anthropologist can find some ana-
logue among the primitive peoples he has studied. The art of
those civilizations sprang from the same primitive needs of
adornment and ritual, and particularly the adornment of the
sacred rituals that held the society together. For a thousand
years the chief works of art in Europe were its churches. The
greatest masterpieces belonged there and not in the museums.

One by one, in each of these areas, we have been departing
from all that. We seem to be headed toward a civilization that
would be the first to break its ties with that primitive being. To
accomplish this would be a step more audacious than the mere
physical leap into space. It would probably be mankind's most
daring adventure yet. Will it succeed? Art seems to say no.

Index

Page numbers in *italics* refer to illustrations

About the Author

William Barrett is one of America's most respected philosophers. He was educated at City College of New York (B.A.,
1933) and Columbia University (M.A., Ph.D., 1938). He has
taught philosophy at University of Illinois, Brown, and, from
1950 to 1979, at New York University, and has been a Distinguished Professor at Pace University in New York since 1982.

He joined the staff of *Partisan Review* in 1945 and was an
editor until 1953, helping to introduce European existentialism
to the U.S. He has written six books, among them a memoir
of *Partisan Review, The Truants: Adventures among the Intellectuals; Irrational Man;* and *The Illusion of Technique*.

He lives in Tarrytown, New York.